Championing Cutting-Edge 21st Century Mentoring and Learning Models and Approaches

Global Education in the 21st Century Series

Series Editor

Tasos Barkatsas (*RMIT University, Australia*)

Editorial Board

Amanda Berry (*Monash University, Australia*)
Andrea Chester (*RMIT University, Australia*)
Anthony Clarke (*University of British Columbia, Canada*)
Yuksel Dede (*Gazi University, Turkey*)
Vasilis Gialamas (*National and Kapodistrian University of Athens, Greece*)
Kathy Jordan (*RMIT University, Australia*)
Peter Kelly (*RMIT University, Australia*)
Huk Yuen Law (*The Chinese University of Hong Kong*)
Patricia McLaughlin (*RMIT University, Australia*)
Juanjo Mena (*University of Salamanca, Spain*)
Wee Tiong Seah (*The University of Melbourne, Australia*)
Dianne Siemon (*RMIT University, Australia*)
Robert Strathdee (*Victoria University, Australia*)
Ngai Ying Wong (*Education University of Hong Kong*)
Qiaoping Zhang (*The Chinese University of Hong Kong*)

VOLUME 4

The titles published in this series are listed at *brill.com/gecs*

Championing Cutting-Edge 21st Century Mentoring and Learning Models and Approaches

Edited by

Tasos Barkatsas and Patricia McLaughlin

BRILL
SENSE

LEIDEN | BOSTON

All chapters in this book have undergone peer review.

The Library of Congress Cataloging-in-Publication Data is available online at http://catalog.loc.gov
LC record available at http://lccn.loc.gov/

Typeface for the Latin, Greek, and Cyrillic scripts: "Brill". See and download: brill.com/brill-typeface.

ISBN 2542-9728
ISBN 978-90-04-44036-4 (paperback)
ISBN 978-90-04-39384-4 (hardback)
ISBN 978-90-04-44037-1 (e-book)

Copyright 2020 by Tasos Barkatsas and Patricia McLaughlin. Published by Koninklijke Brill NV, Leiden, The Netherlands.
Koninklijke Brill NV incorporates the imprints Brill, Brill Hes & De Graaf, Brill Nijhoff, Brill Rodopi, Brill Sense, Hotei Publishing, mentis Verlag, Verlag Ferdinand Schöningh and Wilhelm Fink Verlag.
Koninklijke Brill NV reserves the right to protect this publication against unauthorized use. Requests for re-use and/or translations must be addressed to Koninklijke Brill NV via brill.com or copyright.com.

This book is printed on acid-free paper and produced in a sustainable manner.

Contents

Acknowledgements   VII
List of Figures and Tables   VIII
Notes on Contributors   X

Prologue   1
    Tasos Barkatsas and Tricia McLaughlin

1 The Mentoring Profile Inventory Grid: Thinking Differently about Classroom Teachers Who Work with Pre-Service Teachers in Practicum Settings   6
    Juanjo Mena and Anthony Clarke

2 University Student Peer Tutoring: A Pilot Program to Improve Learning for Both Tutors and Tutees   27
    Peter Saunders, Andrea Chester and Sophia Xenos

3 Championing Peer Feedback on Educational Practice: Partnerships for Learning and Development in Tertiary Teaching   45
    Dallas Wingrove and Angela Clarke

4 Motivators, Challenges and Professional Learning for Australian Classroom Teachers Mentoring Pre-Service Teachers   67
    Kathy Littlewood and Kathy Jordan

5 Choosing the Best Way to Travel in an Unknown Landscape: PhD Supervisors' Perspectives on Their Own Learning in Doctoral Supervision   88
    Mikhail Gradovski

6 Mentoring Based on Many-Facet Rasch Analysis in Evaluating Mathematical Modelling Tasks   104
    Yüksel Dede, Veysel Akçakın and Gürcan Kaya

7 The Teacher Ambassador: Mentoring Colleagues to Adopt Twenty-First Century Teaching, Learning and Pedagogical Practice   121
    Kathy Jordan and Kathy Littlewood

8 Theorising Mentoring for the 21st Century Teaching and Learning: Making Invisible Professional Growth Visible through Action Research   135
   Huk Yuen Law

9 Mentoring Students through Global Experiences: Transformative Learning Abroad   157
   Naomi Wilks-Smith and Darren Lingley

Epilogue   176
   Tania Broadley

Acknowledgements

A warm and heartfelt thanks to all the authors and reviewers who have so kindly donated their time. We have a fantastic network of academics with extensive experience in their respective fields; it was a joy to work with all of you, and your contribution to this book has been valuable.

A special thank you to Professor Tania Broadley for her thoughtful Epilogue.

Figures and Tables

Figures

1.1	A mentoring Profile Inventory Report.	10
1.2	The mentoring profile grid. Four quadrants: Quadrant #1: Partner; Quadrant #2: Advocate; Quadrant #3: Facilitator; Quadrant #4: Nurturer.	13
1.3	An illustration of how the grid scores are calculated.	15
3.1	Peer Feedback on Educational Practice Model.	49
4.1	Highest teaching qualification.	74
4.2	Teacher mentor experience.	75
4.3	Motivations for being a teacher mentor.	76
4.4	Challenges of being a teacher mentor.	77
6.1	Solution of group 3.	113
6.2	Solution of group 3.	113
6.3	Solution of group 3.	114
6.4	Solution of group 2.	115
6.5	Solution of group 1.	116
8.1	The four-stage growth model of mentoring practice.	140
8.2	TTR (TuToRial) as mentoring seminar.	147
8.3	The "growth web" as a graphical interpretation of the protégées' continual growth process.	148
8.4	The "growth curve" as a graphical interpretation of the protégées' perception of performance in the four domains of concern across the seven growth points.	148

Tables

1.1	Number of mentors that have taken the MPI from 2009–2019 (n = 1,950).	16
1.2	Number of mentors within each of the nine grid outcomes.	17
2.1	Marks for PPATS first year peer tutored students and control group.	35
2.2	Academic confidence sub-scale scores for PPATS first year peer tutored students and control group at end of semester controlling for pre-test scores.	36
2.3	First year students' perceptions of the most useful aspects of PPATS.	37
2.4	Pre (Week 1) and post-test (Week 12) scores on all measures for PPATS peer tutors.	38
2.5	Peer tutors' perceptions of the most useful aspects of participation in PPATS.	39

FIGURES AND TABLES

3.1 Guiding principles for developmental feedback. 54
4.1 Responses to the survey question concerning content in teacher mentor professional learning. 80
6.1 Unexpected responses ("Big Foot" model eliciting activity). 111
6.2 Unexpected responses ("Lighthouse" modelling activity). 112
8.1 The growth table showing the growth perceptions of the protégée (J stands for Josephine and C for Ching). 147

Notes on Contributors

Veysel Akçacin
is an assistant professor of mathematics education in the Uşak University, Turkey. He has worked as a coordinator, expert, and trainer in projects supported by various public institutions in Turkey. He has lectured in in-service teacher training and professional development workshops supported by the Ministry of National Education, District Governorates, and Universities in Turkey. His research interests include technology integration in mathematics education, mathematical modeling, mathematics teacher education, socio-cultural factors in the teaching of mathematics (e.g., mathematical thinking styles, values), international comparative studies, and application of advanced statistical techniques in mathematics education.

Anastasios (Tasos) Barkatsas
is a Senior Academic in Mathematics, Statistics and STEM Education and a Quantitative Data Analyst at the School of Education, RMIT University, Australia and has published more than 130 refereed journal and conference research papers, chapters and books and has been a Chief Investigator and Quantitative Research Analyst in a series of competitive grants in Australia and Europe. Tasos is an active researcher and has been the recipient of more than $3M in competitive national and international research grants in the scholarship of Mathematics and STEM learning and teaching as well as multivariate data analysis. Tasos is a Professorial Research Fellow of the Society of Educational Evaluation of Greece and the Series Editor of the Brill | Sense Series 'Global Education in the 21st Century' (this book is Volume 4 of the Series), an Editorial Board member in a number of international research journals and a reviewer in numerous international research journals and conferences.

Tania Broadley
is currently Interim Pro-Vice Chancellor, Design & Social Context and Vice President of RMIT University, Australia. The College consists of 9 schools, 28,000 students and 1100 staff. The College activities reach across three campuses in Victoria and five international locations. Tania's academic background is grounded in Education with research concentrated in the field of teacher education, curriculum, educational technologies, learning spaces, and academic professional development. Her previous leadership roles include Associate Dean (L&T) of QUT's Faculty of Education, one of the largest education faculties in Australia, and Academic Lead of the Curtin Learning Institute re-

sponsible for strategic leadership of academic development, teaching quality and learning space design across Curtin University.

Andrea Chester

is Dean of the School of Education at RMIT University. A passionate and committed educator, Andrea has 25+ years' experience in tertiary education. Andrea brings a background in psychology education and practice to her work as a leader and educator, focusing on the importance of relationships in all she does. Andrea's research focuses on how partnerships can improve learning – partnerships between students, between staff, and between students and staff. Andrea is a Principal Fellow of the Higher Education Academy.

Angela Clarke

is a tertiary teaching specialist, educational scholar and creativity advocate who provides academic leadership on research and teaching in creative disciplines at RMIT University. She has published work on creativity, embodiment, fine art education, professional learning, educational change management, motherhood, and performance philosophy. Most recently she is one of two founding members of a social enterprise called Live Particle that provides live and digital embodied educational experiences to adult learners in multiple settings.

Anthony Clarke

is a Professor at the University of British Columbia (UBC). Prior to UBC he spent 12 years as a classroom teacher in Australia. His two main research interests are: (1) understanding and supporting classroom teachers who act as mentors to teacher candidates on practicum; and (2) conceptualising and promoting teacher inquiry at all levels of the educational system.

Yüksel Dede

is a Professor at the Department of Mathematics Education, Gazi University, Turkey. He worked at Berlin Freie University in Germany with Alexander von Humboldt (AvH) Scholarship and Scientific and Technological Research Council of Turkey (TUBITAK) scholarship respectively. He has worked as a director, expert or consultant in projects supported by various public institutions in Turkey (TUBITAK, Governorships, District Governorates, Provincial Directorates of National Education) and abroad (AvH-Germany, Monash University, Australia). Also he is on the board of editors and editors in many refereed national and international journals. There are numerous articles, book chapters, translation book chapters and conference proceedings published nationally and internationally. His research interests include teaching of mathematics concepts (e.g. algebra teaching), teacher education (mathematics), affective domain in mathematics education (values, motivation, beliefs, etc.), mathematical modeling, international comparative studies, research methods and application of advanced statistical techniques in mathematics education.

Mikhail Gradovski
was born in the Soviet Union. After graduation from the Norwegian University of Science and Technology as doctor rerum politicarum in 2008, Mikhail Gradovski participated in research projects on doctoral supervision, professional supervision, use of dialogue in education, and mental skill development. As a teaching practitioner he is using a dialogical approach based on an understanding both teacher and learner as partners with equal rights to make judgements on what is relevant, important and true.

Kathy Jordan
has been a teacher, teacher educator and researcher for over thirty years. She has a range of research interests including educational technologies in school education, teacher use of ICT, the sociology of ICT, literacy and its teaching, teacher education and professional experience. She has published widely in these fields and presented at numerous national and international conferences. Kathy has led research projects around supporting beginning teachers face the challenges of being new to the profession, and encouraging systemic change in initial teacher education around ICT. Currently, she is leading a research project around partnerships with schools to improve the classroom readiness of graduates.

Gürcan Kaya
is a faculty member at the Department of Mathematics Education in Burdur Mehmet Akif Ersoy University, Turkey. He has attended as an expert, and trainer in University-supported Scientific Research Projects and Scientific and Technological Research Council of Turkey supported projects. He has taught various courses about mathematics and mathematics education. His research interests include affective domain in mathematics education (e.g., values, and beliefs), using technology in mathematics education, mathematical modelling, teacher education, cultural and cross-cultural studies and the use of advanced statistical methods.

Huk Yuen Law
is an Adjunct Assistant Professor at The Chinese University of Hong Kong (CUHK). He obtained his PhD in mathematics education from University

of East Anglia. Dr. Law taught secondary school mathematics for 23 years. Then, he taught mathematics pedagogy courses for both pre-service and in-service teachers, and also taught action research for post-graduate as well as undergraduate education students at CUHK. His research interests include mathematics teacher education, action research in education, mentoring in education, communication in the teaching and learning of mathematics, and values in mathematics education.

Darren Lingley
is Professor of Intercultural Communication and Comparative Culture in the Faculty of Humanities and Social Sciences at Kochi University, Japan. Primary research interests include analysis and assessment of spoken language and intercultural pragmatics. His research explores the concept of 'authenticity' in ELT, and how language teachers pedagogically mediate authentic texts, materials, and experiential learning. Darren also convenes international fieldwork courses on language education and indigenous culture in Australia and Canada. He is the 2016 recipient of the TESOL International Association's Virginia French Allen Award for scholarship and service.

Kathy Littlewood
is a serial teacher, early career researcher, writer and learner who has been fortunate to work across many educational sectors including secondary schools, vocational training and higher education. Most recently, she has been working in the School of Education at RMIT University, as the Program Manager and a lecturer in the Master of Teaching Practice (Primary and Secondary) programs. Kathy's wide range of experiences in the field has allowed her to see the application of mentoring practices first-hand in different contexts. Her current role working with mature age pre-service teachers has afforded insight into the challenges of mentoring this group of learners, both in university and school environments.

Tricia McLaughlin
is an Associate Professor, School of Education, RMIT University, Australia. Tricia is a nationally recognised scholar in the area of lifelong learning and pathways. She has extensive experience in the development of lifelong learning principles and their application in workplaces, educational settings and schools. Tricia is an active researcher and has been the recipient of almost $3M in competitive national research grants in the scholarship of learning and teaching and related areas. She has received a number of university and national teaching awards. Her research publications, including six books, span both her discipline of construction and the practice of learning and teaching.

Tricia is particularly interested in the delivery of learning and most recently has explored the significance of 21st century skills and STEM in changing educational landscapes. Prior to her role in academia, Tricia was employed by the Parliament of Victoria as Executive Officer and consultant to the Economic Development Committee of Victoria. She was the executive officer for the Parliamentary Inquiry into the Building Industry and was consultant to the Minister during the Security of Payments Public Hearings. She has worked in the Australian construction industry and held positions on the Industry Skills Council and industrial associations for many years. Tricia was also employed for a number of years as an advisor to the Federal Minister for Industrial Relations.

Juanjo Mena
is an Associate Professor in the Department of Education at the University of Salamanca (USAL, Spain). He completed his Master degree (with honors) in the Department of Developmental & Educational Psychology in 2004. He obtained his PhD with distinction and special mention of "European Doctor" in 2007. Now he is Treasurer and National Representative of the ISATT. His research focuses on Teaching Practice, Teacher Education, Mentoring, Teacher Development and ICT. He has been a visiting scholar in a number of universities in The Netherlands, Canada, Australia, USA, Finland or Mexico. He also spent 5 years as a classroom teacher before joining USAL as full time professor. At the moment he is an affiliate professor at the University of British Columbia (Canada) and research collaborator at the Kazan Federal University (Russia).

Peter Saunders
is a clinical psychologist and lecturer at the Australian College of Applied Psychology. Peter has over 10 years of experience teaching psychology to individuals within the higher education sector. His current research interests include mentoring, social anxiety and self-presentation online.

Naomi Wilks-Smith
is a Lecturer in the School of Education at RMIT University in Melbourne, Australia. With an extensive career as an educator, she is particularly passionate about language education. Naomi speaks Japanese, has established a partner university and schools in Japan and has led university student global experiences between Australia and Japan. Her research interests include language teaching methodology, bilingualism, second language output, educational technology for language learning, and learning from global experiences. Naomi is also the Co-Founder and Co-Director of EdTech Trends, an educa-

tional technology business, which has developed an innovative app for languages called Voice Story.

Dallas Wingrove
is an Academic Developer working in the College of Design and Social Context at RMIT University in Melbourne, Australia. She has accumulated 20 years experience in higher education providing learning and teaching leadership for professional learning about teaching to deliver quality enhancement. She is currently undertaking a PhD which theorises and advances knowledge of how to foster scholarly professional learning in tertiary teaching through developmental peer observation of teaching. This research contributes to knowledge of how peer observation as praxis can foster development and quality in contemporary tertiary educational practice.

Sophia Xenos
is Associate Professor at RMIT University, Australia, and an experienced academic, clinical educator, and clinical psychologist with extensive experience in teaching employability skills, peer mentoring and building sustainable models of education to empower students of all ages. Her passion for facilitating deeper understanding for both learners and teachers of how students develop their professional identities during their university studies has been the key impetus for the various evidence-based initiatives she has led. Some of these initiatives include the introduction of an evidence-based peer mentoring model, an authentic assessment and reflective practice framework and the introduction and evaluation of online WIL-based assessments.

Prologue

Tasos Barkatsas and Tricia McLaughlin

This exciting addition to scholarly practice, *Championing Cutting-Edge 21st Century Mentoring and Learning Models and Approaches* showcases a range of invited national and international authors who bring together their expertise, knowledge and previous studies to this edition. It is the fourth book in the series "Global Education in the 21st Century" and focuses upon mentoring in education.

The concept of mentoring is not new – it is increasingly recognised as a key strategy in staff development and training across many industries (Peiser et al., 2018). Educators know that mentoring occurs between peers, between pre-service and in-service teachers, between school leaders and teaching staff and between academics and students on a daily basis – sometimes formal, sometimes informally. This mentoring concept of individualised professional support for teachers at various stages of their careers has been much practised and refined to suit different contexts and stages of learning for many years across many diverse settings. However, whilst the word "mentoring" is well known, it is often perceived in different ways by different people. For example Earl and Timperley (2008) talk of the teaching and learning process; Kochan and Pascarelli (2012) talk of the cultural implications of mentoring, whilst others think of mentoring as a coaching process and even as a nurturing, growing and self-actualisation process (Roberts, 2000).

Maynard and Furlong (1995) note that the way in which mentoring is conceptualised depends upon views about learning and learning to teach. They suggest that mentoring can be conceptualised as either a behaviourist approach or a reflective one. A behaviourist approach is often based upon a competency view of mentoring – the mentee may simply adopt the strategies or ideas of the mentor, without understanding the philosophical or conceptual justification for such a strategy. As Peiser et al. (2018) have identified, this may mean the adoption and ongoing use of strategies that lack underpinning beginning teacher knowledge. At the other end of the mentoring scale is a reflective approach which encourages the development of knowledge and skills that are underpinned by a deeper understanding rather than just practical teaching skills.

Most importantly, previous research has established that the adoption of one approach to educational mentoring is unlikely to be effective. For example Harrison et al. (2006) discovered that mentees rated role-modelling behaviour, interpersonal skills and the ability to promote reflective discussion as paramount, whilst Crutcher and Naseem (2016) have noted that good mentoring involves critical reflection, collaborative relationships and knowledge about individuals' needs. Of even more diverse approaches and outcomes, Izadinia (2015) contends that it is the mentor's role to help mentees to develop their teacher voice and identity, further suggesting that humanistic and educative orientations should operate in parallel in the case of mentoring.

There is also wide variation in mentoring practices, most of which are influenced by the multiple mentoring purposes, contrasting settings, and the views of individuals. Brondyk and Searby (2013), for example, have strongly indicated that different professional contexts with their own unique characteristics influence practices in mentoring. Mentoring practices are shaped by complex dynamic relationships within perceived structures – especially when educational contexts are considered.

To harness these diverse perspectives and to ensure that some of the most recent research around the complex themes of mentoring in education is disseminated, a number of authors were invited to submit chapters for inclusion in this volume. All chapter submissions underwent a double-blind peer review process, and in each chapter, the authors have demonstrated contextual understandings and insights into the many avenues of mentoring in education.

Juano Mena and Anthony Clarke in Chapter 1, explore the dimensions of motivators for and challenges to mentoring; separate motivators; and a mentoring profile grid. Using the Mentoring Profile Inventory (MPI) they have distinguished four roles that encompass the work of cooperating teachers within the context of mentoring: partner, advocate, nurturer, and facilitator. The grid provides a useful tool that gives insight into how mentoring could be applied and measured across diverse contexts. The use of the grid to explore mentoring relationships will allow teacher educators to provide appropriate professional development that better meets the needs of mentors according to how the mentors conceptualise their own roles within the practicum setting. This will enable greater exploration of how and why mentors conceptualise their work – which in turn will benefit both the mentor and the mentee.

Müller (2009) has highlighted the role of mentoring in higher education, noting that mentors act as "linchpins" between the domains of higher education (HE) and the workplace. In such contexts mentors then can assist students in the application of what Eraut (2014) labels "codified knowledge" – that is knowledge learnt in the university in particular situations. Saunders, Chester and Xenos, in Chapter 2, give further insights into this use of mentors in higher education and explore the use of student peer tutoring as an attempt to improve learning, satisfaction and retention of first year students at university. Through the use of an embedded model in first year tutorials in a small sample of discipline specific students, they indicate positive outcomes for both mentors and mentees. Their approach illustrates successful intentional curriculum design and transition pedagogy and has significant propositions for future development.

In a similar way, the work of Wingrove and Clarke, in Chapter 3, presents a partnerships model for tertiary educators designed to foster peer to peer feedback on educational practice through an iterative cycle of teaching observations, feedback and critical reflection. Formative peer feedback on teaching partnerships have been shown to provide significant and rich opportunities for improvement in the quality of teaching practice (Daniels, 2017) and their presented model draws upon many years of implementation and development experience, the efficacy of which is demonstrated, in part, through the strong level of voluntary uptake by educators from their own and other universities. The implementation of a peer partnerships model utilising peer feedback has not been without challenges and they present their work against a backdrop of higher education performance metrics which have grown in consistency and discourse in recent years. The authors boldly present their model as a contribution towards mitigating the risks that arise when peer feedback on teaching partnerships are colonised by performance and quality measurement agendas. Such work gives prominence to developmental peer feedback on teaching as a pedagogic practice to enhance and evidence development and quality in tertiary teaching.

Huk Yuen Law in "Theorising Mentoring for the 21st Century Teaching and Learning", explores the way mentoring can be theorised by nurturing prospective teachers' professional growth through action research. He explores the co-construction of the discourse between the mentor and the protégées in the form of imagined dialogue contributes to the theorisation of mentoring. Using the growth model, he concludes that mentoring can be interpreted as encountering, as experiencing, and as relating.

Mentoring has value in terms of supporting student teachers to explicitly reflect on aspects of their developing pedagogy by seeking advice from teachers of a similar experience as themselves as well as from more experienced colleagues. It is therefore timely that Littlewood and Jordan in Chapter 4, select to report upon on a small sample of practicing classroom teacher mentors in Victorian schools who participated in a survey about motivators and challenges when mentoring pre-service teachers on practicum. Their results consider the role of the adult learner in professional learning along with some insights into the types of professional learning these teachers preferred and the sort of information they felt would be important, such as relationships and communication, particularly about providing feedback and having difficult conversations. Their work is pertinent and endorses many of the findings of recent works, in particular Nielson, Mena, Clarke, O'Shea, Hoban, and Collins (2017). This growing body of evidence illustrates the needs for professional learning for mentors as well as mentees.

Yuksel, Veysel and Gurcan further explore the mentoring of pre-service teachers in the area of mathematics education in Turkey. This, along with Jordan and Littlewood in Chapter 7, who explore mentoring in technical schools in Victoria, Australia, provides valuable international comparisons of mentoring challenges and understandings across disciplines, settings and educational systems. Such insights value-add to our knowledge and provide contributions that can lead to international best-practice adoptions.

McNamara et al. (2014) highlighted how high-quality professional learning requires a dialogue and symbiotic relationship between practical and theoretical knowledge. They note that professional learning, such as that occurring in a mentoring relationship requires "integrated ways of conceptualising and articulating and needs support from colleagues" (p. 296). Mikhail Gradovski, from the University of Stavanger, Norway, investigates the evaluation of a PhD supervising course trialled in three Norwegian universities. He discusses the course organisation and learning activities as well as the opportunities it provided for the development of participants' professional agency as doctoral supervisors. His critique is based on the results of the thematic analysis, and by employing the concepts of professional agency and authorial agency, he provides insights into a rare relationship not frequently explored.

Mentors may also help pre-service professionals to make sense of and reconcile contradictions between the different learning communities in which they are situated (Engeström, 2001). In the final chapter of this book, Wilkes-Smith and Lingley report on reciprocal teacher-guided global experiences, which are operationalised in the form of international education practicum and field study courses between Australia and Japan. Focus is placed upon mentoring students through the research-practice nexus as it relates to language education and intercultural understanding. The project sought pre-service teacher participants' reflections on personal and professional learning whilst undertaking a global experience. Their findings highlight the transformative experiences that the students had, and the important role that mentors played in mediating their overall learning prior to and during the global experience.

We hope you will find this book both informative and challenging.

References

Brondyk, S., & Searby, L. (2013). Best practices in mentoring: Complexities and possibilities. *International Journal of Mentoring and Coaching in Education, 2*(3), 189.

Crutcher, P. A., & Naseem, S. (2016). Cheerleading and cynicism of effective mentoring in current empirical research. *Educational Review, 68*(1), 40–55.

Daniels, M. N., Maynard, S., Porter, I., Kincaid, H., Jain, D., & Aslam, N. (2017). Career interest and perceptions of nephrology: A repeated cross-sectional survey of internal medicine residents. *PLoS One, 12*(2).

Earl, L. M., & Timperley, H. (Eds.). (2008). *Professional learning conversations: Challenges in using evidence for improvement* (Vol. 1). Springer Science & Business Media.

Engeström, Y. (2001). Expansive learning at work: Toward an activity theoretical reconceptualization. *Journal of Education and Work, 14*(1), 133–156.

Eraut, M. (2014). Developing knowledge for qualified professionals. In M. Eraut (Ed.), *Workplace learning in teacher education* (pp. 47–72). Springer.

Harrison, K. C., Comeaux, E., & Plecha, M. (2006). Faculty and male football and basketball players on university campuses: An empirical investigation of the "intellectual" as mentor to the student athlete. *Research Quarterly for Exercise and Sport, 77*(2), 277–284.

Izadinia, M. (2015). A closer look at the role of mentor teachers in shaping preservice teachers' professional identity. *Teaching and Teacher Education, 52*, 1–10.

Kochan, F., & Pascarelli, J. T. (2012). Perspectives on culture and mentoring in the global age. In F. Kochan & J. T. Pascarelli (Eds.), *The Sage handbook of mentoring and coaching in education.* (pp. 184–198). Sage.

Maynard T., & Furlong J., (1995). Learning to teach and models of mentoring. In T. Kerry & S. Mayes (Eds.), *Issues in mentoring* (pp. 10–24). Psychology Press.

McNamara, M. S., Fealy, G. M., Casey, M., O'Connor, T., Patton, D., Doyle, L., & Quinlan, C. (2014). Mentoring, coaching and action learning: Interventions in a national clinical leadership development programme. *Journal of Clinical Nursing, 23*(17–18), 2533–2541.

Muller, C. B. (2009). Understanding e-mentoring in organizations. *Adult Learning, 20*(1–2), 25–30.

Nielsen, W., Mena, J., Clarke, A., O'Shea, S., Hoban, G., & Collins, J. (2017). Australia's supervising teachers: Motivators and challenges to inform professional learning. *Asia-Pacific Journal of Teacher Education, 45*(4), 346–368.

Peiser, G., Ambrose, J., Burke, B., & Davenport, J. (2018). The role of the mentor in professional knowledge development across four professions. *International Journal of Mentoring and Coaching in Education, 7*(1), 2–18.

Roberts, A. (2000). Mentoring revisited: A phenomenological reading of the literature. *Mentoring and Tutoring, 8*(2), 145–170.

CHAPTER 1

The Mentoring Profile Inventory Grid: Thinking Differently about Classroom Teachers Who Work with Pre-Service Teachers in Practicum Settings

Juanjo Mena and Anthony Clarke

Abstract

Mentoring is widely acknowledged as an important determinant in the type of support given to pre-service teachers' prior to their entry to the profession. Mentors, as cooperating teachers, provide valuable *in situ* opportunities for professional learning in the practicum settings.

The present study articulates four mentoring roles (or profiles) that arise from research using the 62-item Mentoring Profile Inventory (MPI). The MPI automatically provides a report to the user divided into three sections: (1) dimensions of motivators for and challenges to mentoring; (2) separate motivator and challenge balance charts; and (3) a mentoring profile grid. The grid, which is the focus of this paper, distinguishes four roles that encompass the work of cooperating teachers within the context of mentoring: partner, advocate, nurturer, and facilitator. The grid is a graphic representation of the emphasis that a mentor places on each of the four roles as part of their mentoring practice. These four roles emerged from the analysis of the MPI responses from 1950 cooperating teachers from fifteen countries.

This research adds new insights to the existing body of research on mentoring by articulating an overall profile based on the four roles for a mentor where each role is directly induced from empirical response patterns of mentors (not deduced from an a priori framework). This research may enable teacher educators to better support the professional development of mentors in practicum settings according to an individual mentor's profile or an aggregate profile for a cohort of mentors

Keywords

school mentoring – teachers' supervision – practicum – mentoring roles

1 Introduction

Teacher mentoring is widely considered as the support given by expert teachers (often referred to as cooperating teachers) who invite pre-service teachers from universities into their classroom to undertake their practicum (Malderez, 2009; Hudson & Hudson, 2018). Mentoring has traditionally been promoted as a meaningful way for pre-service teachers to learn about the teaching profession because it provides them with access to the required knowledge and skills to face the complexities of practice (Hobson, Ashby, Malderez, & Tomlinson, 2009). Mentors are also referred to as school advisors, practicum supervisors, or school-based teacher educators (Zeichner, 2010). School-based teacher educators interpret their work from a more holistic viewpoint as mentors who ground any action both theoretically and empirically within the practicum context.

However, the transition between on-campus coursework to the reality of the practicum classroom in pre-service teacher education (and then later in their role as a practicing professional) is always challenging (Kokikokko et al., 2017). In fact, the number of teachers leaving the profession in the early years of their career continues to grow (Ingersoll & Strong, 2011) suggesting that perhaps more could be done to better induct beginning teachers into the profession, especially from a mentoring perspective. One dimension involves the ways in which mentors are prepared for, understand their work with, and act as school-based teacher educators for pre-service teachers.

Young et al. (2006) suggest that understanding and providing the infrastructure for mentoring requires multiple theoretical lenses. For example, traditional models on mentoring place a single pre-service teacher with a single mentor teacher (Grimmett, Forgasz, Williams, & White, 2018) which often follows an apprenticeship model. However, in recent years finding sufficient school-based professional placements, as well as ensuring high quality learning experiences, has become increasingly difficult (Talbot, Denny, & Henderson, 2018). For this reason, some teacher education providers have proposed a community or cohort approach in which a group of pre-service teachers are assigned to single mentor as one alternative model. In this sense relational mentoring functions by using communal norms (Forgasz, 2016; Ragins & Verbos, 2007) including "… relational processes (e.g., reciprocity, mutual learning, and growth), interpersonal attributes (e.g., sensitivity, empathy, compassion, empowerment), and future-oriented developmental networks (e.g., life satisfaction, balance, integration of conflicting roles" (Li, Malin, & Hackman, 2018, p. 5).

Other perspectives on mentoring seek to extend our understanding of the unique role that regular classroom teachers undertake when mentoring pre-service teachers. For example, Orland-Barak (2014) states that mentoring revolves around three key dimensions: (1) behaviors and performance; (2) identity (which includes reasoning, beliefs and roles); and (3) context, which includes culture and discourse. In a similar vein, Mena and Clarke's (2015) review of the literature suggests that mentoring can also be conceptualized around three related components for learning a professional practice; specifically, (1) developing one's professional identity as a mentor (2) in a professional development framework, and (3) within the immediacy of the practice setting.

However, it is not always easy to conceptualize and group the actions of mentoring by types or patterns since much information is needed to capture the various ways acting. For this reason, there is a need to create tools or metrics that can empirically point to particular mentoring roles in relatively efficient and easily administered ways that allow teacher educators to better adjust professional preparation, engagement, and action accordingly.

This chapter focuses on Orland-Barak's (2014) identity dimension as it explores particular roles that cooperating teachers might adopt when supervising pre-service teachers. Importantly, mentor teachers' field experiences with pre-service teachers during the practicum influence the ways in which they perceive their profession and frame their conceptualisations of practice which ultimately leads to constructing and reconstructing their professional identities (Chu, 2019) over time. How and in what ways those identities are developed are central to understanding mentoring as a professional practice in its own right within teacher education.

Varghese, Morgan, Johnson, and Johnson (2005) view mentor identity as a dialogic construction that occurs within the course of conversations with others. They coined the term of "identity-in-discourse" as a way in which individuals think, talk and act with others. Not surprisingly, mentor presence in practicum classrooms affects the ways in which students in the classroom and pre-service teachers interact with one another (Marciano et al., 2019). However, all too often pre-service teachers attempt to unproblematically imitate their mentor's routines and procedures (Rozelle & Wilson, 2012) without fully understanding the complexities involved. In this regard, Jonson (2002) suggests four mentoring tasks that assist pre-service teachers develop as professionals: (a) career management; (b) ensuring pre-service teachers acquire the requisite knowledge and skills; (c) promoting self-reliance; and (d) providing support for learning. Delving into these roles, Fairstein (2016) extends the list to five requirements for effective mentoring: (a) provision of knowledge and experience in teaching; (b) guidance and counseling; (c) attending to the social needs of novice teachers (i.e., relational dimensions); (d) emotional support; and (e) explicit instruction in what 'being a professional' entails. The mentor's role may not be an easy task since advisors are usually required to meet the pre-service teachers on a daily basis (depending on the program), regularly observe their teaching, assist them pedagogically, support them emotionally, and provide timely and constructive feedback throughout the practicum. An undertaking that is not for the faint-hearted!

2 Objective

In furthering our understanding of mentoring, this chapter presents empirical research that aims to describe and justify that addition of a mentoring profile grid to the existing Mentoring Profile Inventory (MPI) which was first developed in 2009 (Clarke, Collins, Triggs, & Nielsen, 2012). The new grid represents four mentoring roles that embody the work of mentors and is based on a international database of mentors' responses to the MPI collected 2010 and 2018.

3 The Mentoring Profile Inventory (MPI)

The MPI is free, online, and available in multiple languages.[1] The MPI is a fully validated survey instrument that is designed to help mentors think about their various roles within the context of mentoring pre-service teachers on practicum. Mentors respond to 62-Likert type items that ask them about various dimensions of their work with pre-service teachers. The MPI also has an additional 13 demographic questions (all fixed-responses). A final item on the survey asks mentors to respond to the following open-ended question: What single piece of advice would you offer to other teachers who wish to work with pre-service teachers on practicum? A mentor's responses to the 62 Likert type items results in an individual Mentoring Profile Inventory report (see Figure 1.1). Responses are automatically grouped into two mentoring categories: motivators (what mentors find attractive and appealing about their profession); and challenges (what mentors find difficult or problematic to deal with). What motivates mentors can be related to personal aspects or benefits accruing to pre-service teachers as a result of their mentoring rendered as eight motivator scales. Challenges can arise from interpersonal problems (e.g., lack of communication and communication) or systemic challenges (e.g., lack of clear policies, guidelines, or procedures) rendered as six challenge scales. These scales are, in turn, represented in the MPI report as, motivator (self or other) and challenge (interpersonal or systemic) balance charts respectively. The motivator and balance charts then lead to four roles that constitute one's mentorship practice:

partner, advocate, facilitator, and nurturer. We admit that there may be other roles but argue that our research indicates that these four are particularly pertinent within pre-service teacher practicum mentoring contexts. A more detailed account of the Mentoring Profile Inventory report is provided below.

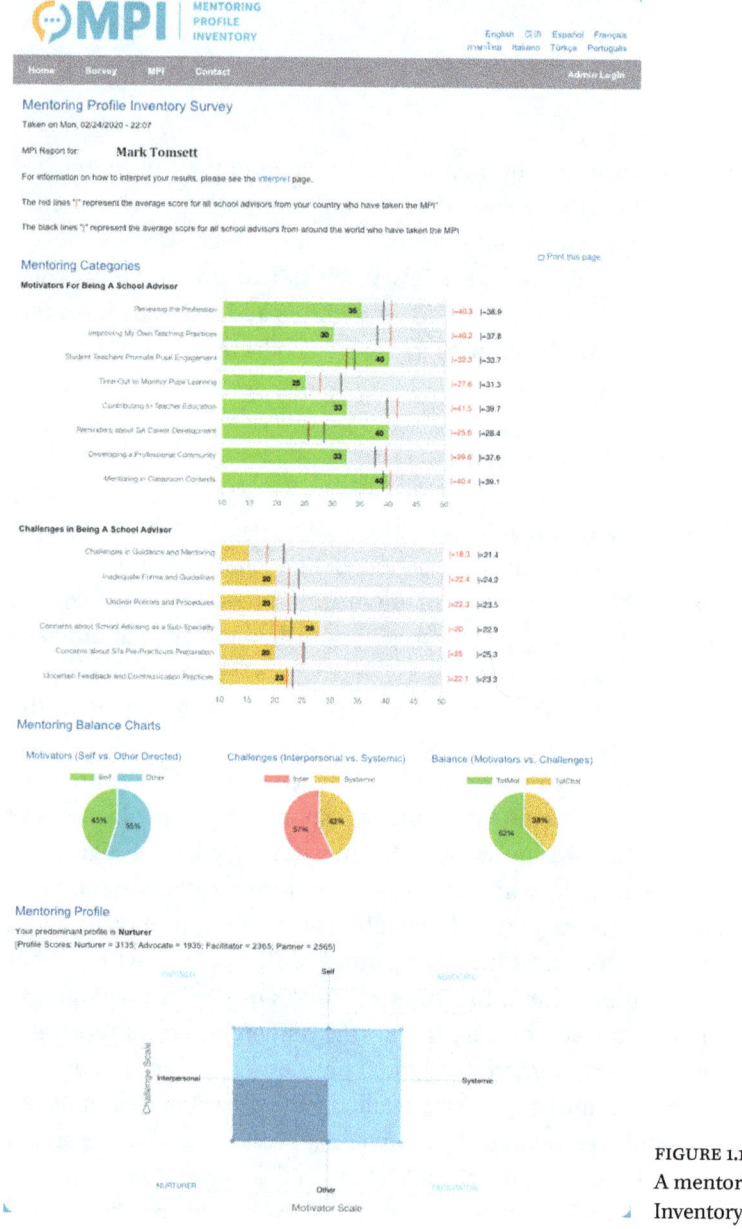

FIGURE 1.1
A mentoring Profile Inventory Report

3.1 The Eight MPI Motivator Scales

The mentors' responses to the 62 items are clustered into 14 scales that represent two 'categories of description': Motivators (i.e., what stimulates mentors in their work with pre-service teachers) and Challenges (i.e., what do mentors perceive as problematic about that work) where higher scores indicate higher levels of motivation or challenge (see Figure 1.1, Mentoring Categories). The definition of the eight motivator scales and six challenges scales is provided below.

Motivator #1: Renewing the Profession. Some mentors declare that they play an important a role by developing the next generation of teachers. They believe that supervising is necessary to renew and replenish the profession of teaching and who recognize that working with pre-service teachers is important to education and to society in general.

Motivator #2: Improving my own Teaching Practices. The mentors see that practicum advising helps to refine their own teaching practices and skills, keep them current with new ideas, and reward them by explaining to their pre-service teachers why they teach the way they do.

Motivator #3: Pre-service teachers Promote Pupil Engagement. Many mentors state that pre-service teachers provide 'new blood' in the classroom, thereby prompting pupil learning, enhancing pupil interest and classroom dynamics, and assisting in addressing pupil diversity in the classroom.

Motivator #4: 'Time-Out' to Monitor Pupil Learning. Mentoring allows classroom teachers to pause and reflect or to have a 'breather' to think and observe the classroom while they work, for example, one-on-one with pupils or while monitoring the classroom learning needs.

Motivator #5: Contributing to Teacher Education. Mentors acknowledge that working with pre-service teachers 'is the right thing to do', is a part of their professional responsibility, and contributes to their own professional development.

Motivator #6: Reminders about Career Development. Mentors acknowledge that school advising is a form of educational leadership. At the same time these advisors are conscious of the dangers of self-aggrandizement and report that working with pre-service teachers provides a window into their own practice as both a classroom teacher and a mentor to others.

Motivator #7: Developing a Professional Community. Mentors find satisfying to work with other adults and to promote collaboration, collegiality and community. They recognize that supervising develops professional relationships with future colleagues and they enjoy the collective learning that arises in student teaching contexts.

Motivator #8: Mentoring Practices in Classroom Contexts. Mentors enjoy helping pre-service teachers connect theory to practice, to help them work through day-to-day issues, to learn and develop, and to understand that there are many 'right ways to teach' in the immediacy of the action setting.

3.2 The Six MPI Challenge Scales

Challenge #1: Challenges in Guidance and Mentoring. Some mentors experience difficulties in addressing and correcting student teacher misconceptions as they arise, in developing more meaningful relationships with their pre-service teachers, or better articulating the evaluation process to their pre-service teachers.

Challenge #2: Inadequate Forms and Guidelines. Mentors perceive unclear evaluation guidelines to differentiate between pre-service teacher successes and failures, vague protocols for providing feedback to pre-service teachers, an absence of evaluation forms.

Challenge #3: Unclear Policies and Procedures. Mentors believe that there is lack of clarity about the roles and responsibilities of university advisors, unclear feedback mechanisms between university advisors and school mentors, a lack of access to university resources for pre-service teachers who are struggling, or an absence of systematic procedures for selecting and preparing school mentors or University Advisors.

Challenge #4: Concerns about School Advising as a Sub-Specialty. Mentors feel that there is an absence of a common set of expectations among mentors, difficulties maintaining communication among these mentors, from problems helping mentors to resolve their own issues and doubts, or from difficulties involving other supervisors in decision-making about the profession.

Challenge #5: Concerns about pre-service teachers' Pre-Practicum Preparation. Mentors feel that there is an absence of agreement about standard practices for advising pre-service teachers, from scanty information about pre-service teachers' coursework or preparation prior to the practicum to advisory handbooks that provide only limited guidelines, scenarios or examples.

Challenge #6: Uncertain Feedback and Communication Practices. Mentors believe that there is an absence of engagement between school and university administrators to inform mentor teachers how well they are assisting pre-service teachers and insufficient feedback practice from pre-service teachers to report on what is working and what is not within the mentoring setting.

3.3 The Three MPI Balance Charts

Using the motivator and challenge scales, it is possible to generate three summary charts (see Figure 1.1, the three pie charts midway through the report).

The first is a motivator balance chart that represents the degree to which a teacher engages in mentoring for the benefits they accrue themselves from working with a pre-service teachers versus the benefits they offer to others in that role. The second is a challenge balance chart that represents the degree to which the problematic aspects of their work arise from either interpersonal issues versus systemic issues within the context of their mentoring. The third is an overall balance chart representing the extent to which mentors are motivated versus challenged in their work with beginning teachers.

3.4 The MPI Grid

Finally, the most recent addition to the MPI report, which is the focus of this chapter, is the mentoring profile grid (Figure 1.1, the final part of the report). The grid uses two axes (motivator and challenge) to differentiate between four possible mentor roles: advocate, facilitator, nurturer, and partner (see example, Figure 1.2).

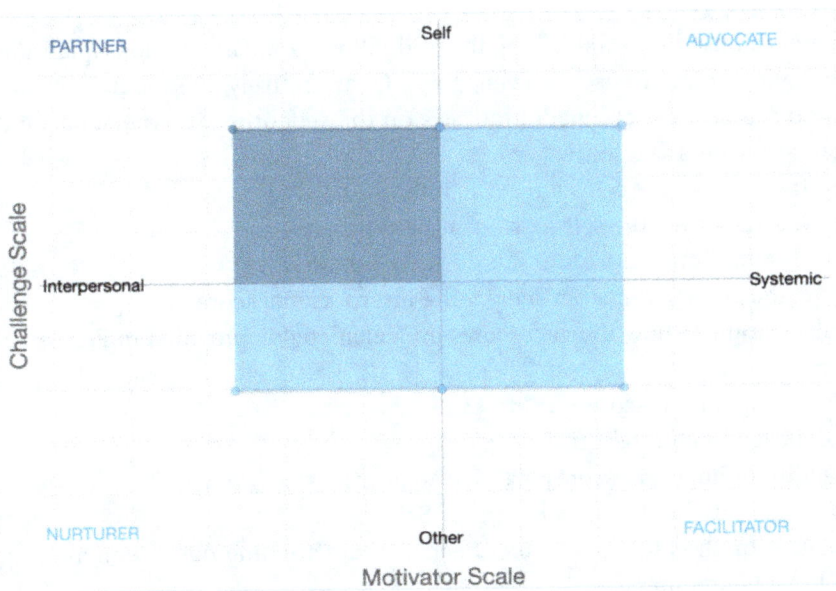

FIGURE 1.2   The mentoring profile grid. Four quadrants: Quadrant #1: Partner; Quadrant #2: Advocate; Quadrant #3: Facilitator; Quadrant #4: Nurturer

The definition of the four roles is provided below:

Quadrant #1: *Partner mentoring role* (the interaction between the self and interpersonal dimensions): Mentors are focused on improving their mentoring practice so that they are well prepared to facilitate pre-service teacher learning within the context of the practicum setting;

Quadrant # 2: *Advocate mentoring role* (the interaction between the self and systemic dimensions): Mentors recognize the importance of 'giving voice' to the importance of the pre-service teacher learning within the context of practicum settings.

Quadrant #3: *Facilitator mentoring role* (the interaction between the other and systemic): Mentors are attentive and respond accordingly to pre-service teachers' professional needs by providing the necessary scaffolding within the context of practicum settings.

Quadrant #4: *Nurturer mentoring role* (the interaction between the other and interpersonal dimensions): Mentors view the personal and relational dimensions of pre-service teacher learning as central to the students' professional development within the context of practicum settings.

4 Methodology

The method used for establishing the grid follows a mixed method (quantitative-qualitative) analysis (Creswell, 2013). Quantitatively, the mentoring profile grid scores for each quadrant draws on the self, other, interpersonal, and systematic scores as follows:
– Partner score = the self score × the interpersonal score
– Advocate score = the self score × the systemic score
– Facilitator score = the other score × the systemic score
– Nurturer score = the other score × the interpersonal score

An illustration of how the grid scores are calculated is provided in Figure 1.2, where:
– Partner quadrant score = $47^*55 = 2585$
– Advocate quadrant score = $47^*45 = 2115$
– Facilitator quadrant score = $53^*55 = 2951$
– Nurturer quadrant score = $53^*45 = 2385$

Using this method for calculating the grid, there are nine possible mentoring profile grid outcomes:
– 4 single-quadrant grid outcomes (i.e., there is one predominant quadrant): Partner (PRT), Advocate (ADV), Nurturer (NUR), Facilitator (FAC);
– 4 dual-quadrant grid outcomes (i.e., there are two quadrants of equal size): Partner/Advocate; Nurturer/Facilitator; Partner/Nurturer; Advocate/Facilitator (N.B.: given the method for calculating the grid, it is impossible to have diagonally opposite quadrants of equal size); and
– 1 equal-quadrant grid outcome (i.e., all four quadrants are of equal size).

Appendix A provides a visual of four different MPI reports to demonstrate how the variation in the bars and charts results in a variety of grid outcomes. This

THE MENTORING PROFILE INVENTORY GRID

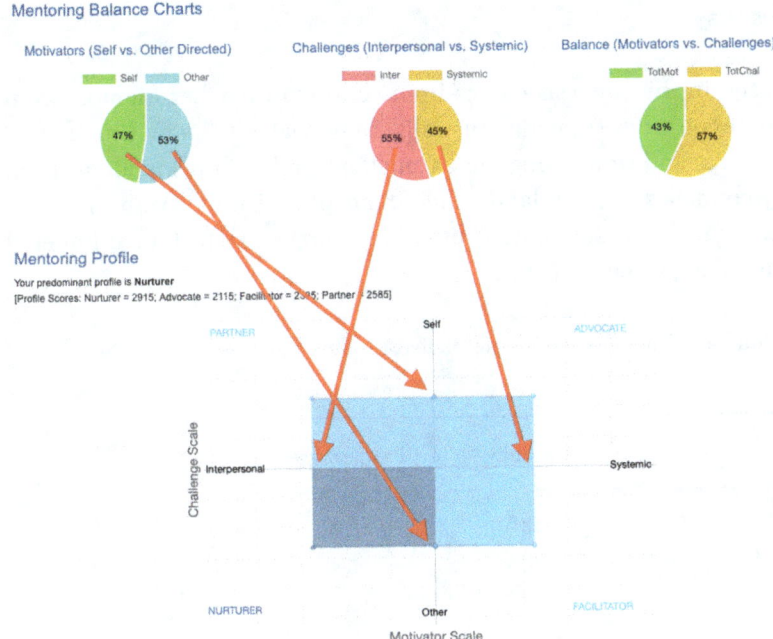

FIGURE 1.3 An illustration of how the grid scores are calculated

method was used to calculate the grid outcomes for all 1950 respondents in this study. This provided the first level of analysis for this study.

While the grid and associated quadrant definitions is intuitively justifiable, of particular interest to this chapter, is the attempt to validate the addition of the grid, and the four roles, to the MPI report. To that end, the second level of analysis was conducted. This was a topic analysis (Strauss & Corbin, 1994) using the mentors' responses to the single open-ended question on the MPI ("What single piece of advice would you offer to other teachers who wish to work with pre-service teachers on practicum?"). This analysis was used to determine if our intuitive construction of the grid and the results from level one were supported by the outcome of the topic analysis.

It is important to note that a limitation of the results reported below is that the degree to which a mentor exhibits each of the four roles is largely based on an arithmetic calculation (drawing on the 62 Likert-type items that constitute the main body of the MPI).

Finally, all those who have completed the MPI have done so voluntarily. This is an important ethical consideration. Thus the data only includes responses from those who have willingly chosen to participate. Further, the authors and administrators of the MPI use pseudonyms at all times in any reports or papers generated from the MPI and deliberately separate names from profiles. At this point in time we regard the grid as a 'work in process.'

5 Results

The data used in this analysis comes from cohorts of teacher mentors from nine different countries (Canada, Australia, New Zealand, Spain, China, USA, Thailand, France and Hong Kong) and a smaller number of respondents from another 15 countries (e.g., Ireland, Chile, Singapore, United Arab Emirates, Austria, Sweden, The Netherlands, United Kingdom, etc.). The total number of respondents is 1,950 (see Table 1.1).

TABLE 1.1 Number of mentors that have taken the MPI from 2009–2019 (n = 1,950)

Country	Frequency	Percentage
Canada	544	16.5
New Zealand	178	5.4
Australia	508	15.4
China	257	7.8
Spain	171	5.2
Thailand	170	5.2
USA	41	1.2
France	31	.9
Hong Kong	30	.9
Ireland	1	.0
Chile	1	.0
Singapore	4	.1
Sweden	1	.0
Netherlands	2	.1
Afghanistan	1	.0
Åland Islands	1	.0
United Kingdom	2	.1
United Arab Emirates	1	.0
Cape Verde	1	.0
Austria	1	.0
Shri Lanka	1	.0
Portugal	1	.0
India	1	.0
Zambia	1	.0

THE MENTORING PROFILE INVENTORY GRID

Five regions are represented in the sample: the Americas (586; 30.05%) Europe (214; 10.97%), Asia (465; 23.84%) and Oceania (686; 35.17%) with a single respondent from Africa (1; 0.51%).

5.1 Mentoring Profiles

An individual MPI grid was generated for all cases (n = 1,950). Table 1.2 shows the number of mentors within each of the nine possible grid outcomes.

TABLE 1.2 Number of mentors within each of the nine grid outcomes

One predominant quadrant				Two equal quadrants				Four equal quadrants	
Partner	Advocate	Nurturer	Facilitator	Partner/Advocate	Nurture/Facilitator	Partner/Nurture	Advocate/Facilitator	Four Quadrant	TOTAL
420	375	275	411	111	96	106	108	48	1950
21.53%	19.23%	14.10%	21.07%	5.69%	4.92%	5.43%	5.53%	2.46%	100%

Single predominant quadrant outcomes account for 1481 (75.9%) respondents. Two-equal quadrant outcomes account for 421 (21.58%) respondents. Four equal quadrant outcomes account for 48 cases (2.46%). Two-equal quadrant outcomes are equally distributed among the profiles. The ranking of single quadrant predominance is as follows: partner (420; 21.53%), facilitator (411; 21.07%), advocate (375; 19.23%) and nurturer (275; 14.1%).

5.2 Open-Ended Question Responses within Profiles

While this analysis is still ongoing given the amount of data collected, the following section provides an initial substantiation of our intuitive construction of the grid and the associated four roles. As noted above, the questionnaire has one open-ended question: "What single piece of advice would you offer to other teachers who wish to work with student teachers on practicum?" From this deliberately broad question, the main utterances from a selection of 40 mentor teachers were selected to verify the four single quadrant roles as defined above.

For example, as per our definition of the partner mentoring role, these mentors reveal that they are more focused on their own role as mentors demonstrating in their responses to the MPI that they want to be current in their knowledge about mentoring (both theoretically and professionally) in order to better respond to teacher candidate learning needs. Examples of partner role open-ended responses include: "Be reflective and ready to learn from people new to the profession" (mentor #571); "Supervising improves your own practice and makes a contribution to the profession" (mentor #638); and "Having a student teacher has helped me refine my beliefs as a teacher. It has provided me with time to work one-on-one with my students. I would definitely work with a student teacher again in the future" (mentor #199). Another mentor whose scores placed them predominantly within this role spoke about the challenging situations regarding his role:

> Being a supervisor or a mentor is a challenge situation. This is because many skills are involved in order to provide practical support to a student teacher or new teacher. I think it is very important to understand student or new teacher's professional and emotional needs in order to help them succeeding and be motivated to be effective teachers. This requires having a clear picture about the mentor responsibilities on supporting and providing practical and effective feedback that may enhance student or new teacher's skills and knowledge to reach their potential. (mentor #121)

In our definition of the *facilitator* role, mentors are more focused on the pre-service teachers than themselves in order to find strategic ways to lead them into a better adaptation to the teaching. They care about their learning needs too as long they fit within the frames of the institution, for example: school facilities, social dynamics, working conditions, etc. Examples of facilitator role open-ended responses include: "Be very clear what is expected of ST in and out of the classroom" (mentor #571); "... make them feel welcome! We must remember how scary walking into our first classroom was and share with them (Mentor#259); and "School Advisors should be very clear of their school and district obligations from the beginning, so the student teacher is aware of how much freedom pre-service teachers will have" (mentor #1029).

As for the *nurturer* role, where mentors feel it is important to attend more to the pre-service teacher needs, the open-ended responses include: "Be patient with a student teacher--they are learning. They are doing something that might be for the first time and like all teachers, need to experience success and disasters like the rest" (mentor #423) and "We need to allow pre-service teachers to learn through their experience and encourage them to develop their own style of teaching. It is too difficult to try to mimic someone else's style if it is not a good fit" (mentor #563).

Finally, within the *advocate* role, more prone to envisage the inconsistencies of the system, school district politics, lack of resources, or school facilities, we found the following declarations (included in full here to capture the essence of their current conceptualisation of the mentor role):

> The Education Department, schools and universities need to work together to create a teaching training course that is relevant and practical. Young graduate teachers should be leaving university with a solid knowledge of educational initiatives and practices. e.g. inquiry learning, thinking, Early Years, middle years, boys education, ICT and especially. (mentor #511)

> The new teachers should forget to have any kind of reward for this task … At least in Spain the mentoring work is totally altruistic, I do not mean that it has to be this way, but it actually is. (mentor #1449)

> I request the educational administration to have pre-service teachers every year, but when working in a rural area, I don't always have someone assigned to my school. I think it is a fundamental phase in terms of future teacher training and I think that having many more hours of practice will be very positive because this experience allows them to better interact with classroom. Besides, it is known that we all learn from committing mistakes. (mentor #1462)

As noted above, these are tentative outcomes based on our initial topical analysis of the open-ended responses. However, they are encouraging in terms of a 'deep dive' into how and in what ways mentors are making sense of their practice and their connection to the grid and the associated role categorisation. All of the comments strengthen the idea that there are some attitudinal and behavioral patterns around the inferred roles which are in consonance with Orland-Barak's (2014) key dimension of mentors' attributes and roles that define supervisory work.

6   Conclusions

This research adds new insights into the existing body of research on pre-service teacher mentoring by exploring mentoring roles that are directly induced from empirical response patterns based on the MPI survey responses. This approach might allow teacher educators to provide appropriate professional development that better meets the needs of mentors according to how the mentors conceptualise their own roles within the practicum setting. Izadinia (2016) states that "… conflicting role expectations, or lack of clarity of such roles, might result in unsuccessful mentoring relationships" (p. 2). Such outcomes are detrimental to the relationship between the mentor teacher and aspiring teacher candidate.

In our study we emphasise that all mentors display aspects of each of the four roles within their overall MPI profile. However, in our analysis there are some roles that are more dominant than other roles suggesting that particular beliefs and practices are more evident that others. For instance, the partner and facilitator roles are the ones that are particularly prevalent among the overall sample of mentors suggesting that being prepared to help pre-service teachers or providing key scaffolding for success in the school settings is particularly important for mentors regardless of their country of origin. Conversely, the nurturer profile has been shown to be the less represented in the overall sample in contrast to some research that indicates that friendliness or emotional support are key components in mentoring new professionals (Beck & Kosnik, 2002). This is something that we hope to address more fully as we move forward with our analysis and continue our work with the MPI. There is clearly a delicate balance between emotional, relational, and professional work in mentoring which relies on the type of connections made between pre-service teachers, mentors, other colleagues, students and staff members within practicum settings (Grimmett et al., 2018).

As we move forward, we are also interested in further exploring cultural differences to determine what might be 'particular' versus what might be 'general' with respect to mentoring within and across contexts. School mentors are individuals and they differ in their thinking, experiences and guiding actions across schools, districts and countries.

Mentoring implies a multidimensional task aimed at professional growth and creating opportunities to help pre-service teachers at a most critical point in their careers. Mentors' roles and beliefs play a determinant role in shaping those experiences (Grimmett et al., 2018). The findings presented in this chapter are an attempt to think more expansively about that work and to explore additional avenues to better understanding how and why mentors conceptualise that work.

Note

1 See www.mentoringprofile.com

References

Clarke, A., Collins, J., Triggs, V., & Nielsen, W. (2012). The mentoring profile inventory: An online professional development resource for cooperating teachers. *Teaching Education, 23*(2), 167–194.

Chu, Y. (2019) Mentor teacher professional identity development in a year-long teacher residency. *Mentoring & Tutoring: Partnership in Learning, 27*(3), 251–271. doi:10.1080/13611267.2019.1630991

Grimmett, H., Forgasz, R., Williams, J., & White, S. (2018). Reimagining the role of mentor teachers in professional experience: Moving to I as fellow teacher educator. *Asia-Pacific Journal of Teacher Education,* 1–14. https://doi.org/10.1080/1359866X.2018.1437391

Hobson, A. J., Ashby, P., Malderez, A., & Tomlinson, P. D. (2009). Mentoring beginning teachers: What we know and what we don't. *Teaching and Teacher Education, 25*(1), 207–216. https://doi.org/10.1016/j.tate.2008.09.001

Hudson, P., & Hudson, S. (2018). Mentoring pre-service teachers: Identifying tensions and possible resolutions. *Teacher Development, 22*(1), 16–30. https://doi.org/10.1080/13664530.2017.1298535

Fairstein, E. (2016). *Developing novice teachers' professional identity through mentoring* (Unpublished doctoral dissertation). State Pedagogical University from Chișinău, Romania.

Izadinia, M. (2016). Teacher candidates' and mentor teachers' perceptions and expectations of a mentoring relationship: Do they match or clash? *Professional Development in Education, 42*(3), 387–402. https://doi.org/10.1080/19415257.2014.994136

Li, S., Malin, J. R., & Hackman, D. G. (2018). Mentoring supports and mentoring across difference: Insights from mentees. *Mentoring and Tutoring: Partnership in Learning.* https://doi.org/10.1080/13611267.2018.1561020

Marciano, J. E., Farver, S. D., Guenther, A., Wexler, L. J., Jansen, K., & Stanulis, R. N. (2019). Reflections from the room where it happens: Examining mentoring in the moment. *International Journal of Mentoring and Coaching in Education.* https://doi.org/10.1108/IJMCE-08-2018-0047

Mena, J., & Clarke, A. (2015). Eliciting teachers' practical knowledge through mentoring conversations in practicum settings. In H. Tillema, G. J. van der Westhuizen, &

K. Smith (Eds.), *Mentoring for learning: Climbing the mountain* (pp. 47–78). Sense Publishers.

Orland-Barak, L. (2014). Mediation in mentoring: A synthesis of studies in teaching and teacher education. *Teaching and Teacher Education, 44*, 180–188. https://doi.org/10.1016/j.tate.2014.07.011

Shalka, T. R., Corcoran, C. S., & Magee, B. T. (2019). Mentors that matter: International student leadership development and mentor roles. *Journal of International Students, 9*(1), 97–110.

Strauss, A., & Corbin, J. (1994). Grounded theory methodology – An overview. In K. D. Norman & S. L. Y. Vannaeds (Eds.), *Handbook of qualitative research* (pp. 22–23). Sage.

Talbot, D., Denny, J., & Henderson, S. (2018). 'Trying to decide ... what sort of teacher I wanted to be': Mentoring as a dialogic practice. *Teaching Education, 29*(1), 47–60. https://doi.org/10.1080/10476210.2017.1347919

Young, A. M., Cady, S., & Foxon, M. J. (2006). Demystifying gender differences in mentoring: Theoretical perspectives and challenges for future research on gender and mentoring. *Human Resource Development Review, 5*, 148–175.

Appendix A: Four Single-Quadrant Outcomes Drawn from the Current MPI Database

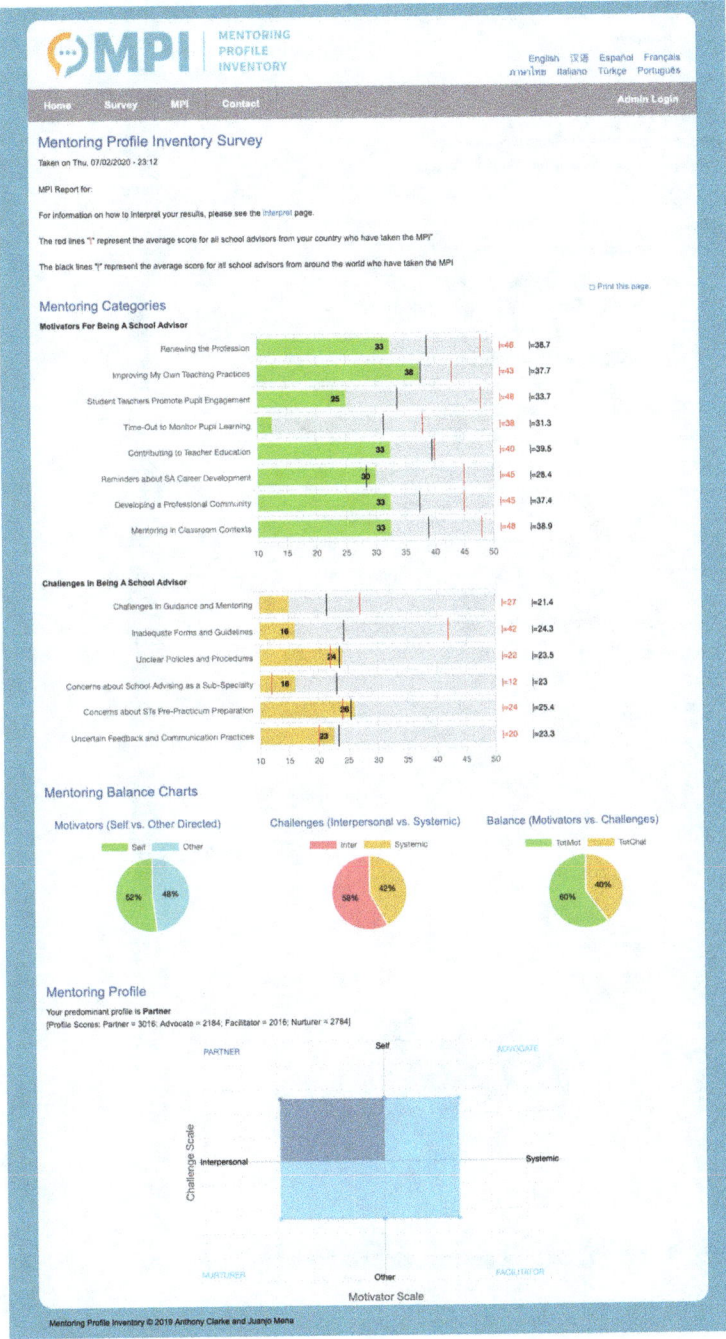

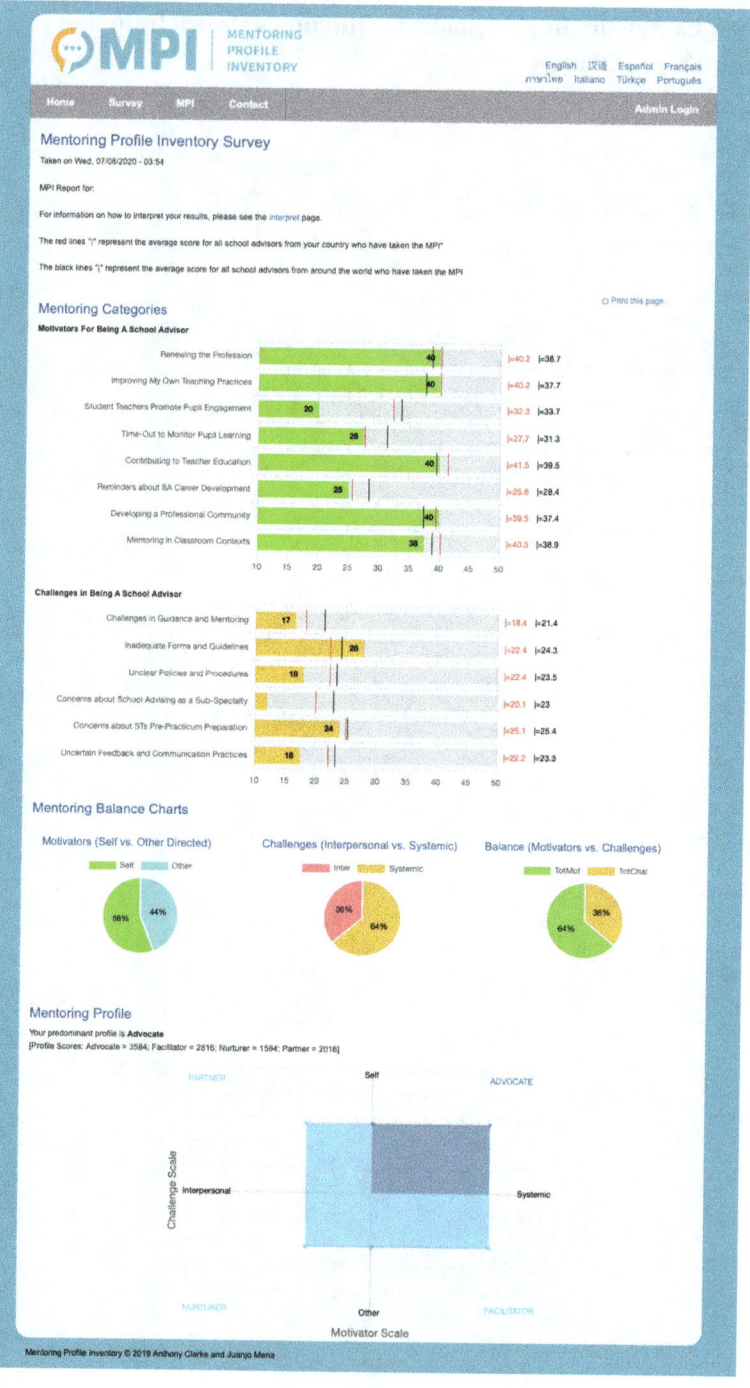

THE MENTORING PROFILE INVENTORY GRID

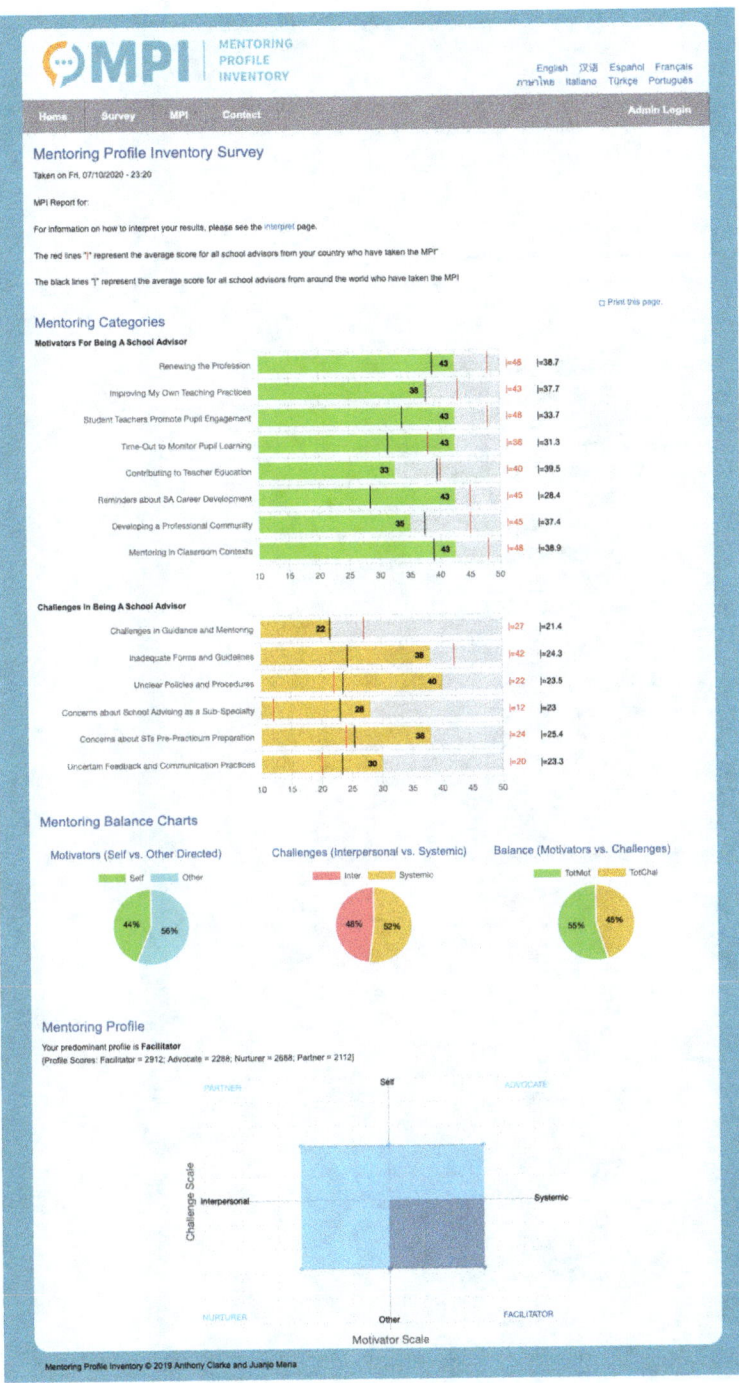

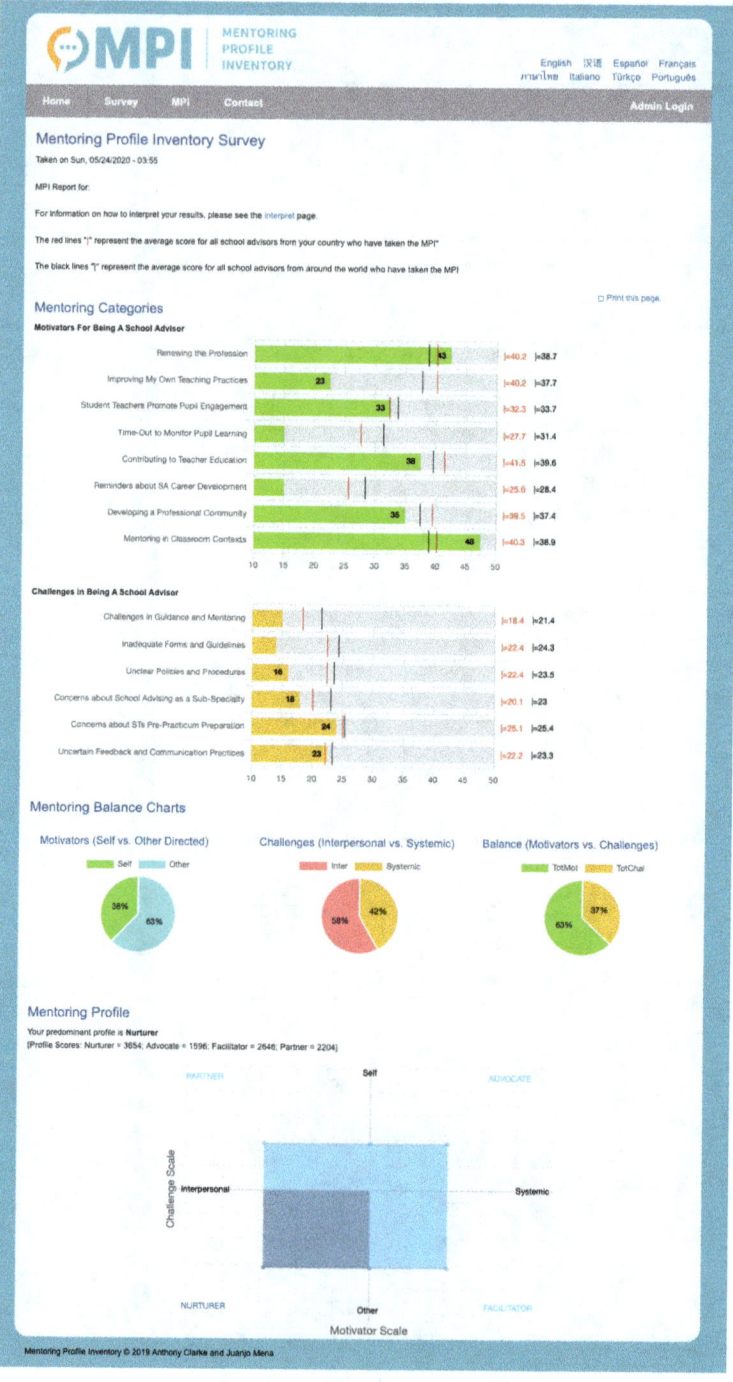

CHAPTER 2

University Student Peer Tutoring: A Pilot Program to Improve Learning for Both Tutors and Tutees

Peter Saunders, Andrea Chester and Sophia Xenos

Abstract

Student peer tutoring provides an evidence-based approach to improve learning, satisfaction and retention of first year students in a range of disciplines. It has also been reported to impact positively on later year peer tutors. In this chapter we describe a number of models of student peer tutoring including Class Wide Peer Tutoring, Supplemental Instruction and Peer Assisted Study Sessions (PASS). Against this backdrop we present data from a pilot program developed to support the transition of first year undergraduate psychology students. Using second year peer tutors, this program used small peer tutoring groups embedded in tutorials. With a focus on assessment tasks the program evidenced a positive impact on academic performance in early assessment tasks as well as improved academic confidence and retention for the first year participants. The quantitative results of this experimental study are presented alongside qualitative data from both first year students and their later-year peer tutors to examine the strengths as well as areas for improvement of the program.

Keywords

peer tutoring – peer learning – peer mentoring – academic learning

1   Introduction

First year students face a range of challenges when transitioning to higher education, including learning how to learn at university, adapting to new systems and processes and finding a place to belong. Not surprisingly, the period of transition to university is associated with high attrition. Research has found that over 16% of Australian undergraduate students do not return in second year and this number has been increasing since 2008 (Cherastidtham, Norton, & Mackey, 2018). The importance of providing support for first year students is well documented and universities have undertaken many strategies to improve first year engagement and retention.

Student peer tutoring has been identified as an evidence-based practice to support first year students. In this chapter we outline some of the major models of peer tutoring and empirical work that supports these approaches. We describe the development and evaluation of our own pilot peer tutoring program created specifically for a first-year psychology course. We discuss the challenges we hoped to address through the program and present quantitative and qualitative findings from a randomised controlled study of the program's effectiveness. Finally, we share a series of recommendations for peer tutoring programs.

2 What Is Peer Tutoring?

Peer tutoring includes a range of approaches in which students support each other's learning. Similar to mentoring, most definitions of peer tutoring involve more skilled or experienced students working with less experienced students (Falchikov, 2001). Peer tutoring and mentoring are both characterised by a supportive and interactive relationship. In contrast to mentoring however, which is often one-to-one, less structured and often has an element of social support, peer tutoring generally takes place in groups, is structured with clear procedures and guidelines, and is usually focused on developing skills associated with an assessment task (Topping, 2005). The approach builds on the social capital that exists within and for the benefit of learners and the learning contexts they are part of (Chester, Johnston, & Clarke, 2019).

Core to peer tutoring programs is effective training of peer tutors (Alzahrani & Leko, 2018). In their review of the literature, Burgess, McGregor, and Mellis (2014) reported that the majority of peer tutor training incorporated facilitator skills training alongside content specific instruction. Examples of the former include: qualities expected of a peer tutor, how to provide feedback and administrative processes. In an experimental study, Fuchs, Fuchs, Bentz, Phillips, and Hamlett (1994) found that peer tutors who had previous training and experience in peer tutoring scored higher on observer ratings measuring effective instructional principles compared to peer tutors with less training and experience.

3 The Benefits of Peer Tutoring

One of the challenges of unpacking benefits of peer tutoring is the breadth of research that sometimes conflates primary, secondary and tertiary peer tutoring programs. We examine some of this evidence below specifying, where possible, the sector.

A growing number of research studies have examined the impact of peer tutoring on student academic outcomes in primary and secondary education. In one of the first meta-analyses of secondary school-based peer tutoring programs, Cohen, Kulik, and Kulik (1982) found a positive impact on both academic achievement and attitude towards study amongst peer tutoring recipients. Similarly, in a later meta-analysis focused on primary school children, Rohrbeck, Ginsburg-Block, Fantuzzo, and Miller (2003) found that peer tutoring had a positive impact on academic achievement. In his list of effect sizes related to student achievement, Hattie (2018) noted peer tutoring has an effect size of 0.55 on learning, above the average effect size of 0.40 for the 190+ interventions examined. Other research that focuses on evidence-based approaches for primary and secondary education (Evidence for Learning, n.d.) describes the support for peer tutoring to be both extensive and consistently positive, noting the approach:

> appears to have a positive impact on learning, with an average positive effect equivalent to approximately five additional months' progress. Studies have identified benefits for both tutors and tutees, and for a wide range of age groups. Though all types of students appear to benefit from peer tutoring, there is some evidence that students who are low-attaining and those with special educational needs make the biggest gains.

Similarly, in higher education contexts multiple benefits have been reported, including improvements in academic achievement (Comfort & McMahon, 2012), retention (Quin et al., 2002), student satisfaction, exam scores and reduction in distress (Fantuzzo, Dimeff, & Fox, 1989). Research suggests that peer tutoring may lead to higher meta-cognitive awareness and self-efficacy, which in turn, leads to an increase in motivation and academic capabilities. Self-efficacy is an individual's belief that they are likely to succeed in a task (Stajkovic & Luthans, 1979). Some research has found that peer tutoring is associated with increased self-efficacy (e.g., Poellhuber, Chomienne, & Karsenti, 2008; Van Keer & Verhaeghe, 2005). Students who have higher self-efficacy are more likely to be confident learners and are more likely to participate, engage and persist with their academic studies (Pajares, 2007). Self-efficacy is also a strong predictor of academic achievement and success (Broadbent, 2016; Chemers, Hu, & Garcia, 2001).

Although studies have tended to focus on the impact of peer tutoring for tutees, research also suggests there are potential benefits for peer tutors (Leung, 2018). Benefits for peer tutors include greater self-regulation, development of meta-cognitive awareness and reinforcement of learned material. Arco-Tirado, Fernández-Martín, and Fernández-Balboa (2011), using an experimental design to investigate the impact of a peer-tutoring program in higher education, reported that peer tutors improved on measures of social skills and cognitive and metacognitive strategies.

Despite the positive results, research on the impact of peer tutoring has been criticised for weak research designs, small sample sizes, and methodological errors. Alzahrani and Leko (2018), in their systematic review, concluded that studies investigating peer tutoring lacked scientific rigor. A randomised controlled trial, sometimes considered to be the gold standard of quantitative research design (Sanders & Halpern, 2014), offers one way in which to test the effectiveness of peer tutoring. Notwithstanding the limitations of such an approach (Clay, 2010), a randomised controlled trial does allow the researcher to control for a range of variables that might otherwise be expected to impact the effectiveness of peer tutoring, such as the motivation of tutee and tutor volunteers.

4 Models of Peer Tutoring

Over the past three decades a number of empirically based peer tutoring models have been developed. In this section, three models of peer tutoring are examined: ClassWide Peer Tutoring (CWPT), Supplemental Instruction (SI) and Peer Assisted Learning (PAL). While described separately below there is significant overlap in terms of strategies employed and benefits obtained from the implementation of each approach.

ClassWide Peer Tutoring (CWPT) was one of the earliest student peer tutoring models to be developed and empirically measured. CWPT was originally developed in the 1980s to develop mastery and accuracy in primary education (Greenwood, 1997). The program uses same-age reciprocal peer tutoring in class. Students work in pairs, alternately taking the roles of tutor and tutee during CWPT sessions, with tutors providing immediate correction of errors (Greenwood, Arreaga-Mayer, Utley, Gavin, & Terry, 2001). Using a gaming format CWPT typically sees the class divided into two teams that compete for points.

Multiple studies, including small and large scale experimental studies, have evaluated the effectiveness of CWPT with a number of strong and positive outcomes. In a 12-year longitudinal study comparing 182 students in an experimental group with those in a comparison group, students in the CWPT group demonstrated increased engagement, higher grades and better retention by the end of grade 11 compared to the control comparison (Greenwood & Delquadri, 1995). These results are promising, however, the authors reported high attrition (68%) in the program. Further, it is unclear whether CWPT is an appropriate strategy for university students as little research has been conducted with older populations.

In comparison, *Supplemental Instruction* (*SI*) was developed in the US to improve student retention, most often in higher education settings. SI typically targets students in high risk courses where there are high rates of failure and withdrawal (Aredale, 1994). Final year students generally assist first or second year students. SI sessions are structured to promote high student interaction. SI sessions encourage feedback and direct interaction between the peer tutors and teacher (Saunders & Gibbon, 1998) and the teacher and peer tutors are encouraged to keep a reflective journal. A limitation of SI is that, due to the highly structured nature of the sessions, preparation for peer tutors can be onerous (Aredale, 1994).

Peer Assisted Study Sessions (*PASS*) is an approach adapted from SI for the UK and comprises study sessions run by student tutors. PASS is used to describe a range of approaches including Peer Assisted Learning (PAL) and Supported Learning Groups (SLG), all of which involve students teaching other students (Kirkham & Ringlestein, 2008). PASS is based on the foundation that higher-level students help lower level students develop their academic and personal confidence. Key to the effectiveness of this approach is the responsive attitude of the peer tutor and the atmosphere generated in the sessions. Sessions typically take place outside formal class time, attendance is voluntary and students themselves decide the agenda (Saunders & Gibbon, 1998). Research has found PASS leads to improvements in achievement across the education continuum, from primary school (Rohrbeck, Ginsburg-Block, Fantuzzo, & Miller, 2003) through to university (Cheng & Walters, 2009).

Some limitations of PASS include challenges with timetabling and lack of consistent tutee participation. As PASS programs are generally run outside of class and use an opt-in approach, first year tutees may not take the program seriously or attend (Saunders & Gibbon, 1998). Further, if the program is conducted outside of class time then students most in need of assistance may fail to take advantage of the program (Heirdsfield, Walker, & Walsh, 2008). An alternative to this approach is to incorporate the peer tutoring program into the curriculum.

Below we describe a pilot peer tutoring program that was embedded into the curriculum to support first year students from the Discipline of Psychology. The name of the peer tutoring program was Psychology Peer Assisted Tutorial Support (PPATS).

5 Background to the PPATS Pilot

As part of a needs analysis, data was collated from a range of sources including student course evaluations, student-staff consultative committee meeting minutes, grades, an informal survey of first year students at the completion of their first year in which they were asked what advice they would offer new first year students for the following year, and anecdotal information from staff. An analysis of this data revealed three major challenges for psychology students.

Firstly, students both reported and demonstrated persistent difficulties learning the skills of scientific writing. Introduced in first year and built upon in subsequent years, scientific writing skills are central to academic success in the psychology program. Even when tutorials were dedicated to scientific writing skills it continued to be identified as difficult for first year students to master. Difficulty acquiring this core skill in first year affected new students' academic career paths and appeared to influence confidence. Secondly, a consistent first year fail rate of around 15% was noted, with a large proportion of these students failing because they did not submit one or more pieces of assessment. Finally, few opportunities existed within the program for communities of learning across year levels, although students who participated in student-staff consultative committees noted how helpful it was to interact with peers at other stages in their degree.

6 Research Aims

The aims of this pilot project were to:
- Develop an empirically validated peer tutoring package to assist first year psychology students to acquire foundational skills of scientific writing, with the potential to be extended to a wider number of courses across the University.
- Support first year students to engage with the course and complete all assessment tasks.

– Establish a learning community within undergraduate psychology to formalise communication and knowledge sharing between new and more experienced students and reduce some of the significant challenges faced by students in the transition to university.

We predicted that peer tutoring would enhance first year students' confidence in their own ability as well as improve retention and grades. We anticipated that peer tutors would also experience benefits.

7 Design of the PPATS Pilot

In contrast to the PASS model of peer tutoring that is often "opt-in" or "add-on", PPATS was designed to be embedded in tutorials, ensuring equal access and requiring no additional commitment from first year students. Peer tutoring was designed to take place in the second hour of tutorial time for 7 weeks of the 12-week semester. In the hour directly after the tutorial peer tutors attended a debriefing of that session as well as a briefing for the following week. First year tutorials were held on days on which the peer tutors had no other classes to enable peer tutors time to commit to the project.

We recruited peer tutors from a pool of second year distinction-average students and allocated pairs of peer tutors to small groups of no more than five first year students. Peer tutoring sessions were designed to use a series of scaffolded activities focused on scientific writing, leading first year students through exercises and discussions on issues including academic integrity, APA style and self-assessment processes to prepare for submission of their first major scientific writing assessment. A PPATS Manual was developed to provide peer tutors with consistent information for each session. Material in the manual was covered in all other first year tutorials by the classroom tutor, all of whom had postgraduate qualifications in Psychology.

Training for peer tutors was also conducted. The training package (presented over two half days) covered information on roles and responsibilities of peer tutors and generic information on group development including building rapport, stages of group development and group roles. Discipline-specific components of the training ensured that all peer tutors were familiar with the material relevant to the first-year scientific writing assessment. In the week following training peer tutors attended the first-year tutorial and were randomly allocated their peer tutoring group. First year students selected their own groups for PPATS.

8 Participants

Students enrolled in an undergraduate psychology program took part in the study. First year students in one tutorial group were chosen randomly as the pilot tutees and students in two other tutorials scheduled at the same time were selected as the control group. There were 21 first year students (13 females, 8 males) in the PPATS group and 46 students (33 female, 13 male) in the control group. First year students were aged from 17 to 40 years ($M = 21.02$, $SD = 2.81$) and were predominantly Australian-born (80.7%).

Peer tutors were 11 second year psychology students (10 females, 1 male).

9 Measures

First-year tutees and second year peer tutors completed the Academic Confidence Scale at the beginning and end of semester. The Academic Confidence Scale (Sanders & Sander, 2007) is a 24-item scale that measures academic confidence on six subscales: studying, grade achievement, attendance, clarification, understanding, verbalising and attendance. The *studying* sub-scale measures a student's confidence that they can prepare appropriately, manage deadlines, and stay motivated. The *grade achievement* sub-scale measures a student's confidence that s/he can not only pass, but produce work of a high standard. The *clarifying* sub-scale reflects a student's confidence to engage in debate. The *understanding* sub-scale measures perceived ability to follow and comprehend material. The *verbalising* sub-scale measures confidence asking and responding to questions as well as engaging in class. *Attendance* measures the student's confidence they will be able to attend classes. The attendance sub-scale is not reported below because confidence in ability to attend classes was outside the scope of influence of the tutoring program. Responses are completed on a five-point Likert scale, from *very confident* (5) to *not at all confident* (1). The Academic Confidence Scale has good construct validity (Sander & Sanders, 2003). The internal reliability of the scale in the present study was good; Cronbach's $\alpha = .823$.

At the start of semester peer tutors were asked about their motivations for engaging in the program and their expectations. In the middle of semester first-year tutees and peer tutors were asked what was going well and what, if anything, they would like to change. At the end of the semester all participants in the pilot were asked what worked best, what was challenging and what impact participation in the pilot program had on their learning. This information was obtained via the online open-ended surveys.

Consent was obtained from all first-year students involved in the study to access their grades. Students were graded on five assessment tasks in this course, three of which were the focus of peer tutoring. These included two short exercises that were low stakes tasks, submitted early in the semester, designed to scaffold scientific writing skills. These skills were used and assessed in the psychology laboratory report, an extended piece of scientific writing.

Ethics approval was obtained for the pilot from the University's Human Research Ethics Committee.

10 Results

Results of the pilot are divided into two sections: outcomes for first year tutees including a comparison of grades, retention and academic confidence and outcomes for peer tutors.

11 Outcomes for First Year Student Tutees

The PPATS program improved first year student grades and retention as well as academic confidence. An analysis of academic grades (summarised in Table 2.1) shows that students who participated in PPATS performed better on the three scientific writing assessment tasks compared to those students who did not participate in PPATS. This difference was statistically significant for Exercises 1 and 2, the first short assessment pieces in the course which provided early feedback on skills relevant to scientific writing, as well as final grade.

TABLE 2.1   Marks for PPATS first year peer tutored students and control group

	PPATS ($N = 21$)		Controls ($N = 46$)			
Marks	M	(SD)	M	(SD)	t	p
Exercise 1 (5 marks)	4.26	(0.83)	3.35	(1.21)	3.11	.003
Exercise 2 (10 marks)	7.58	(1.62)	6.44	(1.40)	2.94	.005
Lab report (20 marks)	11.13	(1.46)	9.33	(2.41)	1.53	.13

Results also highlighted the positive impact of PPATS on student retention rates. The retention rate for students in the PPATS tutorial was 100% and the failure rate 0%. In the control group five students did not complete the course and a further four students failed. In the control tutorials six students did not submit one or more pieces of assessment, compared to only one student in the PPATS tutorial. In the PPATS tutorial 100% of students submitted the major scientific writing assignment. In the control tutorials, 92% (42 out of 46 students) submitted this work.

TABLE 2.2 Academic confidence sub-scale scores for PPATS first year peer tutored students and control group at end of semester controlling for pre-test scores

Scale	PPATS (N = 15)		Controls (N = 23)		f	p
	M	(SD)	M	(SD)		
Studying	3.83	(0.52)	3.42	(0.66)	4.72	.04
Understanding	3.96	(0.41)	3.47	(0.61)	4.40	.04
Grades	3.98	(0.33)	3.58	(0.63)	4.62	.04
Verbalising	3.37	(0.86)	2.97	(0.85)	1.00	.76
Clarifying	4.25	(0.41)	3.68	(0.61)	8.71	.006

In relation to academic confidence, when controlling for scores at the start of the program, PPATS first year students rated themselves significantly higher than the control group on three of the five sub-scales (studying, understanding, grade achievement, and clarifying) at the end of semester, indicating confidence to do well in all these areas. These sub-scales align with the explicit and implicit emphases of the PPATS program. The two areas where no difference was reported were studying and verbalising.

Qualitative data highlighted a range of self-reported benefits of PPATS for first year students. A thematic analysis of this data revealed four major overlapping advantages of PPATS involvement for first year students: direct advice and assistance from the peer tutors; interaction with later year students who had successfully negotiated the demands of first year; a sense of motivation to complete work; and the benefits associated with small group interaction. It is of note that several of these themes complement the quantitative data reported above. These themes are summarised in Table 2.3, together with representative, verbatim examples of each.

TABLE 2.3 First year students' perceptions of the most useful aspects of PPATS

Theme	Examples
Direct assistance/advice	Tutors gave a great insight into their first year experiences, giving us advice on what they found difficult and how they overcame it. I found this to be particularly important and helpful. I found the tutor's help with assignments really useful – it was good to bounce ideas off and get feedback from people with experience.
Relevant experiences	The chance to engage with students who ... had been where we are now recently. The fact that they had already completed much of the same assessment we are facing and so can give us points and help from their experience.
Motivation	They got me to start an assignment earlier than I normally would. Being close to the peer tutor provided more of a motivation, i.e. not wanting to let them down.
Group support	Being in a smaller group enabled me to ask as many questions as I wanted (even if they were small and silly) without being embarrassed. The opportunity to interact with others (both tutors and tutees) in a supportive environment. It was beneficial to be able to discuss concerns and issues relating to the course with them.

Although the overwhelming majority of comments from first year students were positive, challenges were noted. A small number of first year students commented on downtime during the peer tutoring sessions. For example:

Whilst the mentors were helpful with assessment items, sometimes we ran out of things to talk about during our allocated time.

12   Outcomes for Peer Tutors

Unlike the evaluation of PPATS for first year students, the evaluation of PPATS peer tutors did not use a randomised controlled design. Peer tutors were invited to participate in PPATS because of their strong academic record and we were not confident that comparisons with the rest of their cohort would be meaningful. As a result the effectiveness of PPATS for peer tutors was assessed by a within-group analysis, comparing Week 1 and Week 12 scores for peer tutors on the Academic Confidence Scale. Given the small sample size statistically significant differences were not anticipated and none were found. The following summary therefore focuses on trends in the data.

Pre and post-test scores on all measures are summarised in Table 2.4. PPATS positively impacted on the verbalising sub-scale of the Academic Confidence Scale, indicating the peer-tutors' enhanced confidence in their ability to ask and respond to questions, engage in debate and make effective presentations at the completion of the program. This change is consistent with the skills peer tutors used in their PPATS work.

TABLE 2.4 Pre (Week 1) and post-test (Week 12) scores on all measures for PPATS peer tutors

Scale	Pre-test ($N=7$)		Post-test ($N=7$)			
	M	(SD)	M	(SD)	f	p
Studying	4.55	(0.44)	4.26	(0.54)	1.13	.33
Grades	4.49	(0.29)	4.31	(0.40)	0.83	.40
Verbalising	3.61	(0.94)	4.00	(0.65)	0.81	.40
Clarifying	4.71	(0.27)	4.46	(0.47)	1.11	.33
Understanding	4.46	(0.36)	4.25	(0.51)	0.66	.45

When asked what they liked most about participating in PPATS, peer tutors provided a range of responses illustrating three major themes: the opportunity to pass on the knowledge they were developing in their degree, the chance to support the transition of first year students and the sense they were making an important contribution to the learning community of the discipline, connecting both with the first years as well as their peer tutoring partner. Underpinning most of the comments were two overarching features: a level of empathy was evident as peer tutors remembered the challenges of their own first year experience; and the peer tutors' hopes, often expressed tentatively, that their peer tutoring input had been helpful. These themes and verbatim examples of each are summarised in Table 2.5.

TABLE 2.5   Peer tutors' perceptions of the most useful aspects of participation in PPATS

Theme	Examples
Pass on knowledge	Being able to (maybe) help out the first years. I was pretty overwhelmed by the mystical beast the "lab report" in first year so it was good to help them with it and give them tips for understanding etc. Meeting and helping less experienced students with aspects of their course and uni life they wouldn't otherwise get from anyone else.
Social support/ transition	Being able to produce my input to those who are in need. The ability to guide the first years into understanding the roles of psychology undergrad and writing. Meeting other students and helping them (hopefully) make a successful transition from high school to uni.
Contribution to a learning community	I felt a sense of purpose and a sense of responsibility to my tutees and tutoring partner. Being in a position where my opinions/knowledge is appreciated and wanted.

Similarly to the first year students, the peer tutor comments were overwhelmingly positive. Some challenges were noted, including how to manage the session when tutees had not completed tasks for peer tutoring discussion:

> I found it difficult when students hadn't started the work and therefore had no questions to ask us.

> Trying to motivate the group to do assignments. It was hard to help them when the activities were based around work they had not completed.

In addition, some peer tutors noted that there were times when they were unsure what to do. For example:

> It was pretty unstructured so that there were times when I wasn't exactly sure what we should be doing/ how we should be helping more.

It is of note that despite these frustrations and the considerable time commitment required of peer tutors, the retention rate was 100%; all peer tutors who commenced the training completed the pilot.

13   Discussion

Results of this pilot study suggest that PPATS enhanced academic transition, built critical skills and improved pass rates of first year psychology students. The PPATS program improved grades and retention as well as several aspects of the academic confidence of first year students. Pleasingly peer tutoring was associated with gains in understanding (perceived ability to follow and comprehend material), grades (a student's confidence that s/he can not only pass, but produce work of a high standard) and clarifying (confidence to engage in debate). Even though the peer tutors were only one year ahead of the tutees, they were perceived to have valuable, expert experience and were viewed as good role models. The peer tutoring program was described by the first year students as motivating and supportive.

In summary and as predicted, participation in PPATS produced tangible results for first year students. The program also demonstrated benefits for peer tutors who improved their verbal confidence and felt as if they were making a valued contribution. The benefits of the PPATS pilot extended beyond the first year students and their peer tutors. As a consequence of the evaluation conducted throughout the PPATS program, members of the undergraduate psychology teaching team developed a comprehensive understanding of the first year cohort and its specific learning needs and challenges. This information was used to support further curriculum design and pedagogical improvements. PPATS also benefited the program by producing a motivated and skilled group of peer tutors, who indicated an interest in undertaking further tutoring and pursuing academic careers in the future. In particular peer tutors noted that the PPATS program had increased their sense of belonging to a discipline-specific learning community and that this had led to a greater commitment to the discipline.

Interestingly there was one area of academic confidence where PPATS did not produce significant benefit for peer tutees: verbalising (confidence asking and responding to questions as well as engaging in class). We anticipated that PPATS, by providing small group opportunities and more focused and personalised support, would impact positively on this aspect and indeed academic performance suggests the program impacted on outcomes, if not confidence. While it is possible that the lack of significant difference was influenced by the relatively small sample size, verbalising confidence should be prioritised in future iterations of the program. Possible improvements are discussed in the next section.

14   Limitations of the Pilot and Recommendations for Future Peer Tutoring Programs

Supporting first year students in the critical early months of transition is important, but it is unclear whether the benefits often associated with peer tutoring are sustained beyond this period. With the exception of Greenwood and Delquadri (1995) few studies have explored the long-term benefits of peer tutoring. In our pilot we had planned a six-month follow-up to examine whether impact of PPATS continued into the second half of the year. Unfortunately, less than 20 percent of first year students completed the follow-up questionnaire. The timing of the follow-up, after the completion of classes, may have contributed to this low response rate. Analysis of this follow-up data was therefore not included in this chapter. We recommend the timing of follow-up data collection be carefully planned to maximise response rates and ensure the long term impact of such programs is appropriately measured.

A second area for further consideration is explicit training for peer tutors on how to manage lack of initiative and motivation amongst their tutees. Several peer tutors commented that the most frustrating part of peer tutoring was when their students didn't complete tasks on time for peer tutoring sessions and the first year students themselves did not experience an uplift in their confidence to prepare appropriately, manage deadlines and stay motivated. Such training might provide skills to pre-empt this challenge, such as a targeted and integrated focus on time management to maximise the effectiveness of PPATS participation.

In addition, and perhaps sometimes linked to the above challenge, both first year students and peer tutors noted that there were times when it was unclear how to best use the tutoring time. One way to address both this issue would be to provide alternative activities and additional tasks for peer tutors to choose from. Some of these additional tasks might be deliberately social in nature. Anecdotal feedback collected during this pilot suggested that building in social support, such as regular time to check how first year students are managing non-academically (playing a stronger mentoring role), would be a useful addition to the manual, providing a more holistic approach.

A final challenge for the pilot is the question of scaling. While there was benefit in running a pilot project to determine the effectiveness of the program and refine the model, to be of real value to the discipline it needs to operate at scale for all first year students. In scaling up the model the team decided to embed PPATS in all first year tutorials and integrate peer tutoring as a requirement for all final year students.

15 Conclusions

Peer tutoring has a history of effectively supporting students from primary education through to tertiary study. While a number of models have been developed in different parts of the world, core to all is the underlying value of using peers to help support learning. In this chapter we presented data from one small-scale pilot in the discipline of psychology that produced positive outcomes for first year students and their peer tutors. Key to the model was the embedded nature of the tutoring program. This distinguishes the pilot from other widely implemented approaches that provide drop-in sessions or opt in support. Integration of PPATS into the first year tutorial curriculum ensures that all students have access to the program without additional effort or time commitment. As such the model is an example of successful intentional curriculum design and transition pedagogy (Kift & Field, 2009). With positive impact for the peer tutors the program extends its impact beyond transition. Opportunities exist for continued refinement and application in other disciplines.

References

Alzahrani, T., & Leko, M. (2018). The effects of peer tutoring on the reading comprehension performance of secondary students with disabilities: A systematic review. *Reading and Writing Quarterly, 34*(1), 1–17.

Arco-Tirado, J. L., Fernández-Martín, F. D., & Fernández-Balboa, J. M. (2011). The impact of a peer-tutoring program on quality standards in higher education. *Higher Education, 62*(6), 773–788.

Arendale, D. R. (1994). Understanding the supplemental instruction model. *New Directions for Teaching and Learning, 60*, 11–21.

Burgess, A., McGregor, D., & Mellis, C. (2014). Medical students as peer tutors: A systematic review. *BMC Medical Education, 14*(115).

Cheng, D., & Walters, M. (2009). Peer-assisted learning in mathematics: An observational study of student success. *Australasian Journal of Peer Learning, 2*(1), 23–29.

Cherastidtham, I., Norton, A., & Mackey, W. (2018). *University attrition: What helps and what hinders university completion?* Grattan Institute.

Chester, A., Johnston, A., & Clarke, A. (2019). Partnerships for learning and belonging in tertiary education: A social capital analysis. In B. Tynan, T. McLaughlin, A. Chester, C. Hall-van den Elsen, & B. Kennedy (Eds.), *Transformations in tertiary education* (pp. 11–26). Springer.

Clay, R. A. (2010). More than one way to measure. *Monitor on Psychology, 41*(8), 52.

Cohen, P. A., Kulik, J. A., & Kulik, C. C. (1982). Educational outcomes of tutoring: A meta-analysis of findings. *American Educational Research Journal, 19*(2), 237–248.

Comfort, P., & McMahon, J. J. (2012). The effect of peer tutoring on academic achievement. *Journal of Applied Research in Higher Education, 6*(1), 168–175.

Evidence for Learning (n.d.). *Peer tutoring.* Retrieved from https://evidenceforlearning.org.au/teaching-and-learning-toolkit/peer-tutoring/

Falchikov, N. (2001). *Learning together: Peer tutoring in higher education.* Routledge Falmer.

Fantuzzo, J. W., Dimeff, L. A., & Fox, S. L. (1989). Reciprocal peer tutoring: A multimodal assessment of effectiveness with college students. *Teaching of Psychology, 16,* 133–135.

Fuchs, L. S., Fuchs, D., Bentz, J., Phillips, N. B., & Hamlett, C. L. (1994). The nature of student interactions during peer tutoring with and without prior training and experience. *American Educational Research Journal, 31*(1), 75–103.

Griffin, N. M, & Griffin, B. W. (1998). An investigation of the effects of reciprocal peer tutoring on achievement, self-efficacy, and test anxiety. *Contemporary Educational Psychology, 23*(3), 298–311.

Greenwood, C. R. (1997). Classwide peer tutoring. *Behavior and Social Issues, 7*(1), 53–57.

Greenwood, C. R., Arreaga-Mayer, C., Utley, C. A., Gavin, K. M., & Terry, B. (2001). Class wide peer tutoring learning management system: Applications with elementary-level English language learners. *Remedial and Special Education, 22*(1), 34–47.

Greenwood, C. R., & Delquadri, J. (1995). Class wide peer tutoring and the prevention of school failure. *Preventing School Failure, 39*(4), 21–25.

Hattie, J. (2018). *Hattie's 2018 updated list of factors related to student achievement: 252 influences and effect sizes (Cohen's d).* Retrieved from https://visible-learning.org/hattie-ranking-influences-effect-sizes-learning-achievement/

Heirdsfield, A. M., Walker, S., & Walsh, K. M. (2008, November 25–29). *Enhancing the first year experience – Longitudinal perspectives on a peer mentoring scheme.* Paper presented at Australian Association for Research in Education. Research impact: Proving or improving, Fremantle, Australia.

Kift, S. M., &Field, R. M. (2009, 29 June–1 July). Intentional first year curriculum design as a means of facilitating student engagement: Some exemplars. In *Proceedings of*

12th Pacific Rim First Year in higher education Conference: Preparing for tomorrow today: The first year experience as foundation. Townsville, Queensland. Retrieved August 30, 2019, from https://www.researchgate.net/publication/41150093_Intentional_first_year_curriculum_design_as_a_means_of_facilitating_student_engagement_some_exemplars

Kirkham, R., & Ringelstein, D. (2008). Student Peer Assisted Mentoring (SPAM): A conceptual framework. *E-Journal of Business Education & Scholarship of Teaching, 2*(2), 39–49.

Leung, K. C. (2015). Preliminary empirical model of crucial determinants of best practice for peer tutoring on academic achievement. *Journal of Educational Psychology, 107*(2), 558–579.

Leung, K. C. (2018). An updated meta-analysis on the effect of peer tutoring on tutors' achievement. *Social Psychology International.* Retrieved from https://journals.sagepub.com/doi/abs/10.1177/0143034318808832?journalCode=spia

Poellhuber, B., Chomienne, M., & Karsenti, T. (2008). The effect of peer collaboration and collaborative learning on self-efficacy and persistence in a learner-paced continuous intake model. *Journal of Distance Education, 22*(3), 41–62.

Rohrbeck, C. A., Ginsburg-Block, M., Fantuzzo, J. W., & Miller, T. R. (2003). Peer-assisted learning interventions with elementary school students: A meta-analytic review. *Journal of Educational Psychology, 95*(2), 250–257.

Sanders, M., & Halpern, D. (2014, February 3). Nudge unit: Our quiet revolution is putting evidence at the heart of government. *The Guardian.*

Saunders, D., & Gibbon, M. (1998). Peer tutoring and peer-assisted support: Five models within a new University. *Mentoring and Tutoring, 5*(30), 3–13.

Topping, K. J. (2005). Trends in peer learning. *Educational Psychology, 25*(6), 631–645.

Underwood, J., Underwood, G., & Wood. (2000). When does gendermatter? Interactions during computer based problem-solving. *Learning and Instruction, 10,* 447–462.

Van Keer, H., & Verhaeghe, J. P. (2005). Effects of explicit reading strategies instruction and peer tutoring on second and fifth graders' reading comprehension and self-efficacy perceptions. *The Journal of Experimental Education, 73*(4), 291–329.

CHAPTER 3

Championing Peer Feedback on Educational Practice: Partnerships for Learning and Development in Tertiary Teaching

Dallas Wingrove and Angela Clarke

Abstract

Research demonstrates that developmental models of peer feedback on teaching can improve educational practice and foster professional learning to support excellence in tertiary teaching. In this chapter, we present a partnerships model for tertiary educators designed to foster peer to peer feedback on educational practice through an iterative cycle of teaching observations, feedback and critical reflection. Our model is based upon contemporary theories of adult professional learning, including critical theory, and is underpinned by three educational practice-based concepts: situated learning, reflective practice and conceptual expansion. We draw upon the substantial research that demonstrates the efficacy of developmental peer observation practices, along with our professional learning and scholarship. Our expertise in this field stems from our successful co-leadership of a peer feedback on teaching program, known as Peer Partnerships. Peer Partnerships was implemented across all faculties within our university between 2013 and 2017 and resulted in 312 voluntary peer partnerships. Its evidence base affirms the critical importance of personal agency, professional autonomy, and intrinsic motivation in adult professional learning. Our model is designed to support educators to: work cooperatively, collaboratively and independently to reflect upon educational practice; critically question their teaching practices and the practices of others; be open to peer feedback on their teaching; be flexible and open to change; and to be supported to expand conceptions of educational practice through scholarship. It is a model that is designed to create partnered, authentic, needs-based, professional learning for development and improvement in tertiary educational practice.

Keywords

peer feedback – peer observation – professional learning – partnerships – tertiary teaching

1 Partnerships for Professional Learning

Partnerships matter. In tertiary education they are central to the academy and core to enabling the university's vision and mission. In this chapter we focus specifically on partnerships between tertiary educators involving peer feedback on educational practice. We present a *Peer Feedback on Educational Practice Model* that is designed to facilitate the process of sharing and critically reflecting on teaching for developmental purposes. Our model draws upon the well-established evidence base which demonstrates the efficacy of formative peer feedback approaches for improvement in tertiary teaching (Bell, 2005; Bell & Cooper, 2013; Bell & Mladenovic, 2008). It also draws upon our five years of practice-based research and professional learning arising through our leadership of a developmental program of peer feedback on teaching, Peer Partnerships. Peer Partnerships involved the voluntary reciprocal peer observation of teaching for developmental purposes.

Our new *Peer Feedback on Educational Practice Model* is purposefully designed to guide and facilitate collegiate, outcomes-focused developmental peer feedback on educational practice. It does so through a supported process of reciprocal peer observation and guided critical reflection. As Brookfield (2005) theorises, critically reflective practice entails standing outside our practice and viewing our practice from another perspective. As a complement to educators' self-reflections and student feedback, our model creates a third space, which gives prominence to reciprocal peer feedback on teaching.

Formative peer feedback on teaching partnerships have been shown to provide significant and rich opportunities for improvement in the quality of teaching practice (Bell, 2005; Bell & Mladenovic, 2008; Daniels, 2017; McMahon Barret & O'Neill, 2007; Peel, 2005; Shortland, 2010), delivering useful professional learning about teaching (Wingrove, 2019). Our model acknowledges and harnesses this evidence base to guide and facilitate voluntary, partnered and outcomes focused developmental peer feedback on educational practice. In developing our model we also draw upon our five years of experience in co-leading Peer Partnerships to create structured learning experiences whereby educators can elect to participate in reciprocal peer feedback on teaching partnerships.

2 Peer Partnerships: An Evidence Based Case for Developmental Peer Feedback on Teaching

In collaboration with a third academic from our university, we designed the Peer Partnerships model in 2012 (Wingrove, Hammersley-Fletcher, Clarke, & Chester, 2018). Our three-way collaboration was the culmination of our shared experiences of implementing peer to peer observation programs within our university. We came together energised by the prospect of raising the value of peer feedback on teaching by creating a formal place to foster, recognise, support and grow peer to peer feedback on teaching partnerships across our university.

Peer Partnerships was purposefully underpinned by adult learning principles as devised by Speck (1996) to ensure a voluntary, confidential and reciprocal engagement in peer observation of teaching. These guiding principles also underpin our *Peer Feedback on Educational Practice Model* and are detailed further in this chapter (see Table 3.1). These principles seek to cultivate the cultural conditions required for critical reflection and developmental professional adult learning. We further harness and build upon our learning from Peer Partnerships in key ways which includes to ensure that our model locates learner agency as central to the peer feedback process.

The efficacy of Peer Partnerships is demonstrated, in part, through the strong level of voluntary uptake by educators from our university. With more than 300 partnerships, from across our university, our Peer Partnerships principles appear to have resonated with educators. Our partnerships are also testament to educator's intrinsic motivation to share and reflect on practice for developmental purposes.

The participant experience of Peer Partnerships is further demonstrated in Wingrove's (2019) analysis of post participant feedback data, qualitative and quantitate, captured via 181 surveys. This research examined participants' experiences of the Peer Partnerships program and what they perceived they gained from their engagement. Findings evidence useful practical learning about teaching including enhanced confidence. Seventy-two qualitative responses to open-ended prompts confirmed that perceived benefits also included that participants valued that Peer Partnerships provided a low stakes process, along with opportunities to learn collaboratively through the exchange of practice whereby new collegial relationships were fostered.

3. Peer Feedback on Educational Practice: Partnerships for Developmental Learning about Teaching

Given that our new model builds on Peer Partnerships, it is important to provide details about its design and intent. Peer Partnerships was purposefully designed to provide partnered, structured learning experiences for educators to engage in formative reciprocal peer observation. The process encouraged critical reflection on practice for development and improvement and created opportunities for educators to voluntarily partner with a peer, reflect on peer feedback and then integrate this feedback with their own reflections and practice, student feedback and educational theory.

The process of peer feedback on teaching and reflection on learning was moderated through an induction and debrief workshop. These workshops were moderated by us in our roles as Academic Developers in recognition of the importance of moderation to ensure process integrity (Drew, Klopper, & Mallitt, 2015).

Like Peer Partnerships, our new model is also designed so that the process of peer feedback is guided by a teacher education expert. The role of the teacher education expert is to provide good practice resources and relevant educational literature. We do so in recognition of the importance in providing contextualised good teaching practice resources for educators and in recognition of the importance of the role of scholarly led teaching as an enabler of good teaching practice.

Our model comprises three workshops commencing with a group induction and concluding with a group debrief where learning and reflections on practice are shared. As a point of difference to Peer Partnerships, our model includes a new second stage mid-point check-in workshop. Further, whilst Peer Partnerships was designed to facilitate a cycle of observation and feedback over one semester, our model is designed to provide for participation in the process of peer feedback over a two-semester cycle. We do so to provide for enhanced opportunities for critical reflection and learning and to ensure a deeper engagement with learning and teaching scholarship (Barnard, Croft, Irons, Cuffe, & Bandara, 2011).

We also extend the peer observation life cycle over two semesters to support the integration of student feedback. Along with peer feedback and educator's own reflections, student feedback can be harnessed to enhance reflection on practice and inform goal setting and actions for development and improvement. Our model importantly provides staged opportunities for participants to implement and evaluate a change in practice as they revisit the process of peer feedback on teaching. A visual representation of our five-stage

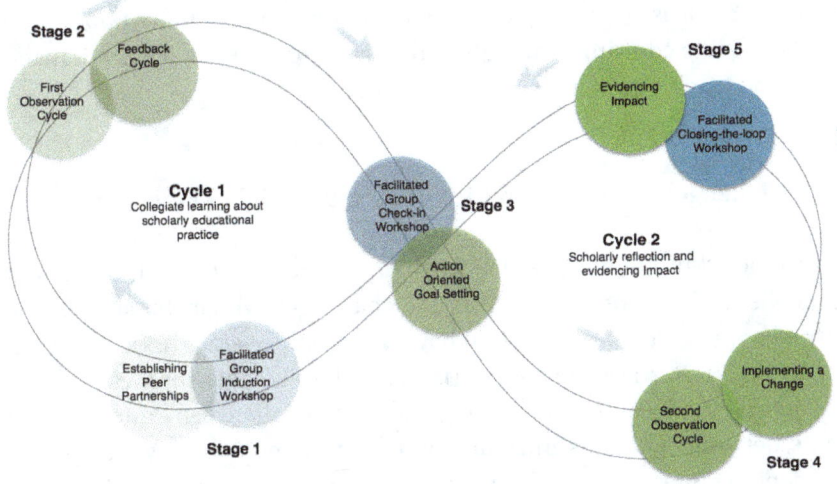

FIGURE 3.1 Peer Feedback on Educational Practice Model

model is provided in Figure 3.1. The five stages are described in detail later in the chapter.

Reciprocal exchange of practice represents a core feature of our model since it is well established that reciprocal peer feedback is most useful in promoting critical reflection for developmental learning (McMahon et al., 2007; O'Leary, 2012; Peel, 2005). Further benefits of reciprocal peer observation practices have been widely documented including by Hendry and Oliver (2012) who found that when undertaken for developmental purposes, reciprocal peer observation delivers benefits for both the observer and observee. Their findings evidence the importance of creating a confidential, non-judgmental environment. Reciprocal partnerships importantly facilitate opportunities for observational learning (Baduara, 1987) and work to mitigate against power disparities between partners (McMahon et al., 2007). Regardless of experience or seniority, all educators bring to a teaching partnership a breadth of experiences, including their experiences as a learner and as an educator, along with conceptions of good practice, which are shaped by key factors including enculturated disciplinary ways of knowing.

As the literature identifies (Drew, Klopper, & Mallit, 2015), models of successful peer feedback on teaching partnerships feature a structured and supportive framework. We recognise the importance of these features and argue that, to be successful, programs should be informed by principles of adult learning which value academic agency (Schön 1983; Speck 1996) and recognise that adult learners bring to the learning context a broad life experience and potential to "reflect critically on their world views and assumptions"

(McDougall & Davis, 2010, p. 435). Our model purposefully draws upon these elements to guide educators through a process of a partnered exploration and reflection on teaching practice.

4   Challenges and Opportunities: Teaching in Higher Education

Before we detail in full our peer feedback on teaching model, it is important to acknowledge key contextual factors and challenges, which characterise the tertiary education sector. Partnerships have commonly operated as a key organising principle in tertiary education, (manifest for example through collaborations between educators for teaching and research, between educators and students, between educators and industry and community), however, as Collyer (2015) identifies, in recent decades the tertiary sector has undergone significant changes due to the "influx of market principles into the traditions and practices of the academy" (p. 328). This marketisation is manifest in a number of ways which includes: the massification of the tertiary sector; the ever increasing casualisation of the tertiary teaching workforce with casually employed educators often not fully integrated into Faculty nor the teaching team; along with increases in academic workload (Collyer, 2015; Nethsinghe, 2017). Combined, these factors work against the time needed for relationship building.

As Trust, Carpenter, and Krutka (2017) identify, the siloing of teaching practice in higher education is further compounded by the nature of higher education practice itself which they note is "often highly specialised and competitive in nature" (p. 1), contributing to "an isolating environment that hinders the growth of faculty and staff" (p. 1). We argue that one way to mitigate against such isolation for educators is to foster and nurture teaching partnerships.

This includes to harness partnerships that occur informally and to formalise these through professional development programs including peer feedback on teaching, which fosters reflection on practice. We further note the current unrealised potential of reflective practice to foster and enhance professional learning in higher education. As Harvey and Vlachopoulos (2018) identify that whilst "a growing body of research supports the learning and teaching of reflective practice in higher education" the development and use of reflection for the purposes of professional development, remains "underdeveloped" (p. 1).

In response to the imperative to deliver measurable improvement in teaching quality, recent decades have given rise to universities increasingly focusing on professionalising tertiary teaching (Bell, 2005; Bell & Mladenovic, 2013). This move toward the professionalisation of teaching has been paralleled by increasing accountability for the quality of tertiary teaching (Klopper & Drew,

2015; O'Leary, 2013). Within the complex tertiary landscape, universities are challenged to design and deliver effective, needs-based adult professional learning programs, which build teaching capability in ways which ensure buy-in from the academy, and which deliver developmental learning for improvement in teaching.

In the Australian tertiary context, similar to the UK and elsewhere, accountability to quality and performance measurement acts as a powerful driver in shaping university practices and policies, which are designed to improve quality in teaching. The imperative to deliver quality teaching in tertiary education has given rise to a suite of mandated performance measurement orientated approaches to improvement in teaching. Such approaches include mandatory peer observation for evaluative and performance driven managerialist purposes.

Performance and quality measurement driven tertiary teaching policies and practices feature in the higher education discourse, reinforced through relations of power (Ball, 2003; Fairclough, 1989; O'Leary, 2012; Shortland, 2010). Our model offers a counterpoint to such practices. It recognises the benefits of voluntary, reciprocal peer feedback on teaching partnerships (Gosling, 2014) that are undertaken for developmental purposes. We highlight that when framed as a mechanism for quality and performance measurement peer feedback on teaching, through the process of peer observation, can be viewed, experienced and resisted by educators who perceive it as a means of ensuring a surface level compliance with quality performance agendas (Ball, 2003; Peel, 2005; Shortland, 2010).

More recent shifts in funding and regulatory requirements have resulted in the need for universities to achieve and demonstrate the quality of learning and teaching (Klopper & Drew, 2015). This quest for quality has resonated in a number of ways, which includes through the emergence of competitive league tables with "universities compared in the quest for international and local students" (Drew, Klooper, & Mallitt, 2015, pp. 35–36). Within a climate of "increasing regulation and market driven student demand" (Klopper, Drew, & Nulty, 2015, p. 28), the measurement of teaching quality via student surveys has come to occupy a prominent place in tertiary teaching. (Klopper, Drew, & Nulty, 2015, p. 12; Smith, 2005). This shift has resulted in a student-oriented approach to quality indicators in teaching, (Drew, Klopper, & Nutlty, 2015), with student evaluations commonly used summatively rather than in ways, which can foster learning and development in teaching. By creating a third space, our model provides a balance to the student perspective. It gives voice to feedback on educational practice by creating a lens through which practice can be viewed, reflected upon and theorised supported by feedback from a peer.

5 Theories of Adult Professional Learning

Our model gives emphasis to Brookfield's concept of critical theory (1998, 2005) and is designed to promote critical reflection (Brookfield, 1998, 2005) through the exchange of teaching practice. Critical theory provides a lens through which we can see, understand and examine our world. As Brookfield theorises, critical theory offers a perspective which strives for improvement in our world through enhanced democracy (Brookfield, 2005). We invoke this concept as "a reflective theory which gives agents of a kind of knowledge inherently productive of enlightenment and emancipation" (Brookfield, 2005, p. 26). We view adult learning as a social practice, and in line with Brookfield, argue that its ultimate goal, as emancipatory, is to foster a philosophical and social view of the world that is democratic, fair and just. As Brookfield (2001) describes, "A critical theory of adult learning should have at its core an understanding of how adults learn to recognise the predominance of ideology … how adults learn to challenge ideology that serves the interests of the few against the wellbeing of the many. Such a theory is inevitably a theory of social and political learning" (pp. 21–22).

Brookfield's conception of critical theory strikes at the heart of the current quality paradigm. It importantly recognises that we can contest and reframe dominant discourses. We invoke his theorising to challenge prevailing dominant quality discourses where performance and quality measurement and competitive league ranking tables can drive the design and implementation of professional development practices in tertiary teaching, and where student evaluations are positioned as "the sole arbiter of quality" (Drew, Klopper, & Mallitt, 2015, p. 35). We challenge the limitations of this paradigm to reimagine a more holistic and integrated approach to evidencing and enhancing development and quality in tertiary teaching.

We thus propose a triangulated approach that takes account of student's reflections, educator's reflections and a third space, peer feedback on teaching. We have intentionally designed a holistic and integrated model to give voice to the academy. Our model is designed to ensure that tertiary educators are supported to engage in voluntary peer feedback on educational practice partnerships which: respect diverse ways of knowing; give prominence to academic agency; and which recognise and evidence development and improvement in teaching through the partnered process of peer feedback and reflection on practice.

We further acknowledge, as Brookfield (1998) importantly identifies, that "few of us can get very far doing this on our own" (p. 197). "We find it very difficult to stand outside ourselves and see how some of how our most deeply held values and beliefs lead us into distorted and constrained ways of being" (p. 197).

Here we see the fundamental importance and rich potential of educator partnerships. Drawing upon Brookfield's concept of critical reflective theory (1998, 2005) we have designed our model to facilitate partnerships whereby educators hold a mirror to their practice; standing outside their practice, seeing their practice from the view of a different perspective (Brookfield, 1998). It is through this third space that new perspectives on educational practice are shared to encourage reflection on practice for development. Brookfield (1998, 2005) and others including Cranton (2011) acknowledge that critically reflecting on an experience and implementing new ways of working, which are in turn reflected upon, can foster developmental professional learning. Reflective practice is further acknowledged as central to the scholarly development of educators (Hall & Sutherland, 2013).

To contribute to understandings of the potential of peer to peer feedback on educational practice through teaching partnerships it is also useful to acknowledge Senge's (2011) theorising, which gives prominence to professional conversations as a catalyst for critical reflection and learning. Senge theorised that conversations which are focused upon reflection and which lead to professional learning can be viewed as "learningful". Senge describes the "learningful conversation" as one whereby reflection encompasses a focus on mental models. These mental models relate to our assumptions and beliefs, our worldview and our actions which arise from our world view. Senge conceptualises the "learningful conversation" as a precursor to professional learning. We see such conceptions of professional conversations as enablers of learning as occupying an important place in the adult professional learning literature (Candy, 1996; Haigh, 2005; Liaurillard, 2001). As theorised by Haigh (2005), professional conversations can foster critical reflection which contributes to professional and scholarly learning.

A further key feature of our model is that it fosters situational (Lave & Wegner, 1992) and experiential learning (Kolb, 1984). In line with Lave and Wegener's theorising, our model facilitates learning that is collaborative, involving sharing ideas and strategies through educator partnerships where there is a common interest, learning about teaching. Our model also foregrounds Kolb's (1984) concept of experiential learning, where learning is by doing, where learning occurs in authentic teaching practice contexts through the process of peer observation and feedback. We also acknowledge Vygotsky's (1978) socio-cultural theory, which identifies social interaction as critical to the development of cognition.

In summary, our key practice-based concepts, which include situated learning, reflective practice and conceptual expansion aim to support educators to make changes to their teaching practice that support student learning. What draws these concepts and practices together is that they are developmental in their orientation. They underpin our intent to foster an adult professional learning environment in which educators are active agents in their decision-making and where learning is situated; constructed collaboratively through social interactions, which are integrated as part of a community of practice (Lave & Wenger, 1992). Our adopted principles of adult professional learning importantly foreground respecting and harnessing academic agency and fostering ownership and trust (McMahon et al., 2007; Speck, 1996). These principles are explored further in the following section.

6   Peer Feedback on Educational Practice Model: An Iterative Peer Feedback Learning Cycle

Our model recognises the need, beyond formal student evaluations, to evidence and promote quality and development in teaching. Our seven guiding principles recognise the importance of ownership, trust, reciprocity, confidentially, and responsibility of all participants.

TABLE 3.1   Guiding principles for developmental feedback

Peer feedback on educational practice	Aligned with adult learning principles[a]
Builds relationships	Learning is supported and facilitated through peer collaboration
Fosters learning	Learning is practical, applied and guided
Encourages reciprocity	Learning is co-created and values life experience and knowledge
Values voluntary participation	Learning is voluntary: internally motivated and directed (intrinsic motivation)
Ensures confidentiality	Learning is private and respects confidentiality in the peer feedback process
Respects ownership	Learning is realistic and relevant to needs and aspirations, recognising learner agency in goal setting and actions
Enhances quality	Learning supports scholarly developmental learning that is evidenced and goal oriented

a Adapted from Speck (1996) and McMahon, Barrett, and O'Neill (2007).

7 The Process

We have adapted Brookfield's (1998) four reflective lenses as a way of supporting educators to critically reflect on practice as they cycle through our peer feedback on teaching process as follows:

- autobiographies as learner and educator (self)
- colleagues' perspectives (peers)
- learners' perspectives (students)
- theoretical literature (self and peers). (pp. 198–200)

These lenses are complementary and non-linear. They are intended to foster reflective practice that, as critical, goes beyond exploring what we do, to reflect in the following ways on why we make the choices we do in our educational practice.

1. *Self:* Educators reflect on their own learning journey. As Brookfield (1998) identifies, "Recalling dimensions of our autobiographies as learners helps us understand why we gravitate towards certain ways of doing things and why we avoid certain others" (p. 198). Educators also reflect on their experiences of teaching. These reflections are shared with a peer. We encourage a reflexive perspective to explore beliefs and assumptions which define and shape our professional roles and identity
2. *Peers:* Educators engage in reciprocal peer observation partnerships. This lens acknowledges that "participating in critical conversation with peers opens us up to their versions of events we have experienced" (Brookfield, 1998, p. 200).
3. *Students:* Educators reflect on student feedback, noting the critical importance of anonymity in student feedback (Brookfield, 1998, p. 199).
4. *Self & Peers Theory:* Educators view practice through a theoretical lens, to advance scholarly led teaching and to as Brookfield (1998) identifies, "help us name our practice ..." (pp. 200–201). In this way we create opportunities for educators to integrate educational theory as well as pedagogical knowledge to enhance practice.

Participants move through a five-stage, flexible program facilitated by a teacher education expert and tailored to career and professional learning needs. Professional learning partnerships are underpinned by three critical elements: (1) educational learning and teaching leadership provided by the university; (2) staged, intrinsically motivated, opt-in/opt-out process; (3) opportunities for educators to engage in reciprocal peer partnerships.

The process of giving and receiving is designed to facilitate collaborative relationships between educators. The peer feedback cycle is staged over two semesters and involves three facilitated workshops and two peer observation and feedback cycles.

Reciprocal peer partnerships are undertaken with a peer from within or across disciplines. In a reciprocal exchange, both educators observe, share and reflect on one another's practice to inform future goal setting for the purposes of continuous improvement and evidencing effective teaching practice.

The process of peer feedback on teaching is enacted through the following five stages. All workshops are faciliated by a teacher education expert.

7.1 Stage 1: Facilitated Group Induction Workshop, Establishing Peer Partnerships

Participants are inducted into an iterative cycle of action learning that involves planning, observing, reflecting, implementing and evaluating. This workshop includes a focus on supporting participants to reflect on their auto biographies as learners, and educators, and to articulate their teaching values and philosophies of learning. To support this process, educators engage with the *Characteristics of Effective Teaching Practice* (Appendix A) that we have adapted from Drew, Klopper, and Nulty (2015). Participants explore examples of the type and range of evidence that might be observed in each characteristic of effective educational practice. This workshop also draws upon broader scholarly literature in tertiary teaching including Biggs and Tang (2011), Chickering and Gamson (1987) and Ramsden (1992).

Participants integrate self-reflections and student feedback (e.g., mid-course polling, one-minute papers, university administered student surveys) to inform their foci for their first observation. Participants may observe face-to-face teaching, or choose to focus on other aspects of educational practice which include course and program design, and learning and teaching resources. Participants workshop scenarios to promote constructive, evidenced-based feedback strategies. Giving and receiving feedback is supported by our *Guidelines for Giving and Receiving Feedback* (Appendix B). Templates to guide participants through the five stages are provided (Appendix C). By the end of this workshops participants have either self-selected a peer partner or they have been paired with a colleague based on areas of interest and/or observation foci. To guide this stage participants also use the *Focus Template* (Appendix C, Stage 1).

7.2 Stage Two: First Observation of Educational Practice and Feedback Cycle

Partnerships are undertaken within or across disciplines enabling educators to observe one another's practice, share and reflect on practice through a professional dialogue to inform goal setting and enhance future practice. Written and verbal feedback and feed forward is shared between peers. To guide this process, participants use the *Observe Template* (Appendix C, Stage 2).

7.3 Stage Three: Facilitated Group Check-in Workshop

This workshop occurs mid-way through the feedback process and is facilitated by a teacher education expert. By this stage participants have engaged in their first peer observation and feedback cycle. In this workshop, participants are guided to reflect on their experience and formulate goals for future practice based on their first round of peer feedback and reflection. This process fosters agency and empowers participants to play an active role in the process of peer feedback, co-creating knowledge through guided scholarly reflection. Scholarly teaching practice is further explored in relation to accepted good practice principles for example Biggs and Tang (2011), Shulman (1987), with goal setting informed by educational literature. Participants document their reflections and goals, using the *Reflection and Set Goals Template* (Appendix C, Stage 3).

7.4 Stage Four: Second Observation and Feedback Cycle and Implementing a Change

Participants engage in a second cycle of peer observation and feedback. The focus is on implementing and evaluating a change in practice based on reflections and peer feedback and feed forward from the first peer feedback cycle. Participants implement their action-oriented goals for improvement and evidence impact on the student experience captured via institutional course experience surveys and/or other course polling mechanisms. To guide this process, participants use the *Implement and Evaluate Template* (Appendix C, Stage 4)

7.5 Stage 5: Debrief: Closing the Loop

The closing the loop workshop provides an opportunity for final reflections on the process of giving and receiving feedback, goal setting, implementing a change and evaluating impact. Educators evidence the impact of their teaching on student learning captured via informal subject polling tools and/or institutional subject experience surveys.

This workshop supports participants to utilise their reflections on their peer and student feedback, along with their own reflections and student feedback, to consolidate and develop ideas/strategies to enhance ongoing teaching practice. Through a guided process, educators share and reflect on their learning and are supported to situate and reflect on their practice in relation to relevant educational literature. Appropriate and needs-based literature is provided by teacher education experts.

8   Conclusions

This chapter has presented a *Peer Feedback on Educational Practice Model* designed to harness the intrinsic value of teaching partnerships in tertiary education. It offers a way forward for universities to realise the rich potential of such partnerships to foster learningful conversations and communities.

Our model speaks to the critical importance of establishing guiding principles which harness and support educator's intrinsic motivation and agency. It also draws upon research demonstrating the efficacy of developmental peer feedback on teaching for improvement in teaching and upon prominent theories of adult professional learning.

We acknowledge, as O'Leary (2013) does, the all-powerful relationship between the purposes of peer observation (whether undertaken for quality measurement or developmental purposes) and its outcomes, impact and risks. We trust that our model will go some way towards mitigating the risks that arise when peer feedback on teaching partnerships are colonised by performance and quality measurement agendas. That it will give prominence to developmental peer feedback on teaching as a pedagogic practice to enhance and evidence development and quality in tertiary teaching. We thus advance our model as one that will give life to Brookfield's conception of emancipatory adult professional learning to ultimately create a learningful community for all.

References

Ball, S. J. (2003). The teacher's soul and the terrors of performativity. *Journal of Education Policy, 18*(2), 215–28.

Barnard, A., Croft, W., Irons, R., Cuffe, N., & Bandara, W. R. P. (2011). Peer partnership to enhance scholarship of teaching: A case study. *Higher Education Research and Development, 30*(4), 435–448.

Bell, A., & Mladenovic, R. (2008). The benefits of peer observation of teaching for tutor development. *Higher Education, 55*(6), 735–752.

Bell, A., & Mladenovic, R. (2013). How tutors understand and engage with reflective practices. *Reflective Practice, 14*(1), 1–11.

Bell, M. (2005). *Peer observation partnerships in higher education*. HERDSA.

Bell, M., & Cooper, P. (2013). Peer observation of teaching in university departments: A framework for implementation. *International Journal for Academic Development, 18*(1), 60–73.

Biggs, J., & Tang, C. (2011). *Teaching for quality learning at university: What the student does* (4th ed.). Open University Press.

Brookfield, S. (1998). Critically reflective practice. *Journal of Continuing Education in the Health Professions, 18*(4), 197–205.

Brookfield, S. (2001). Repositioning ideology critique in a critical theory of adult learning. *Adult Education Quarterly, 52*(1), 7–22.

Brookfield, S. (2005). *The power of critical theory: Liberating adult learning and teaching*. Jossey-Bass.

Candy, P. (1996). Promoting lifelong learning: Academic developers and the university as a learning organisation. *International Journal for Academic Development, 1*(1), 7–18.

Chickering, A. W., & Gamson, Z. F. (1987). Seven principles for good practice in undergraduate education. *AAHE Bulletin, 6*(39), 3–7.

Collyer, F. M. (2015). Practices of conformity and resistance in the marketisation of the academy: Bourdieu, professionalism and academic capitalism, *Critical Studies in Education, 56*(3), 315–331.

Cranton, P. (2011). A transformative perspective on the scholarship of teaching and learning. *Higher Education Research & Development, 30*(1), 75–86.

Daniels, J. (2017). Professional learning in higher education: Making good practice relevant. *International Journal for Academic Development, 22*(2), 170–181.

Drew, S., Klopper, C., & Mallitt, K. (2015). PRO-teaching: Sharing ideas to develop capabilities. In C. Klopper & S. Drew (Eds.), *Teaching for learning and learning for teaching: Peer review of teaching in higher education* (pp. 35–52). Sense Publishers.

Drew, S., Klopper, C., & Nulty, D. (2015). Defining and developing a framework for the peer observation of teaching. In C. Klopper & S. Drew (Eds.), *Teaching for learning and learning for teaching: Peer review of teaching in higher education* (pp. 13–34). Sense Publishers.

Fairclough, N. (1989). *Language and power*. Longman.

Gosling, D. (2014). Collaborative peer-supported review of teaching. In J. Sachs & M. Parsell (Eds.), *Peer review of learning and teaching in higher education* (pp. 13–31). Springer.

Haigh, N. (2005). Everyday conversation as a context for professional learning and development. *International Journal for Academic Development, 10*(1), 3–16.

Hall, M., & Sutherland, K. (2013). Students who teach: Developing scholarly tutors. In F. Beaton & A. Gilbert (Eds.), *Developing effective part-time teachers in higher education: New approaches to professional development* (pp. 82–93). Routledge.

Harvey, M., & Vlachopoulos, P. (2018). What a difference a day makes: Reflection retreats as academic development in higher education. *Journal of Further and Higher Education*, 1–15.

Hendry, G. D., & Oliver, G. R. (2012). Seeing is believing: The benefits of peer observation. *Journal of University Teaching & Learning Practice, 9*(1), 1–9.

Klopper, C., & Drew, S. (2015). Teaching for learning and learning for teaching. In C. Klopper & S. Drew (Eds.), *Teaching for learning and learning for teaching: Peer review of teaching in higher education* (pp. 1–11). Sense Publishers.

Kolb, D. A. (1984). *Experiential learning: Experience as the source of learning and development*. Prentice Hall.

Lave, J., & Wegner, E. (1992). *Situated learning: Legitimate peripheral interpretation*. Cambridge University Press.

McDougall, J., & Davis, W. (2010). Role reversal: Educators in an enabling program embark on a journey of critical self-reflection. *Australian Journal of Adult Learning, 51*(3), 432–435.

McMahon, T., Barrett, T., & O'Neill, G. (2007). Using observation of teaching to improve quality: Finding your way through the muddle of competing conceptions, confusion of practice and mutually exclusive intentions. *Teaching in Higher Education, 12*(4), 499–511.

Nethsinghe, R. (2017). Confronting the challenges of massification surge in higher education: Sustaining the academic workforce and its excellence in Australia. In D. E. Neubauer, K. H. Mok, & J. Jiang (Eds.), *The sustainability of higher education in an era of post-massification* (pp. 59–71). Routledge.

O'Leary, M. (2012). Exploring the role of lesson observation in the English education system: A review of methods, models and meanings. *Professional Development in Education, 38*(5), 791–810.

O'Leary, M. (2013). Surveillance, performativity and normalized practice: The use and impact of graded lesson observations in further education colleges. *Journal of Further and Higher Education, 37*(5), 694–714.

Peel, D. (2005). Peer observation as a transformatory tool? *Teaching in Higher Education, 10*(4), 489–504.

Ramsden, P. (1992). *Learning to teach in higher education*. Routledge.

Schön, D. (1983). *The reflective practitioner: How professionals think in action*. Basic Books.

Shortland, S. (2010). Feedback within peer observation: Continuing professional development and unexpected consequences. *Innovations in Education and Teaching International, 47*(3), 295–304.

Shulman, J. (1987). Knowledge and teaching: Foundations of the new reform. *Harvard Educational Review, 57*(1), 1–23.

Senge, P. (2011). *The fifth discipline fieldbook: Strategies and tools for building a learning organisation*. Nicholas Brealey Publishing.

Smith, R. (2005). Dancing on the feet of chance: The uncertain university. *Educational Theory, 55*(2), 139–150.

Speck, M. (1996). Best practice in professional development for sustained educational change. *ERS Spectrum, 14*(2), 33–41.
Trust, T., Carpenter, J. P., & Krutka, D. G. (2017). Moving beyond silos: Professional learning networks in higher education. *The Internet and Higher Education, 35*, 1–11.
Vygotsky, L. S. (1978). *Mind in society*. Harvard University Press.
Wingrove, D. (in press). *Enhancing educational practice: A five-year journey of tertiary peer observation.*
Wingrove, D., Hammersley-Fletcher, L., Clarke, A., & Chester, A. (2018). Leading developmental peer observation of teaching in higher education: Perspectives from Australia and England. *British Journal of Educational Studies, 66*(3), 365–381.

Appendix A: Characteristics of Effective Educational Practice

Data adapted from Drew, Klopper, and Nulty (2015).
1. Teacher provides explicit, challenging and achievable learning objectives.
2. Teacher uses advanced content knowledge to create clear explanations and address student questions.
3. Teaching style effectively engages students in active learning.
4. Teacher seeks feedback on students' understanding and provides appropriate assistance.
5. Teacher designs learning activities which demonstrate students' understanding and are adapted to further develop understanding as needed.
6. Teacher encourages students to reflect upon and share their prior knowledge and experience and integrate this with their current learning.
7. Teacher designs learning activities and/or assessments in a structured and coherent manner that assists students to achieve the stated learning objectives.
8. Teaching makes effective use of the environment, resources and technologies to enhance the student learning experience.
9. Teaching is inclusive and caters for student diversity.
10. Teaching creates opportunities for students to share and reflect on their learning.
11. Teaching creates opportunities for collaborative learning.
12. Teaching is informed by the scholarship of learning and teaching.

Appendix B: Guidelines for Giving and Receiving Peer Feedback on Educational Practice

Source: Boud, D. (2010) Assessment Futures. Retrieved May 11, 2011, from http://www.iml.uts.edu.au/assessment-futures/elements/Giving-and-Receiving-Feedback.pdf

Giving Feedback

There are many characteristics of worthwhile feedback but the most important is the way in which it is given. Helpful feedback makes a conscious distinction between the person, who is always valued, and particular acts or specific work, which may be subject to critical comment. The tone, the style and the content should be consistent and supportive. If you wish to give helpful feedback, you should:

Be Realistic

Direct your comments towards matters on which the person can act. Don't make suggestions which are entirely outside the scope of what the person can do. Constructive comments can be helpful so long as they respect the other person's individual way of doing things.

Be Specific

Base your comments on concrete observable behavior or materials and provide specific examples. The person should be given sufficient information to pinpoint the areas to which you are referring and have a clear idea of what is being said about those specific areas.

Be Sensitive to the Goals of the Person

Link your comments to your partner's goals; listen carefully to what they wanted to achieve in the session.

Be Timely

Respond promptly when your feedback is requested. Feedback is most effective when it happens soon after the event.

Be Descriptive

Describe your views and give specific examples of what you observed.

Be Consciously Non-Judgmental

Offer your personal view: do not act as an authority even if you may be one elsewhere. Give your personal reactions and feelings rather than value-laden statements. One way of doing this is to use comments of the type "I feel ... when you ...".

Don't compare
Be cautious about giving feedback in a context in which the comments which you give one person will be compared with those of another.

Be Diligent
Check your response. Is it an accurate reflection of what you want to express? Have you perceived the contribution accurately?

Be Direct
Say what you mean. Don't wrap it up in fancy words or abstract language.

Be Positive
Say what you appreciate. However, try to find something which is genuinely felt, rather than being positive because you feel it is required.

Be Aware
Note your own emotional state before you give feedback. If you are anxious or defensive you may well distort otherwise helpful comments.

Receiving Feedback
There is no point in asking others to give you feedback unless you are prepared to be open to it and to consider comments which differ from your own perceptions. As a receiver of feedback:

Be Explicit
Make it clear what kind of feedback you are seeking. If necessary indicate what kinds you do not want to receive.

Be Attentive
Concentrate fully on what is being said. Focus on what the person wants you to know, not on what you would like to hear.

Be Aware
Notice your own reactions, both intellectual and emotional. Particularly notice any reactions of rejection or censorship on your part. If the viewpoint from which the other is speaking is at variance with your own do not dismiss it: it can be important to realise the misapprehensions of others. Some people find

it useful to partially dissociate or distance themselves in this situation and act as if they were witnessing feedback being given to someone else.

Be Silent

Refrain from making a response. Don't begin to frame a response in your own mind until you have listened carefully to what has been said and have considered the implications. Don't use the excuse of correcting factual errors to avoid hearing and resonating with the substance of what has been said. Don't be distracted by the need to explain: if you continue to feel that you need to give an explanation do it later after the feedback session once you are sure you have attended to all that has been said.

Appendix C: Peer Feedback on Educational Practice Model: Process Templates

The following templates have been condensed due to space requirements of this publication. In practice, each template is formatted as a single page so that participants can use them as worksheets during the process.

Stage One: Focus Template

The purpose of this template is to help guide the first stage in the peer partnership cycle. It is an opportunity to clarify your own focus and it will provide important information for your partner. You should give a copy of this completed template to your partner in preparation for the observation. Your partner will look at your course guide prior to the observation.

> Name of Teacher:
> Name of Partner:
> Subject Name/Code:
> Year Level:
> Day, time and location of class:
> Relevant context for your partner: (e.g. information about courses, students, teaching team, etc.)

Focus of the Observation

On which aspects of your teaching are you seeking feedback? We recommend you identify one or two aspects of your teaching to focus on e.g. large class teaching, giving students feedback, managing group work, facilitating class discussions, assessment design, use of technologies etc.

Focus 1:
Focus 2:

Stage Two: Observe Template

The purpose of this template is to help guide the second stage in the Peer Feedback process –observe. As well as meeting with your partner to share your feedback it is important to provide some written feedback. This template may help you to synthesise your feedback into a form that will be useful for your partner.

Teacher:
Peer Partner:
Class Observed:
Observation Focus:
Further observations Feedback:

Stage 3: Reflect and Set Goals Template

The purpose of this template is to help guide the third stage in the peer feedback cycle – reflect and set goals. Thinking about the verbal and written feedback you have received from your partner, and your own reflections on your practice, what are the three most important reflections you have made about your teaching at this stage?

Reflection 1:
Reflection 2:
Reflection 3:

Based on your reflections, what changes do you plan to make? We encourage you to articulate at least one goal to work towards in your teaching. The best way to achieve goals is to make sure they are SMART goals.

Specific: What are you going to do? How are you going to do it?

Measurable: Choose a goal that has measurable outcomes so you can note your progress. How will you know when you have attained your goal?

Attainable: A goal should be achievable, but challenging.

Realistic: Do you have the skills and resources to achieve your goal? If not, your goal in the first instance may be to acquire these skills and resources.

Timely: Set a time frame. This gives you a clear target to work towards. You may plan to make changes this semester or next time you teach the subject.

Prompts:
My teaching goal is:

My strategy for achieving this goal is:
My time frame is:

Stage 4: Implement and Evaluate Template

The purpose of this template is to help guide the fourth stage of the peer feedback cycle – implement and evaluate. In this stage you are encouraged to try something new in your teaching and then evaluate how effective this change has been for you and your students. It is advisable to make incremental and achievable changes over time rather than making large and whole scale changes to every aspect of your curriculum.

Prompts:
The goal I implemented was:
I can measure the achievement of my goal by:
I know I have attained by goal because:

Stage 5: Future Directions Template

The purpose of this template is to help guide the fifth stage of the peer feedback cycle – Future Directions. In this stage you are encouraged to revisit and reflect upon the feedback you have received from students and peers and to build upon your own reflections. The following prompts are designed to guide you to utilise your reflections and integrate this learning with the scholarship of learning and teaching.

Prompts:
I have learnt that, as an educator, I value:
The key principles that underpin my practice are:
I have reflected upon the following scholarly article/case study to inform and validate my educational practice:
My goals moving forward are to:
I need the following support to action my goals:

CHAPTER 4

Motivators, Challenges and Professional Learning for Australian Classroom Teachers Mentoring Pre-Service Teachers

Kathy Littlewood and Kathy Jordan

Abstract

There is considerable evidence in educational research literature that teacher mentors have an important role when mentoring pre-service teachers. The Australian Institute for Teaching and School Leadership (2016), recommends that teacher mentors need "access to professional learning" in order to "develop mentoring skills" (p. 6), to enable the provision of high-level support to pre-service teachers. This chapter reports on survey data from 22 classroom teachers in Victorian schools. The survey design drew on the Mentoring Profile Inventory (MPI) (Clarke, Collins, Triggs, & Nielson, 2012) which identified and described motivators and challenges in the work of teacher mentors. The current research also examined teachers' experiences of professional learning related to mentoring. Recommendations for future practice in the mentoring of pre-service teachers conclude this chapter.

Keywords

teacher mentor – practicum – pre-service teacher

1   Introduction

Researchers in Australia and internationally agree that teacher mentors have a very important role to play in supporting Initial Teacher Education (ITE), particularly assisting in the education of pre-service teachers during practicum (professional experience) in schools (Teacher Education Ministerial Advisory Group [TEMAG], 2014; Zeichner, 2010). Pre-service teachers view the practicum experience, or time in schools developing practical teaching skills and knowledge, as the most important, exciting and challenging aspect of their program

(Darling-Hammond, 2006). This experience is organised by the universities in partnership with schools and is dependent on the schools providing access to their classrooms, their students and their experienced teachers, to assist in the pre-service teacher's development of teaching skills and knowledge in the classroom environment.

Yet, exactly what the role involves is open to considerable interpretation (House of Representatives Standing Committee on Education and Vocational Training, 2007). The experienced teachers who work with pre-service teachers are known by different names. A scan of current terminology used by some Australian universities who deliver ITE programs, reveals a variety of names for the role including: Supervising Teacher (University of Sydney, UNSW, UTS, Macquarie University, University of South Australia), Associate Teacher (Charles Sturt University) and Mentor Teacher (Melbourne University, Monash University, RMIT University and Flinders University). This range of nomenclature potentially leads to some confusion around what is expected of the teacher mentor and the nature of the interaction between the pre-service teacher and the teacher mentor. It is generally agreed that promoting a "culture of learning" (House of Representatives Standing Committee on Education and Vocational Training, 2007) in the school environment and supporting the development of the pre-service teacher towards being graduate ready, should be key outcomes of the mentoring process. In this chapter, we use the term "teacher mentor", as it implies that the relationship is "significant" and "enduring" (Irby, 2018, p. 116) and conjures a more supportive, equal and productive practicum experience (van Ginkel, Verloop, & Denessen, 2015).

However, it is interesting to note that while recognised as an important role, it is often assumed that mentoring is straight-forward and simple, undertaken by experienced teachers, which can lead to certain assumptions about the position. The predominant model in Australian ITE, is to assign mentors to pre-service teachers without any specific mentor training and a lack of any particular support whilst undertaking the role (Betlam, Clary, & Jones, 2018). This presumes that "if one is a good teacher of elementary or secondary students, this expertise will automatically carry over to one's work with novice teachers" (Zeichner, 2005, p. 118).

While the significant role of the teacher mentor is well researched in the literature and considered of high value, there is a lack of clarity about what the role actually is and this can therefore make it difficult to measure the effectiveness of a mentoring relationship and the mentoring practice being enacted. The assumptions and lack of clarity about the mentoring role, along with a deficiency of mentor voice in the literature, "Little is known about the act of mentoring from the lens of the teacher-mentor" (Betlam et al., 2018, p. 2), provides the impetus for this research into what motivates and challenges teacher mentors and the opportunities for professional learning to support their work with pre-service teachers.

2 Motivators and Challenges

Australian and international research has a lot to say about mentoring from the point of view of the pre-service teacher or the University but the view of the teacher mentor is not often interrogated and their motivations for mentoring and the challenges they face in the role, have only more recently started to be examined (Ehrich, Hansford, & Ehrich, 2011; Betlam et al., 2018). Ehrich et al. (2011), in a comprehensive review of Australian and international studies concerning mentoring across selected professions, found that in the field of education, collegiality and networking, reflection on own practice, personal professional development and personal satisfaction were the top four cited positive outcomes (motivations) for mentoring. In a similar vein, findings from a Netherlands study of 726 secondary school teacher mentors undertaken by van Ginkel et al. (2015), revealed that the main motivations to mentor were for personal learning and to contribute to the profession. They categorised motives as "self-focused" or "other-focused" with other-focused motives including "a desire to help and pass along information to others and to build a competent workforce" and "self-focused motives included a desire to increase learning and to feel gratification" (p. 5). The authors suggest that these results could be used as "potential strategies for the selection and preparation of mentor teachers for programs that intend to foster collaborative inquiry approaches for novice teacher support" (p. 3). Neilson et al. (2017), who reported on the results of Australian research using the Mentoring Profile Inventory (Clarke et al., 2012), which was adapted for the current research, found that the strongest motivators for this cohort were: "Renewing the Profession, Contributing to Teacher Education, Improving own Teaching Practice, Developing a Professional Community and Mentoring in Classroom Contexts" (p. 354). Thus, it is evident that the findings from these studies are similar in nature, with high motivators for mentoring pre-service teachers generally being of an altruistic nature in the desire to build a competent future workforce and to give back to the profession, as well as the more personal driver of increasing one's own learning opportunities through the mentoring of others.

Ehrich et al. (2011) found the most frequently cited challenges for teacher mentors were "lack of time, and professional expertise and/or personality mismatch" (p. 11). Other highly rated challenges from this study included a "lack of training or understanding of program goals and the extra burden or responsibility as problematic outcomes associated with mentoring" (p. 14). From research undertaken in Zimbabwe, similar challenges for teacher mentors were identified, including lack of mentor training, personal differences between the mentor and the mentee, and limited resources available to mentors (Samkange, 2015). Other challenges reported in this research included interpersonal relationship issues, lack of clear procedures for selecting mentors and lack of teacher mentor role clarity. Nielson, Mena, Juanjo, Clarke, O'Shea, Hoban, and Collins, (2017) reported that the highest identified challenges for the Australian cohort they surveyed were "Concerns about Student Teacher Pre-Practicum Preparation and Unclear Policies and Procedures" (p. 358). As with the motivators to mentor, there were similarities across the identified challenges such as inadequate time to mentor, personality and relationship issues, lack of clarity around university policies and the mentor role, lack of university information about pre-service teacher coursework, mentor selection procedures and lack of mentor training.

3   Professional Learning

Mentoring pre-service teachers on placement in schools is not a new phenomenon and has been seen in ITE around the world "from the early 1980s" (Sorenson, 2012, p. 4). However, professional learning to support these teacher mentors has been limited and is more often undertaken voluntarily. In contrast, in Australia, there has been specific professional learning developed to support the mentors of new graduates. For example, new graduates in Victoria have been supported by a dedicated, experienced teacher mentor in their first year of teaching. In part, this is to assist graduate teachers navigate the registration process (moving from provisional as a new graduate, to fully registered after teaching a minimum of 80 days in an Australian or New Zealand school setting). In part also, such support for mentoring, including the recently developed Mentoring Capability Framework (Department of Education and Training Victoria, 2019) in Victoria, is a strategy to "counteract the high attrition rate of new teachers" and also to "encourage educational reform through professional development opportunities for experienced teachers" (Rajuan, 2012, p. 4).

Recent reports from Australian state and federal governments acknowledge the importance of the practicum in the development of graduate ready teachers. The Teacher Education Ministerial Advisory Group (TEMAG, 2014) report notes that "highly skilled supervising teachers" are crucial to "demonstrate and assess" (p. 7) the requirements of effective teaching. Recent revision to the accreditation of ITE programs have now stipulated that provision should be made for professional learning for teacher mentors (AITSL, 2018). In general, teacher mentors volunteer for the role and undertake it with little training, not much formal knowledge of mentoring and limited support for the task (Betlam et al., 2018; van Ginkel et al., 2014). Interestingly, although the practicum experience is highly valued by pre-service teachers and acknowledged as important by government bodies, the worth placed on practicum and the role of the teacher mentor is perhaps underplayed by teachers and principals in the schools and also by university practicum partners (Zeichner, 2005).

This chapter reports on data that formed part of a larger study on the mentoring of pre-service teachers and aims to further understand the role of the teacher mentor. The current study was set up as a small-scale pilot to test the questions for the larger study and to enable input from the participants about the clarity of the questions. The pilot survey also enabled the researcher to identify any gaps in the questions, or problems with the flow of the survey, of which several were discovered. This allowed the researcher to address these issues before the large-scale survey was implemented. The pilot study examined the motivators and challenges for teachers when they mentor, including those related to postgraduate and undergraduate pre-service teachers during practicum in schools, and in addition looked at the opportunities for teacher mentor professional learning in a Victorian school context. Specifically, this study examined:
– Teacher mentor motivators to support pre-service teachers during practicum.
– Teacher mentor challenges to support pre-service teachers during practicum.
– Teacher mentor opportunities to undertake professional learning related to mentoring pre-service teachers during practicum.

4   Method

This study focused on teacher mentor motivators and challenges in supporting pre-service teachers during placement and their experiences of teacher mentor professional learning. The survey instrument was adapted from Nielsen et al. (2017) and modified to suit the research focus. The survey used a set of Likert-style questions that generated both quantitative and qualitative data.

Participants were asked to indicate to what extent each of the items, categorised as motivators (10 items) and challenges (9 items), influenced them, using a five point scale where participants indicated motivators from being most important to least important, or challenge being from most challenging to least challenging similar to that used in the Nielsen et., (2017) survey. The Mentoring Profile Inventory [MPI] (Clarke et al., 2012) has 62 items, divided between eight motivation sub-scales (containing four items each) and six challenge sub-scales (containing five items each). The psychometric properties of the MPI are described in Clarke et al. (2012). The motivation sub-scales are: Renewing the profession; Contributing to teacher education; Improving own teaching practice; Developing a professional community; Mentoring in classroom contexts; Time out to monitor pupil learning; ST (student teacher) promotes pupil engagement; Reminders about career advancement. The challenge sub-scales are: Concerns about student teacher pre-practicum preparation; Unclear policies and procedures; Inadequate forms and guidelines; Uncertain feedback and communications; Concerns about school advising as a sub-specialty; Challenges to guidance and mentoring. These categories broadly framed the survey used in this study, which was adapted to pre-test the items to ensure that they were meaningful to the target audience and provided the focus required for the subsequent larger study. The 12 sub-scale headings were used as items in this small pilot study to generate broad information on motivators and challenges for teachers when mentoring pre-service teachers.

Regarding the adaptation of the instrument, Boateng, Neilands, Frongillo, Melgar-Quiñonez, and Young (2018), explained that pre-testing, or piloting questions allowed for revision of items that were not clearly worded, to enable clarity of the phrases used. In addition, the authors stated that pre-testing the survey questions made the final survey instrument easier for participants to understand and allowed the targeted group to contribute to the research through the development of the survey items. The researcher acknowledges that the adapted instrument used in this chapter has not been validated and is therefore a limitation of this research. In addition, the adapted survey used several open-ended questions to gather further information around motivators and challenges in mentoring pre-service teachers and experiences related to teacher mentor professional learning and supporting postgraduate pre-service teachers.

The adapted survey was divided into three sections. The first section focused on participant demographical information such as teacher qualification, years of teaching and number of pre-service teachers mentored. The second section focused on participant views of the motivators and challenges to mentoring pre-service teachers. It used the closed items and scale discussed previously. As well, this section included open-ended questions seeking further information about motivators and challenges not listed in the closed item questions and one question seeking to discover if participants discerned any differences between motivators and challenges concerning mentoring postgraduate as compared to undergraduate pre-service teachers – "Please write in the space below any different motivations and/or challenges you experience when mentoring undergraduate level (Bachelor) and postgraduate level (Diploma or Master) pre-service teachers? The third section focused on professional learning associated with mentoring.

The university professional experience office administered the practicum experiences for students within the Faculty of Education. The administration involved liaising with partner primary and secondary Victorian schools and securing placements for pre-service teachers in education degree courses at the university. The professional experience office database provided a list of the names of current teacher mentors at the university partner schools. Participants were selected to represent a cross section of Victorian teachers with varied length of teaching experience, and employment across government, independent and Catholic school sectors. The survey was administered via Microsoft Forms and sent to the teacher mentor work email addresses. The survey took on average, 15 minutes for participants to complete. The survey data was read and analysed. For ease of analysis, the five response categories were collapsed into three broad categories representing strong endorsement, moderate endorsement and little endorsement. In line with the six-phase process for thematic analysis (Braun & Clarke, 2006), open-ended questions were schematised by what participants said, rather than what the question had asked. This was done by firstly reading the responses and then creating some initial codes to help sort the information into broad emerging themes. The themes were reviewed to check for accuracy and then defined and named for the purposes of this research.

5   Findings

The findings are presented in three subsections. Section 5.1 relates to the 22 respondent's teaching experience. Section 5.2 examines their experiences of mentoring pre-service teachers including motivations and challenges of the role and any differences in mentoring postgraduate compared to undergraduate pre-service teachers. The third and final subsection, Section 5.3, explores the professional learning respondents had undertaken to support their mentoring of pre- service teachers and their ongoing professional learning needs.

5.1 Teaching Experience

Years of teaching experience amongst respondents ranged from 5 to 40 years, with a mean of 23.1 years. For the purpose of further analysis respondents were grouped into three categories of teaching experience: early career teachers with five years of teaching experience (3 respondents), mid-career teachers with more than 5 and less than 20 years teaching experience (5 respondents) and very experienced teachers with 20+ years teaching experience (14 respondents).

As shown in Figure 4.1, the largest group of respondents had a Graduate Diploma of Education as their highest qualification.

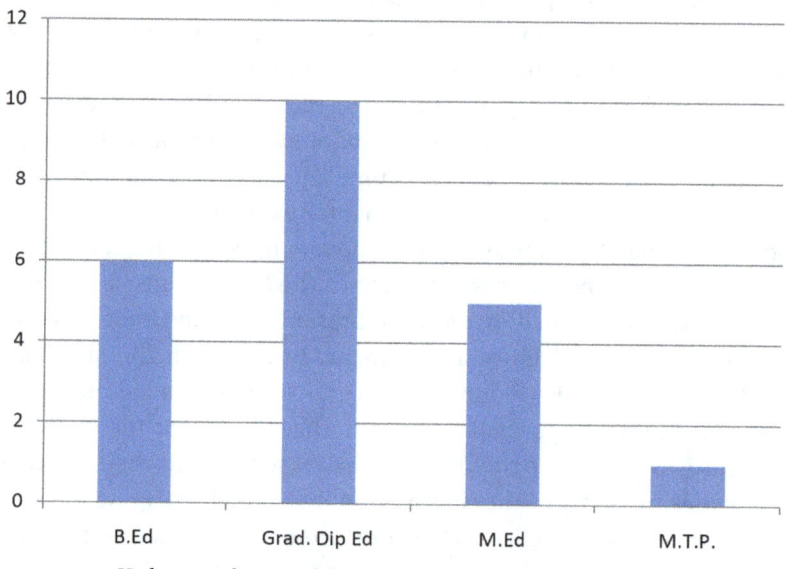

FIGURE 4.1   Highest teaching qualification

With respect to school sector, 17 of the 22 respondents were employed in the government school sector, 3 in independent and 2 in Catholic schools.

5.2 Mentoring Experience

All respondents had previously mentored pre-service teachers, however, experience as a teacher mentor varied considerably from 2 to more than 20 mentoring partnerships (see Figure 4.2). For the purpose of further analysis teacher mentoring experience was coded as beginning (experience with 2 to 3 pre-service teachers), experienced (between 6 to 10 pre-service teachers) and very experienced (for those who had worked with more than 10 pre-service teachers).

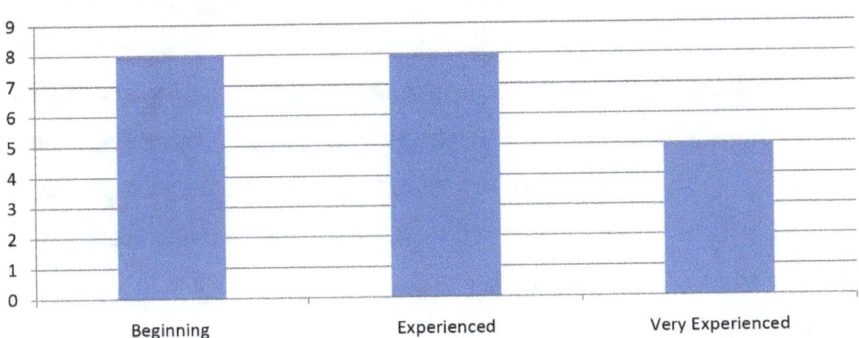

FIGURE 4.2   Teacher mentor experience

Most teachers had mentored 10 or fewer pre-service teachers. A small number of respondents had more experience, with the most experienced teacher mentor stating they had supervised more than 50 pre-service teachers. Not surprisingly, the very experienced teachers had mentored the most pre-service teachers. However, years of teaching practice was not always predictive of mentoring experience; some of the very experienced teachers with 20+ years in the classroom were beginning teacher mentors. The majority of respondents (60%) had mentored both undergraduate and postgraduate pre-service teachers.

5.3   *Motivations for Being a Teacher Mentor*

Respondents were asked to indicate to what extent each of the identified factors motivated them to take on the role of teacher mentor. As shown in Figure 4.3, respondents were highly motivated to take on the role of teacher mentor as a way of feeding back into the teaching profession and contributing to teacher education. Balancing these altruistic motivations was a clear desire to improve their own teaching practice. Least important as an incentive was career progression.

Mirroring own teaching practice as a motivation for working with pre-service teachers evenly divided respondents, with as many respondents noting

FIGURE 4.3   Motivations for being a teacher mentor

this as an important motivation as those that noted it as not at all important. Teachers with more mentoring experience typically rated this aspect as more important than those with less mentoring experience.

6   Challenges of Mentoring Pre-Service Teachers

Teacher mentors were asked to indicate to what extent each of the identified factors challenged them when mentoring pre-service teachers. As can be seen in Figure 4.4, the biggest challenges for teacher mentors were in relation to communication with universities, specifically in the areas of providing assessment and reporting assistance to help determine the success or failure of pre-service teachers, building relationships with university staff and understanding university policy and procedure information. These findings speak to the commonly perceived "theory-practice divide" referred to extensively in the literature (Zeichner, 1990; Zeichner, 2010; Korthagen & Lagerwerf, 2001). It is of interest that the two categories that relate to gaining feedback about their mentoring practice, "Feedback from own school administration" and "Feedback from pre-service teachers", as shown in Figure 4.4, found participants being divided on how challenging these aspects are. There is some indication that both aspects were considered to be greater challenges amongst more experienced teachers.

In response to an invitation to identify additional challenges, "Please write in the space below other challenges not listed above, that you face when

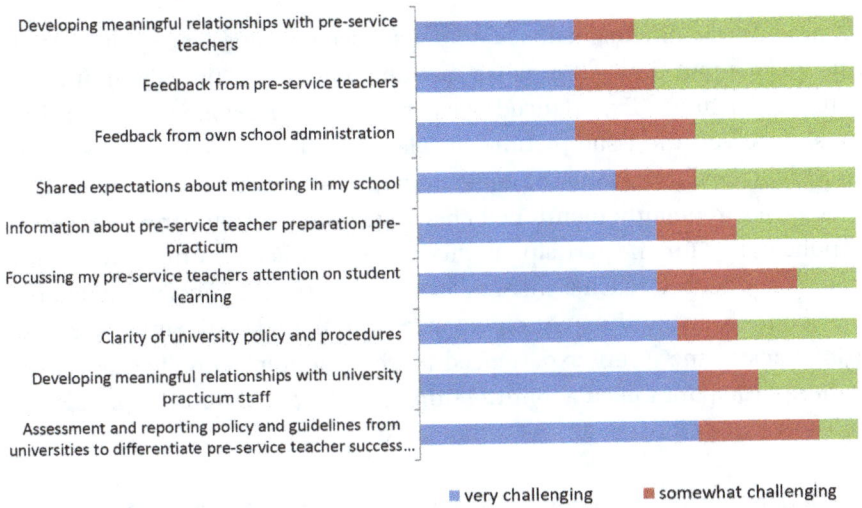

FIGURE 4.4 Challenges of being a teacher mentor

mentoring pre-service teachers", 17 participants responded and provided comments. Almost half the participants identified specific challenges relating to mentoring pre-service teachers, although the nature of the challenge related either to the organisational skills or personal capacity of the pre-service teachers. For example, one participant commented that "Ensuring lesson plans are completed and shown to the teacher prior to lesson" (Experienced teacher mentor, government school) was a challenge they had encountered. Another remarked on making sure that the pre-service teacher "commits to the tasks and follows through with meaningful delivery of tasks" (Very experienced teacher mentor, Catholic school). Still another noted that ensuring the pre-service teacher can juggle work and life adding "they find it extremely stressful and it sometimes impacts on planning for classes" (Experienced teacher mentor, government school).

In relation to personal qualities, participants commented on the pre-service teachers' abilities to take on board feedback, as well as managing expectations. As well, several participants mentioned the variable ability of pre-service teachers to cope with the challenges of catering for difficult students, interruptions to routine and tailoring programs to suit the varied needs of students. Finally, one experienced teacher mentor commented on the language capacity of pre-service teachers, referring specifically to international students.

Another common challenge identified by teacher mentors was the concept of time. For most participants, this referred to a lack of time "to fully support" and "provide meaningful feedback" to pre-service teachers. One of the participants spoke about time issues when mentors "have other time commitments when not teaching" (Experienced teacher mentor, government school). Two others discussed the issue of time in relation to the school administration giving "dedicated time" to have "professional conversations".

The other frequently mentioned challenge related to university processes and policies and for one participant, this related to a lack of contact by the university (Experienced teacher mentor, government school). This was similar to the response from another participant who commented on the university "not getting back to me" (Very experienced teacher mentor, Catholic school). Yet another participant talked about the timing of the practicum the pre-service teacher was undertaking. As was commented:

> Depending on the length of the placement, the pre-service teacher may only be teaching lessons or units you have already prepared, not ones that they have had to develop themselves. This does not give them a deep understanding of development of units/lessons and how this guides student learning, assessment and future lessons or areas for further learning or extension. (Beginning teacher mentor, Independent school)

Still another commented in relation to not knowing what had been taught at the university, specifically "knowing whether or not the PST has been explicitly taught how to teach using school preferred pedagogy e.g. direct and explicit instruction v inquiry-based learning" (Experienced teacher mentor, Independent school).

7 Professional Learning

Of the 22 participants in this survey, only five had undertaken any professional learning related to mentoring, with three participants undertaking the Victorian Institute of Teaching Effective Mentor Training Program (VITEMTP) (2018), which consists of two days of face to face professional learning and one participant undertaking the AITSL (2014) Supervising Pre-Service Teachers online program. One other participant had undertaken mentor training related to a university professional experience (practicum) program that was provided by the university. In terms of how useful the training was to the mentoring role, responses to the VIT Mentor Training included:

> It was helpful in so far as providing advice on how to put a folio together. (Experienced teacher mentor, Government school)

It allowed me to develop coaching conversation skills in supporting pre-service teachers to set goals on placement and provide meaningful feedback to assist with their development. (Beginning teacher mentor, Independent school)

It alerted me to new standards in teaching. (Experienced teacher mentor Independent school)

The participant who had undertaken the AITSL training, when responding to the question about the usefulness of this stated, "I found the AITSL modules very specific and feel the best PD is that which caters for the needs I have at the time". The other participant who had undertaken training provided by the university felt that it was useful in terms of providing "Greater understanding of how the students had been prepared for placement, and the expectations for successful placement. Greater understanding of the students' expectations and the great diversity of their experiences in placements". It is of interest to note that the VIT professional learning is directed at mentors of graduate teachers. The university professional learning and AITSL program were specifically for teacher mentors who would be supporting pre-service teachers during practicum. When asked about any specific practices they had implemented as a result of having undertaken mentor professional learning, responses mainly related to strategies for relationship building including "Giving direct encouragement against all odds", "Building up a rapport with the pre service teacher and developing their trust", "Setting goals with pre service teachers" and "Making time available".

When considering the mode of training delivery, the majority preferred face to face training with one participant preferring online and no one preferencing applications. The reasons given for preferring face to face training related mostly to the relational aspects of working with others including the opportunity to participate in discussions and to feel more engaged with the learning, with typical responses including "I'm a people person and prefer direct contact" (Beginning teacher mentor, Independent school) and "You always learn better through engagement and interactions-questioning and discussions" (Very experienced teacher mentor, Catholic school). This comes as no real surprise, given the relational nature of teaching. The one person who preferred online learning liked this mode as "You can do it as self-paced when it suits you. Rather than missing classes or attending after hours" (Experienced teacher mentor, Government school).

The final question relating to professional learning asked participants to suggest what they would find useful in training designed for mentoring pre-service teachers. This produced a range of suggestions as seen in Table 4.1.

TABLE 4.1 Responses to the survey question concerning content in teacher mentor professional learning

Theme	Responses
Relationships	"Opportunities to meet with others in similar roles" "Teacher student relationships. How to deal with developing young adults and their psychology. How to develop meaningful working relationships with others. Collaborative ownership of learning and nurturing of young minds"
Communication	"How to have difficult conversations" "Challenging conversations" "Growth conversations" "How to support a pre-service teacher who is floundering" "Attention on dealing with underperforming/failing students" "How to deal with pre-service teachers who aren't up to scratch in a way that will support them to grow, instead of dishearten them"
Feedback	"What is the right amount of feedback" "Providing feedback" "Providing meaningful feedback" "Appropriate feedback strategies" "What effective feedback for pre-service teachers would look like"
Expectations	"University expectations, managing the mentee's expectations" "Common understanding of performance standards"
Pre-service teacher university coursework	"Understanding the training the preservice teacher's go through at the university"

Another response to the professional learning content question stated that professional learning needed to be tailored to suit different contexts:

> Information included would need to be pitched differently, depending upon what stage the prospective pre-service teacher is in the degree

and also the type of degree they are working towards. It may also vary depending on the tertiary institution and what is required by that facility.

Only one participant responded negatively to the suggestion of professional learning with, "I'm not in favour of this at all. Teachers will be less likely to mentor if they are forced into further training. Enough demands as is!"

8 Discussion

This chapter has reported on 22 practicing teachers in Victorian schools, who undertook an online survey about their perceptions of the challenges and what motivates them when mentoring pre-service teachers on practicum, as well as their experiences concerning professional learning to be a mentor. For reader ease, we frame this discussion in three parts: demographics, motivators and challenges and professional learning.

8.1 *Demographics*

The age, teaching experience and sector where employed of the participants in this study reflected those in Nielson et al. (2017) and represented the typical profile of Australian teacher mentors across all school sectors. However, the qualifications of the participants in this study, differed from those in Nielson et al. (2017), with one year postgraduate qualifications being most common, rather than the four-year undergraduate program. Previous research has tended to consider teacher mentors as a single entity and for the most part has not considered the possible impact of their qualification on their capacity to mentor and the relationship they have with the mentee. This study found that 75% of the participants had a one-year qualification. Therefore, they would be mentoring some pre-service teachers with a higher Master level qualification. While this study did not investigate this finding further, future research could consider this in further detail.

8.2 *Motivators and Challenges*

The closed survey items that asked participants to rate the impact of various motivators generally aligned with those reported in the earlier Nielson et al. (2017) study. "Communicating with the university" was presented as the greatest challenge overall in both Nielson et al. (2017) and our study. It was interesting to note however that the item, "mirror own teaching practice" resulted in an interesting response pattern in our study; an equal distribution at both ends of the scale ("Very important" or "Not important"). Furthermore, that more experienced teachers were more likely to rate this item of higher importance. This is of interest when we consider that the role of the teacher mentor through the lens of a more traditional supervisory or apprenticeship model, where pre-service teachers are expected to follow the style of teaching demonstrated by the teacher mentor is dominant. As discussed earlier, however, there are now more emerging roles of mentoring as a collaborative partnership, (where both the teacher mentor and the pre-service teacher are equal partners in the learning process) that could possibly be impacting on this identification. According to Ambrosetti (2014), the teacher mentor needs to "nurture, advise, encourage and facilitate learning experiences for developmental growth" (p. 30). Ambrosetti (2014) added "In the absence of preparation or training, many classroom teachers revert to their own experiences as pre-service teachers, or duplicate the methods used by their own supervising teachers" (p. 33).

When it came to identifying challenges to mentoring my study tended to reinforce the findings of Nielson et al. (2017), with the biggest challenge identified as communication with universities. This challenge could relate to the commonly expressed concern around the "theory-practice divide" between schools and universities; in particular, the lack of communication between the theory taught in pre-service teacher coursework and the practical application of teaching in the classroom. As has been suggested in the TEMAG (review), there is considerable concern around the types of documentation universities send out to schools to inform the mentors about the expectations and responsibilities of all parties involved in the practicum experience. Often this documentation is weighty, and each university sends similar but different documents to schools, as each university has a different perspective on each practicum. AITSL has responded by stipulating that mechanisms used by universities to communicate with schools about practicum expectations, need to be clearly stated in accreditation documentation.

Some of the more experienced teachers identified seeking feedback on their own mentoring performance as a challenge. Teacher mentors are not generally observed by other practising teachers when they mentor pre-service teachers, unless in a team-teaching situation. There currently exists a general lack of opportunity to receive feedback on performance as a mentor, as the activity is carried out in the teacher mentor's classroom with just the pupils and the pre-service teacher, who is unlikely to provide constructive feedback on performance as they need to maintain the relationship to pass the practicum. This raises the question as to how teacher mentors reflect on their performance with no external feedback processes in place. Le Cornu (2015) states that encouraging reflective and evidence-based practice by providing explicit feedback" (p. 15) is a "high level commitment from school leadership"

(p. 15). A teacher mentoring a pre-service teacher in their classroom is possibly the only role in teaching that is not observed, or feedback provided. The challenge identified by participants around obtaining feedback on their mentoring performance is interesting, particularly with the current emphasis and expectations on reflective practice in teacher education. It is to be noted that teacher mentors generally undertake their role without the benefit of a community of practice or without other experienced teachers observing their mentoring of pre-service teachers.

In this study, having enough time to perform the mentoring role effectively, was another important challenge identified by several of the participants. This was not specifically noted as a challenge in the previous Nielson et al. (2017) survey. Le Cornu (2015) recommends as a key component for effective professional experience, that school leadership prioritise "opportunities for collaboration and critical dialogue" (p. 15), which would certainly require an adequate allowance of time. Therefore, as feedback, further investigation of the impact of time warrants further study.

As mentioned earlier, one question asked about differences in motivators and challenges when supporting postgraduate as compared to undergraduate pre-service teachers. Comments from the participants were mixed and at times contradictory. When working with adult learners, as with children, learning occurs through the "acquisition of three domains: knowledge, skills and attitudes" (Taylor & Hamdy, 2013, p. 1562). The degree to which each of these domains is enacted or needs to be addressed may originate from each pre-service teacher's "different learning preferences, teaching concerns, stages of development, readiness levels regarding various teaching competencies, tensions in professional identity formation, images and beliefs about teaching, and goals and expectations concerning the mentoring relationship" (Hobson, Ashby, Malderez, & Tomlinson, 2009). As has been stated by Zeichner, (2005); Ambrosetti, (2014); Darling-Hammond, (2005) and others, teaching is a people-focused, relational business that depends on the building of relationships at all levels. The success or otherwise of a practicum experience for all parties depends largely upon how well the participants get along with each other, or how effectively they build a mutually respectful relationship.

Although only a small element of this survey, the results of this section revealed some distinct points of difference from some participants, such as the greater maturity of postgraduate pre-service teachers having a positive impact in the classroom and some points of contradiction, such as content knowledge of pre-service teachers, being identified as greater in undergraduates by some participants and the opposite viewpoint of postgraduates having greater knowledge of content by other survey participants. These differing points of view may be explained by interpersonal interactions on an individual level and do not necessarily hold as overall generalisations, given the small sample undertaken in the research. It is of interest however, that these points were raised as being important by the respondents in this survey and differences between mentoring undergraduate and postgraduate pre-service teachers would benefit from greater examination in future research, as many factors could influence the various views.

8.3　　*Professional Learning*

With only 5 out of the 22 teachers surveyed having undertaken any professional learning about mentoring and that learning relating to the mentoring of graduates, not pre-service teachers, the results from this research support the assertion made by Nielson et al. (2017) that there is currently low availability and uptake of professional learning for teacher mentors in general. As clearly stated by Nielson et al. (2017), when discussing the findings from their Mentoring Profile Inventory "… we need to find ways to enhance the process and develop teacher knowledge for supervision" (p. 349). In addition, there is a need for future teacher mentor professional learning to be informed by the evidence from surveys such as this, that identify the motivators and challenges to mentoring pre-service teachers, by the mentors themselves. It might also be useful for this larger study to consider learning as being on a continuum "which stretches throughout life" (Taylor & Hamdy, 2013, p. 1561) and that pre-service teachers will have "their own individual constraints, experiences and preferences" (Taylor & Hamdy, 2013, p. 1561) in terms of the ways in which they learn and prefer to gain information.

9　　Conclusion

This chapter has reported on 22 practicing classroom teacher mentors in Victorian schools who participated in an online survey about motivators and challenges when mentoring pre-service teachers on practicum and their professional learning. In relation to the closed survey items, the teachers identified a range of challenges and motivating factors, with university communications presenting as the greatest challenge overall and renewing the profession being the greatest motivator. These results aligned with those reported in the earlier Nielson et al. (2017) survey. In relation to mentoring undergraduate and postgraduate pre-service teachers, these teacher mentors were less consistent in their views, with at times some contradictory comments around content knowledge and forming relationships with students in the classroom.

This chapter suggests several implications for future practice. First, as this study has only been a small one, a larger study of more teacher mentors across the Victorian teaching sector, could add to our knowledge of the research area. Second, given that this study has indicated inconclusive views around mentoring undergraduate and postgraduate pre-service teachers, this larger study could have this as a focus. Third, given that this study has shown that most teacher mentors had not undertaken professional learning, a further study that considers the impact of such learning could be warranted. In particular, it could consider the role of the adult learner in such professional learning. In addition, as this study has provided some insights into the types of professional learning these teachers preferred (face to face) and the sort of information they felt would be important (such as relationships and communication, particularly concerning providing feedback and having difficult conversations), these could be investigated in later research.

References

Ambrosetti, A. (2014). Are you ready to be a mentor? Preparing teachers for mentoring pre-service teachers. *Australian Journal of Teacher Education, 39*(6). http://dx.doi.org/10.14221/ajte.2014v39n6.2

Australian Institute for Teaching and School Leadership (AITSL). (2014). *Supervising preservice teachers (module)*. Retrieved from http://www.aitsl.edu.au/initial-teacher-education/supervising-preservice-teachers

Australian Institute for Teaching and School Leadership (2018). *Accreditation of initial teacher education programs in Australia, AITSL, Melbourne*. Retrieved from https://www.aitsl.edu.au/docs/default-source/national-policy-framework/accreditation-of-initial-teacher-education-programs-in-australia.pdf?sfvrsn=e87cff3c_22

Betlam, E., Clary, D., & Jones, M. (2018). Mentoring the mentor: Professional development through a school-university partnership. *Asia-Pacific Journal of Teacher Education*. https://doi.org/10.1080/1359866X.2018.1504280

Boateng, G. O., Neilands, T. B., Frongillo, E. A., Melgar-Quiñonez, H. R., & Young, S. L. (2018). Best practices for developing and validating scales for health, social, and behavioral research: A primer. *Frontiers in Public Health, 6*. Retrieved September 24, 2019, from https://www.frontiersin.org/article/10.3389/fpubh.2018.00149

Braun, V., & Clarke, V. (2006). Using thematic analysis in psychology. *Qualitative Research in Psychology, 3*, 77–101. http://dx.doi.org/10.1191/1478088706qp063oa

Clarke, A., Collins, J., Triggs, V., & Nielson, W. (2012). The mentoring profile inventory. *Teaching Education, 23*(2), 167–194. https://doi.org/10.1080/10476210.2011.625086

Darling-Hammond, L. (2005). Teaching as a profession: Lessons in teacher preparation and professional development. *Phi Delta Kappan, 87*(3), 237–240.

Darling-Hammond, L. (2006). Constructing 21st-century teacher education. *Journal of Teacher Education, 61*(1–2), 35–47.

Department of Education and Training Victoria. (2019). *Mentoring capability framework*. Retrieved from https://www.education.vic.gov.au/Documents/school/teachers/profdev/mentoringcapabilityframework.pdf

Ehrich, L., Hansford, B., & Ehrich, J. F. (2011). Mentoring across the professions: Some issues and challenges. In J. Millwater & D. Beutal (Eds.), *Practical experiences in professional education: A transdisciplinary approach* (pp. 93–113). Post Pressed. Retrieved September 21, 2019, from https://ro.uow.edu.au/cgi/viewcontent.cgi?article=2385&context=edupapers

Hobson, A. J., Ashby, P., Malderez, A., & Tomlinson, P. D. (2009). Mentoring beginning teachers: What we know and what we don't. *Teaching and Teacher Education, 25*, 207–216. https://doi.org/10.1016/j.tate.2008.09.001

House of Representatives Standing Committee on Education and Vocational Training. (2007). *Top of the class*. Report on the Inquiry into Teacher Education. Retrieved from https://www.aph.gov.au/parliamentary_business/committees/house_of_representatives_committees?url=evt/teachereduc/report.htm

Irby, B. J. (2018). Editor's overview: Differences and similarities with mentoring, tutoring and coaching. *Mentoring & Tutoring: Partnerships in Learning, 26*(2), 115–121. https://doi.org/10.1080/13611267.2018.1489237

Korthagen, F. A. J., & Lagerwerf, B. (2001). Teachers' professional learning: How does it work? In F. A. J. Korthagen et al. (Eds.), *Linking theory and practice: The pedagogy of realistic teacher education* (pp. 175–206). Lawrence Erlbaum.

Le Cornu, R. (2015). *Key components of effective professional experience in initial teacher education in Australia*. Australian Institute for Teaching and School Leadership (AITSL).

Nielson, W., Mena, Juanjo, M., Clarke, A., O'Shea, S., Hoban, G., & Collins, J. (2017). Australia's supervising teachers: Motivators and challenges to inform professional learning. *Asia–Pacific Journal of Teacher Education, 45–54*, 346–368. https://dx.org/10.1080/1359866X.2017.1304527

Rajuan, M. (2012). Mentoring student teachers in professional development schools in Israel. In *The Sage handbook of mentoring and coaching in education*. Sage Publications. http://dx.doi.org/10.4135/9781446247549.n22

Sorenson, P. (2012). Mentoring and coaching for school teachers' initial teacher education and induction. In S. J. Fletcher & C. A. Mullen (Eds.), *The Sage handbook of mentoring and coaching in education*. Sage Publications. http://dx.doi.org/10.4135/9781446247549.n14

Taylor, D. C., & Hamdy, H. (2013). Adult learning theories: Implications for learning and teaching in medical education: AMEE Guide No. 83. *Medical Teacher, 35*(11), e1561–e1572. https://doi.org/10.3109/0142159X.2013.828153

Teacher Education Ministerial Advisory Group. (2014). *Action now: Classroom ready teachers*. Commonwealth of Australia.

van Ginkel, G., Verloop, N., & Denessen, E. (2015): Why mentor? Linking mentor teachers' motivations to their mentoring conceptions. *Teachers and Teaching*. doi:10.1080/13540602.2015.1023031

Victorian Institute of Teaching Effective Mentoring Program. (2019). Victorian Institute Teaching Publishers. Retrieved from https://www.vit.vic.edu.au/registered-teacher/how-to-train-as-a-teacher-mentor

Zeichner, K. (1990). Changing directions in the practicum: Looking ahead to the 1990s. *British Journal of Teacher Education, 16*(2), 105–132.

Zeichner, K. (2005). Becoming a teacher educator: A personal perspective. *Teaching and Teacher Education, 21*, 117–124. Retrieved from https://www.academia.edu/25556146/Becoming_a_teacher_educator_a_personal_perspective

Zeichner, K. (2010). Rethinking the connections between campus courses and field experiences in college-an-university-based teacher education. *Journal of Teacher Education, 61*(1–2), 89–99.

CHAPTER 5

Choosing the Best Way to Travel in an Unknown Landscape: PhD Supervisors' Perspectives on Their Own Learning in Doctoral Supervision

Mikhail Gradovski

Abstract

This chapter reports on the evaluation of a course for PhD supervisors that was organised by three Norwegian universities between 2013 and 2018. Drawing on the results of seventeen qualitative interviews across three universities with course participants, the author discussed participants' own perspectives on their learning processes during this course. The focus of the discussion is on opportunities that were created for the development of participants' own professional agency during this course. Based on findings from interviews, the author reflects on how to organise such a course in the future in such a way that its participants experience greater learning efficacy in the development of their own professional agency. The course organisation and learning activities as well as the opportunities it provided for the development of participants' professional agency as doctoral supervisors are discussed and critiqued based on the results of the thematic analysis, and by employing the concepts of professional agency and authorial agency.

Keywords

doctoral supervision – Norway – course for PhD supervisors – thematic analysis – authorial agency

1   Introduction

This chapter reports on part of an evaluative study of the course for PhD supervisors organised by three Norwegian universities between 2013 and 2018. Based on the results of the thematic analysis, I discuss how this evaluated course provided opportunities for the learning and development of participants' professional agency as PhD supervisors, and how such courses should be organised so that their participants can experience better learning and development of professional academic agency in the area of doctoral supervision.

Evaluation of courses for both PhD students and PhD supervisors is a growing research area. Most evaluation studies are focused on PhD students and their learning outcomes (Sampson, Johnson, Comer, & Brogt, 2015; Pearson & Kayrooz, 2004; Zuber-Skerritt & Roche, 2004). There are very few evaluation studies of courses for PhD supervisors. This can be explained by the fact that doctoral supervision as a research area is relatively new (McCulloch, 2018). Evaluation of courses for PhD supervisors conducted over time has taken place in Australia (McCulloch & Loeser, 2016) and South Africa (Bitzer, Trafford, & Leshem, 2013), and conducted based on a quantitative approach where data was collected with the help of a survey. This type of evaluation is most popular when evaluating learning outcomes in the higher education sector (Roth, Ogrin, & Schmitz, 2016). The latter evaluation (Bitzer, Trafford, & Leshem, 2013) is an explorative study that reports descriptive and analyitical results from three African countries based on a mixed-method approach.

The course for PhD supervisors that was evaluated in this study was organised in such a way that approximately half of the lectures were devoted to the theme of doctoral supervision. The content of these lectures was mainly various supervision styles that were previously described in a book written by the main lecturer. In addition to the book, the course's reading list consisted of research papers published in English between 1997 and 2017. The other half of the course was devoted to lectures on the organisational sides of PhD education and its ethical challenges. Course activities consisted for the most part of lectures. In 2013, 2014, and 2015, participants had an opportunity to ask questions after lectures, while no time was allocated for discussions among participants. This changed in 2016, and in both 2016 and 2017 participants could discuss lecture content among themselves. In 2016, participants were asked to complete a task that required them to cooperate on a group project. This task can be characterised as an active learning form, and its sole required output was either an article or a written report.

2   Learning as a Part of Professional Academic Agency

Learning as an activity in the higher education sector can be defined in different ways. I have chosen to base my analysis of the learning that was experienced by course participants on the definition of learning by Akkerman and Bakker (2011). They define learning as an activity that includes appearances of new understandings, development of identity, change in practice, and contributions to organisational development. Akkerman and Bakker write the following on learning grounded on a constructivist foundation:

> Whether we speak of learning as the change from novice to expert in a particular domain or as the development from legitimate peripheral participation to being a full member of a particular community (Lave & Wenger 1991), the boundary of the domain or community is constitutive of what counts as expertise or as central participation. When we consider learning in terms of identity development, a key question is the distinction between what is part of me versus what is not (yet) part of me.

Akkerman and Bakker (2011) distinguish between four types of learning: identification, coordination, reflection, and transformation. The first type, identification, has two sub-types: othering and legitimating coexistence. Akkerman and Bakker (2011) define othering in the following way:

> First, the identification processes occur by defining one practice in light of another, delineating how it differs from the other practice. This dialogical process of identification can be called *othering*.

Bogenrieder and van Baalen (2007) define the process of legitimating coexistence in the following way:

> ... *legitimating coexistence* [...] describe[s] how people, when working simultaneously in different organizational groups, have to consider the interference between their multiple participations to be able to pursue each one and be accepted in this multiple membership by others in the respective groups.

The mutual characteristic of learning as a process within both sub-types of identification is that learning happens when one acquires new insight from being exposed to new ways of doing things, and thus develops one's own professional identity. Coordination as a type of learning concerns the layering that happens due to the manipulation with the tools, and thus this type of learning does not occur in doctoral supervision settings.

Reflection as a type of learning happens when one understands the differences between how one handled things before and now, and thus acquires new insight into one's own practice and the practice of others. Reflection can also occur as a creative process (perspective making), where one acquires new insight into one's own understanding and knowledge of a particular issue

(Akkerman & Bakker, 2011). Another type of reflection as a learning process occurs when one takes the other's perspective. To take the other's perspective is to try to understand how the other sees a subject or an issue, and in so doing discovers new sides of the subject or issue not previously known. Akkerman and Bakker (2011) point out that reflection and identification have similar mechanisms but different foci. While identification is about first focusing on newly discovered insight in praxis and then focusing on the reconstruction of one's own professional identity, the focus of reflection is directed towards the new set of perspectives. Through these, a new future construction of one's own professional identity is created.

Transformation, the fourth type of learning, is about learning that occurs due to intervention. Transformation is characterised by major changes in praxis due to confrontation, provocation, and discussion of differences. Transformation is possible only when learners have opportunities to discover and discuss others' praxis. Akkerman and Bakker (2011) describe transformation as the process that starts with a confrontation that appears to be about a lack of something, or as a problem that requires learners to reevaluate their own praxes and relations. The transformation ends with new insight that occurs due to the differences and plurality of opinions, understandings, and experiences among learners.

The learning of attitudes, knowledge, expertise, and skills among course participants can further be characterised by the concept of professional academic agency. Eteläpelto, Vähäsantanen, Hökkä, and Paloniemi (2013), and Ursin, Vähäsantanen, McAlpine, and Hökkä (2018) point out that professional academic agency happens when professionals or groups of professionals have the opportunity to influence, make choices, and position themselves in ways that directly change their own professional praxes and professional identities. In this study, I understand the participants' attitudes, knowledge, expertise, and skills to be necessary attributes that must be in place so that activities inherent in doctoral supervision can happen. I thus consider these to be attributes that constitute supervisors' professional academic agency.

I understand professional academic agency to be a part of personal authorial agency. Matusov, von Duyke, and Kayumova (2016) define authorial agency as something that is always personal and cannot be collective. This definition of agency implies an Aristotlean understanding of practice as praxis, an activity in which its goals, values, definition, and quality emerge in the activity itself and do not preexist it. Matusov et al. (2016) believe that men make their own history, but they do not make it as they please; they do not make it under circumstances chosen by themselves, but under circumstances directly encountered, given, and transmitted from the past. Further, they define authorial agency as the transcendence of the given and write that the notion of agency revolves around two important dichotomies: the dichotomy of the given versus the innovative and the dichotomy of the individual versus the social. The first dichotomy is resolved because the given shapes agency by situating agency, and by providing material for transcendence (Matusov et al., 2016). Material for transcendence includes natural causes, necessities, ready-made culture, social dynamics, nature, and logic. The innovative emerges in the process of socially-recognised transcendence of the given culture and practice. The innovative in turn consists of new goals, new definitions of quality, new motivations, new wills, new desires, new commitments, new skills, new knowledge, and new relationships (Matusov et al., 2016). The second dichotomy is resolved because within the notion of authorial agency, our personal transcendence has to be recognised by relevant others and/or by the self. Thus, this recognition calls for dialogicity and responsibility. Further, Matusov et al. (2016) write that a bid for social recognition of a person's transcendence of that which is culturally given transforms an individual's action into a personal deed, and the act of individual transcendence into a social event, and thus changes social relationships in communities and society. This means that professional academic agency based on a concept of authorial agency consists of personal attitudes, goals, values, knowledge, competences, and skills. Any professional academic agency is a dynamic entity that goes through changes, as a professional, the holder of the agency—thanks to the process of transcendence, opportunities for responsivity and dialogicity learns and unlearns new knowledge and skills.

As an activity, the process of doctoral supervision can be viewed as metonymically related to the process of travelling in an unknown landscape. As when travelling in an unknown landscape with its first unique impressions and reflections, supervision of each PhD student is a unique endeavour that can never be replicated, as each student and each supervisor's collaboration is unique. Travelling in an unknown landscape encourages an inner dialogue between prior experiences and impressions of the unknown landscape, and thus provides an opportunity for recognition of similarities and disparities. To supervise a PhD student always requires a dialogue between the supervisor and the PhD student, and this dialogue will always be unique and situated as both the supervisor and the student each have his or her own authorial agency.

3   Methodological Approach, Design, Data Collection, Analysis, Outer Validity, and Ethical Issues

This is a qualitative study based on an investigative design described by McGregor (2018). Participants' understanding of their experienced learning is considered to be the result of inner persuasive discourse that appears due to outer persuasive discourse and their own inner persuasive discourse (Bakhtin, 2012). An inner persuasive discourse can be defined as the sum of internal thoughts, approaches, and points of view that are in constant dialogue with each other. The inner persuasive discourse appears due to the authoritarian discourse that comes from outside (from others) and represents points of view that one can agree or disagree with. The inner persuasive discourse is in constant development, never finalised, and always changing, due to the fact that it always relates itself to new contexts, new people, new requirements, and new conditions. In this study, the points of view of the lecturers in this course are considered to be a part of the authoritarian discourse on doctoral supervision, while the participants' reaction to these, their agreement and disagreement with and their internalisation of these points of view, either fully or partially, are part of their inner persuasive discourse. The participants' learning is defined as a part of their inner persuasive discourse.

Data was collected with the help of interviews between the fall of 2017 and the spring of 2018. The list of all course participants from the three universities was obtained from the administration of one of the universities. The first step was to finalise the sample of possible interview participants. Altogether, there were 130 participants on the list. The criteria to qualify for the pool of possible interview participants included three requirements: employment at one of the three universities, completion of the entire course, and active participation as either a main or a secondary PhD supervisor. Some of these participants changed employer, and some did not complete the entire course. The ultimate pool of possible interview participants included 102 participants from the three universities. All participants were sent an email with an invitation to participate in an individual interview. Of the 102 participants, seventeen answered positively, so the final sample included five participants from University 1, six from University 2, and six from University 3. The final sample of interview participants who had completed the course for PhD supervisors between 2013 and 2017 included novices in the field of doctoral supervision, experienced PhD supervisors, and experienced research leaders with doctoral supervision experience. These interview participants had various positions in the power hierarchies in their universities: two participants were institute leaders, three were research leaders with responsibility for huge externally-financed research projects, and twelve were ordinary tenure-track members of the staff who had research related tasks as a part of their contracts. Further, the final sample consisted of professors and associate professors and includes ethnic Norwegians and people with non-Norwegian ethnic backgrounds. All the faculties of the three universities were represented. All interview participants were sent an interview guide and information on how the collected data will be used in the future. The details on when and how each interview would take place were discussed and agreed on with each participant. Some participants wanted to be interviewed on Skype, while others wanted to be interviewed face-to-face. All the interviews were transcribed and sent to the participants for comments. Transcripts were anonymised to make it impossible to trace the identities of participants, and plotted in the NVIVO software programme where a thematic analysis was conducted.

The interview guide was produced in three versions: Norwegian (bokmål), New Norwegian (Nynorsk), and English. The guide consisted of twelve questions and had four main parts (introduction, general information, content and learning at the course, and concluding remarks). The first four questions dealt with facts about participant's employment and experience with supervision, while the rest of the questions were about various aspects of experienced learning and were formulated as open questions. The result of the thematic analysis was the appearance of two main categories: "What was learned?" and "What could have resulted in better learning outcomes?" In this chapter, I report only the results of the analysis of the second category. Within the second category, my thematic analysis resulted in the following five themes: participants' desire for discussion of self-introduced themes, participants' desire for sharing their own experiences, participants' desire for simulator training and role-playing opportunities, a requirement for insight into the Norwegian higher educational context, and a requirement for the provision of information on course content.

The outer validity in this study concerns first and foremost only our interview participants. However, the data collection method, number of interview participants, and positioning of these participants allow me to believe that the opinions expressed by participants were also held by other course participants. The collected data was anonymised in such a way that it would not be possible to recognise the identity of the participants.

4   What Could Have Resulted in Better Learning Outcomes?

The thematic analysis resulted in five themes, where the first three concern various forms of activities that participants felt should be organised to develop their professional agency. The first three themes are participants' desire for discussion of themes chosen by the participants, participants' desire to share their own experiences of PhD supervision and simulation, and participants' desire to learn by role-playing. The two last themes are the requirement for the lecturers to have knowledge of the Norwegian higher educational context and disparity between information on the course's content provided prior to the start of the course and the actual content of the course.

4.1 Discussion of Themes Chosen by Participants

All interview participants from University 3 pointed out that though the content of the main book written by the main lecturer served as an introduction to the discussion of the role of a supervisor, they felt they would have learned more if they could have shared their own knowledge on doctoral supervision. They believed that they would also have learned more if there had been room for participants to suggest themes for discussion. The participants from University 3 wanted to learn more about sharing various responsibilities and tasks connected to doctoral supervision activities, including assessment of a PhD thesis. All interview participants from University 3 believed that a course such as this one should provide room for recognition of participants' experience and prior knowledge.

Participants from University 1 expressed a desire for a very experienced supervisor who could introduce and lead a discussion on how to solve conflicts that could appear in supervision practice. They also expressed that such a course should allow room for discussion of the use of various pedagogical approaches to supervision and PhD students' capabilities and skills that needed to be developed. They believed that there was much new insight to be found if there were organised discussions on what was good and what could be better in connection with the formal requirements for written texts and other profession-related requirements that PhD students must meet in their respective professional fields. They believed that designing the course in a way that allows group discussion among PhD supervisors representing the natural and technical sciences, and the humanities and social sciences, would result in better and deeper learning outcomes. One example of a theme that could be discussed only by representatives of a particular branch of science is written and unwritten rules connected to post-graduate education that exist in each branch of science or a profession. Interview participant A, who completed the course in 2016, said the following:

> I would like such a course to have a focus on technicalities. Every PhD programme has formal requirements that should be met, but what should be done with the unwritten requirements? What is "good enough" in relation to the formal requirements? We need discussions that stem from the traditions developed around various professions. There is a pronounced lack of discussion on what we should require from a PhD student.

Interview participants from University 2 wanted such courses to allow more group discussion and group work. Such group discussion could take place in multi-professional settings and could be done both in Norwegian and English so that both Norwegian speakers and non-Norwegian speakers could be included and have an opportunity to contribute to discussions.

The three participants from University 3 would have learned more if discussion groups for novices in the field of doctoral supervision and experienced supervisors were separate. Themes for discussions in these groups could include conflicts, motivation of a PhD student, co-authorship, and the publication process. Like the interview participants from University 1, the participants from University 3 wanted the opportunity to share their own experiences and room for the exchange of knowledge between experienced supervisors and novices.

4.2 *Learning through Sharing One's Own Experience and Simulation*

Another point connected to better learning outcomes that was raised by the participants was the sharing of learning stories between novices and experienced PhD supervisors. To listen to a story from real practice is considered to be a possible source of inspiration and information that can come in handy when a supervisor is planning activities to motivate PhD students and with the goal of positive efficacy feelings.

Participants also expressed a desire to have a course based on the dialogical approach, where it would be possible to allow PhD students to have a voice. PhD students could, according to interview participants from University 1, share their own stories and experiences of collaboration and cooperation with their supervisors. Themes for such stories and experiences could touch on co-authorship of articles and simulated training and learning. Novice PhD supervisors could learn even more and better if there were a follow-up mentor programme where novices could be mentored by experienced supervisors.

Interview participants from University 2 believed that they would benefit learning-wise if there were an opportunity for sharing their own experiences on the relation between teaching, supervision, and their own research activity. These participants wanted discussions on various supervision traditions that had developed in various branches of science, involving both challenges in and future development of doctoral supervision. Sharing of experiences should also, according to the interview participants, include simulated learning opportunities, where a course participant could learn to function well in conversations between a supervisor and student. The aim of simulated learning for such conversations should be to provide the student with the empowerment and motivation to work with the project. Participant E from University 2, who completed the course in 2016, said the following:

> I would want to learn even more about the role of supervisor. I would want to have simulated training sessions where I could take the role of a listener instead of an expert, and reflect on how I could motivate the PhD candidate more. All in all, I would learn more if there were practical training sessions aimed at developing my skills in assessment and in my capability to be open and ready to motivate a PhD candidate. It's important that our PhD students feel empowered when they finish their PhD theses. It is important for me that supervision happens in such a way that PhD students' interests are known and properly addressed. I would also have learned more if there had been content that was related to present-day challenges and if this content had included an introduction to good conversation tools.

4.3   *Learning by Role-Playing*

The need for role-playing activities was pointed out by five participants across all three universities. They believed that they would have learned more if there were opportunities for role-playing and tasks where the participants could solve situations from real doctoral supervision practice. Such role-playing activities could have been followed by other activities aimed at sharing one's own reflections and follow-up discussions on the themes touched on in the particular scenarios.

4.4   *Knowledge of the Norwegian Higher Educational Context*

A very important point that was mentioned by three course participants from University 2 is the knowledge and expertise of those who lecture at the course. They believed that the lecturers should have insight into the current Norwegian academic context. This requirement is justified by the fact that lecturers who had little understanding of the cultural and academic context of Norwegian higher education were unable to provide relevant knowledge to those who were supposed to supervise PhD students in Norway. Interview participant B from University 2, who completed the course in 2014, said the following:

> The two foreign lecturers had very little to offer. They showed a pronounced lack of knowledge of the Norwegian context. This resulted in the fact that the content of their lectures was not relevant, as it concerned and grew from their own, unknown to us, contexts. Another point that I felt was lacking was orientation towards the future. All in all, cultural

competence and understanding are important pieces of knowledge that the lecturers at such courses should have, as they are teaching people who will be working with the cream of the crop of this country's students [PhD students].

4.5 *Disparity between Information about Course Content Provided Prior to the Start of the Course and the Actual Content of the Course*

Several interview participants from University 2 felt that the requirements for the tasks the participants were asked to do were not thought through well enough, as these were made with the experienced PhD supervisors in mind. Thus, novices in the field of doctoral supervision did not have an opportunity to learn or develop any important skills, as performing well in these tasks required supervision experience, something they did not have. Interview participant C, who completed the course in 2017, and D, who completed the course in 2018, had to participate in a group project where the goal was to do research on various aspects of doctoral supervision. This part of the content was not communicated well enough to the participants-to-be prior to the course. This resulted in an expectation that the course would be devoted only to learning about doctoral supervision, and not research on doctoral supervision. When the requirements for this group task became clear, the disparity between expectation and reality created a motivational challenge for both participants.

Interview participants from University 3 who had long experience as PhD supervisors and those with responsibility for research projects believed that the group project task could have resulted in better learning outcomes if it was formulated in a less ambitious way. The goal, which was to produce an article that could be published in a peer-reviewed journal, was considered disrespectful, as participants in the course were not informed of this requirement before the course started. Participants had been informed that the course was designed for those who wanted to become better supervisors, not researchers on doctoral supervision.

Two of the interview participants from University 3 felt that there was a disparity between prior expectations of what the course was supposed to be about and the actual content of the course. In contrast to what was promised in the information sent out by the organisers of the course, they experienced few opportunities for reflection on the role of supervisor, and thus, their own professional agency and identity as PhD supervisors were not given opportunities to be developed as they had hoped. These interview participants from University 3 asked for more opportunities to be active course participants and wished that there had been more forms of active learning.

5 How Did This Course Provide Opportunities for the Participants' Learning and the Development of Professional Agency in the Field of Doctoral Supervision?

In relation to the types of learning that participants experienced, it is possible to conclude that interview participants experienced identification in the form of othering and reflection. Participants' desire to learn more about conflict resolution, to use learning stories with both positive and negative scenarios as well as cases designed by experienced supervisors can be interpreted as a desire to experience legitimating coexistence, a form of identification. Another type of learning that this course could have provided is transformation. This type of learning can often happen when the learners' prior experience and knowledge of a particular theme or field of praxis were acquired in varying environments.

Interview participants developed parts of their professional agency that can be directly related to doctoral supervision either as PhD students or as both PhD students and PhD supervisors. Eteläpelto et al. (2013) and Ursin et al. (2018) write that professional agency can be practiced and developed when participants have opportunities to influence, make choices, and choose positions that can directly change their own professional environments and professional identities. What opportunities to influence, make choices, and choose positions were provided? The short answer to this question is just one, and this opportunity was provided only to those who attended the course during the last two years. Only interview participants who completed the course in 2017 and 2018 were provided with an opportunity to position themselves within a group, and thus define some of the course content and actively participate in their own professional agency development in a group setting.

The results of the thematic analysis show very clearly that participants wanted to influence and make choices related to knowledge content and forms of teaching. Participants' desire for discussion, to decide the themes of such discussions, and their desire to share their own experiences testify to the fact that they wanted to influence the knowledge content of the course, while their desire to learn by simulation and role-playing show that they wanted to make choices related to forms of teaching and learning. Interview participants who were experienced doctoral supervisors believed that they would have had better opportunities for the development of their own professional agency if such a course had an in-built flexibility in connection to the tasks that the participants had to complete.

The fact that interview participants believed that they would have benefitted more if the lecturers had had better insight into the Norwegian higher education context means that these participants understand that the future development of their own professional agency will take place in the Norwegian educational context. Thus, the content of the course should reflect their ontological and epistemological reality. Further, it is possible to see this requirement as a clear expression of the desire for respect and recognition of their professional agency, including participants' own experience, knowledge, and skills. This desire can stem from the fact that participants consider their own previously acquired and developed knowledge, expertise, and skills as valuable, and the Norwegian academic context that they represent, with its cultural and social values, as an important source of further development of their own professional agency.

Further, it is possible to conclude that interview participants believed that such a course would have provided more benefits for their own professional agency development if it had been organised differently. The organisation and design of this course were done in a very instrumentalist way: the lecturers were ascribed the role of those with more knowledge, who taught participants who were a priori considered to be those with less knowledge. Thus, all teaching activities were organised and carried out within a course structure where only the professional agency of the lecturers, their knowledge, expertise, and skills related to the field of doctoral supervision were recognised, respected, and appreciated. A course designed with this understanding of learning and teaching in mind could provide good learning outcomes in cases when the content of the course is taught to completely inexperienced participants. In this case, however, the participants had both experience and knowledge of the field of doctoral supervision, and some had had successful experiences as both PhD students and PhD supervisors prior to the course. The fact that some of the participants reported that they experienced a disparity between the information given prior to the course and the content of the course that was actually taught testifies to the fact that the participants were not recognised as responsible learners with authorial agency.

All in all, interview participants at the course experienced that their prior knowledge, expertise, skills, and experiences related to the field of doctoral supervision as praxis were not fully recognised, respected, or appreciated. They were not provided with opportunities to position themselves as authorial learners whose desire to develop their own professional agency in the field of doctoral supervision was respected and recognised. It seems as if the teaching and learning activities were organised to colonise and indoctrinate the participants into a predetermined structure where knowledge content, aims, and outcomes had already been decided for the participants.

6 How Should One Organise a Course for Phd Supervisors so that Its Participants Can Experience Development of Their Own Professional Agency?

Matusov et al. (2016) define authorial agency as the transcendence of the given and write that the notion of agency resolves two important dichotomies: the dichotomy of the given versus the innovative and the dichotomy of the individual versus the social. As the first dichotomy is resolved because the given shapes agency by situating agency and by providing the material for transcendence, it is important for participants of such courses to experience recognition of their own ontological and epistemological realities, i.e., their prior knowledge, expertise, and skills. The same applies to the physical contexts where this knowledge, expertise, and skill has been acquired and will be developed. This includes everything that constitutes material for transcendence, i.e., natural causes, necessities, ready-made culture, social dynamics, nature, and logic. In such courses, one has to provide an opportunity for the emergence of the innovative defined by Matusov et al. (2016), which consists of new goals, new definitions of quality, new motivations, new wills, new desires, new commitments, new skills, new knowledge, and new relationships. Opportunities for the emergence of the innovative can be provided by letting participants define parts of the knowledge content, forms of activities, and structure of the course. This requires a certain form of flexibility and a high level of experience as educators. Ample knowledge of the local educational context of doctoral supervision as praxis will develop from the organisers and teachers responsible for such courses, as not every detail in a courses' structure and content can be determined and decided prior to its start.

The second dichotomy mentioned as part of the concept of professional agency is resolved because our personal transcendence has to be recognised by relevant others and/or by the self, and thus, this recognition calls for dialogicity and responsibility (Matusov et al., 2016). This means that it is important to provide participants in such courses with opportunities for discussion and for sharing their own experiences. The thematic analysis' results show that there is a desire to share one's own experiences in the field of doctoral supervision, both with those who have similar, comparable experiences and within groups consisting of people with various levels of experience, expertise, and skills. This also requires a model for the course where organisers, lecturers, and learners are positioned and recognised as both those who learn and those who are learned from.

Providing participants with opportunities to form and change their own educational processes, share experiences, and participate in deciding outcomes and tasks does not only mean that the organisers respect participants' authorial agency and encourage its development, but also allows various types of learning. For example, as previously mentioned, this course could have provided its participants the opportunity to experience the type of learning called transformation, as the participants came from different branches of sciences.

Choosing to supervise PhD students is choosing to travel in an unknown landscape. This unknown landscape is not the landscape of a geographical location, but rather the landscape of one's own and the others' authorial agency. This journey can result in rewarding and successful experiences for both supervisor and supervisee, it can bring about bitter and miserable experiences, or bits of both. Either way, the decision to choose to supervise a PhD student will influence and change a supervisor's authorial agency, as every meeting with the unknown landscape of the other's authorial agency will produce new knowledge and insight if the supervisor is able to keep both his or her own inner dialogue and the dialogue with the PhD student going. I believe that opportunities for dialogue between participants on their prior understandings, knowledge, and expectations related to doctoral supervision should be provided as an integral part of any course for PhD supervisors; such dialogues will encourage the development of every participant's professional academic agency.

7   Conclusion

On the whole, the interview participants believed that if the course had been organised differently, they might have learned more. This concerns primarily the content and teaching forms that could have been used. The results of the thematic analysis show that participants want such courses to recognise their own prior experiences, knowledge, and skills related to the field of doctoral supervision. Participants want such courses to allow discussions, forms of active learning, learning by simulation, and role-playing. In addition, participants want to share their own experiences and discuss cases from real life, both positive and negative scenarios.

References

Akkerman, S. F., & Bakker, A. (2011). Boundary crossing and boundary objects. *Review of Educational Research, 81*(2), 132–169. doi:10.3102/0034654311404435

Bakhtin, M. (2012). Slovo v romane [Word in a novel]. In *Completed works* (Vol. 3). Yazyki Slavyanskih Kultur.

Bitzer, E., Trafford, V., & Leshem, S. (2013). 'Love it when you speak foreign': A transnational perspective on the professional development of doctoral supervisors in South Africa. *South African Journal of Higher Education, 27*(4), 781–796.

Bogenrieder, I., & van Baalen, P. (2007). Contested practice: Multiple inclusion in double-knit organizations. *Journal of Organizational Change Management, 20*, 579–595.

Eteläpelto, A., Vähäsantanen, K., Hökkä, P., & Paloniemi, S. (2013). What is agency? Conceptualizing professional agency at work. *Educational research review, 10*, 45–65.

Matusov, E., von Duyke, K., & Kayumova, S. (2016). Mapping concepts of agency in educational contexts. *Intergrative Psychological and Behavioral Science, 50*, 420–446.

McCulloch, A. (2018). The disciplinary status of doctoral education. *Higher Education Review, 50*(2), 86–104.

McCulloch, A., & Loeser, C. (2016). Does research degree supervisor training work? The impact of a professional development induction workshop on supervision practice. *Higher Education Research & Development.* doi:10.1080/07294360.2016.1139547

McGregor, S. L. T. (2018). Understanding and evaluating research. Sage Publications.

Pearson, M., & Kayrooz, C. (2004). Enabling critical reflection on research supervisory practice. *International Journal for Academic Development, 9*(1), 99–116.

Roth, A., Ogrin, S., & Schmitz, B. (2016). Assessing self-regulated learning in higher education: A systematic literature review of self-report instruments. *Educational Assessment, Evaluation and Accountability, 28*(3), 225–500. doi:10.1007/s11092-015-9229-2

Sampson, K., Johnson, L., Comer, K., & Brogt, E. (2015). Developing evidence for action on the postgraduate experience: An effective local instrument to move beyond benchmarking. *Higher Education Research and Development.* doi:10.1080/07294360/2015.1087469

Ursin, J., Vähäsantanen, K., McAlpine, L., & Hökkä, P. (2018). Emotionally loaded identity and agency in Finnish academic work. *Journal of Further and Higher Education.* doi:10.1080/0309877X.2018.1541971

Zuber-Skerritt, O., & Roche, V. (2004). A constructivist model for evaluating postgraduate supervision: A case study. *Quality Assurance in Education, 2*(2), 82–90.

CHAPTER 6

Mentoring Based on Many-Facet Rasch Analysis in Evaluating Mathematical Modelling Tasks

Yüksel Dede, Veysel Akçakın and Gürcan Kaya

Abstract

Mentoring, which has a significant potential in the learning of pre-service teachers, continues to increase in teaching programs. However, mentoring in teacher education – especially in the area of mathematics education – is usually focused on teaching processes. Only few studies have been conducted on mathematical modelling. However, there are no studies in the literature on mentoring support in the process of evaluating mathematical modelling tasks. In this context, this chapter explored the mentoring support based on Many-Facet Rasch Analysis in the context of evaluating mathematical modelling tasks. In the present study, mentoring support for evaluating modelling tasks is considered as one-to-one support by the experienced person to the inexperienced person. Thus, the mentee tried to specialise in the profession in terms of evaluating mathematical modelling tasks.

Keywords

Many-Facet Rasch Analysis – mentoring – preservice mathematics teachers – mathematical modelling – competencies

1   Introduction

In the 21st century, the skills that are desired in individuals are different than those required decades ago. In this context, many countries – especially in mathematics teaching – are updating their curriculums (e.g. Turkey, England, and Sweden). Especially, in Turkey, mathematics programs at different levels (secondary, high school, etc.) were updated considering 21st century skills. In these updates, particular emphasis was placed on the development of students' mathematical modelling skills. Because, parallel to technological developments, the need for individuals who can use mathematical modelling skills in real-world problems is increasing in order to solve new problems caused by changes in our lives (see Turkey Ministry of National Education [in Turkish: MEB], 2018). Mathematical modelling is a process that involves solving problems in real-world situations or other disciplinary areas (English, 2006). In this context, MEB has pointed out the importance of mathematical modelling in solving problems encountered in daily life (MEB, 2018).

Similarly, mathematical modelling is also emphasised in The Program for International Student Assessment (PISA) exams (The Organisation for Economic Co-operation and Development [OECD], 2016) and in this respect, while achieving solutions to real life problems, student achievement is measured in the context of skills (formulating, employing, interpreting and verifying) and processes (e.g. mathematics, reasoning, using formal and technical language) used by students (OECD, 2014).

In mathematics curriculum in recent years in Turkey; mathematical modelling is included under the headings of mathematical competences and skills, common skills and process skills, and through mathematical modelling, it is stated that students' mathematical thinking skills will develop, they can associate mathematics with real life more easily and they will value mathematics (MEB, 2013). In this context, the mathematics curriculum in Turkey, last updated in 2018, highlighted the importance of mathematical modelling is as follows:

> In order to solve new problems caused by changes in our lives, especially technological developments; there is a greater need for individuals who value mathematics, develop mathematical thinking power, and use mathematics in modelling and problem solving more than ever. (MEB, 2018, p. 11)

Similarly, OECD (2016) emphasises the importance of students' ability to use mathematics in real-life situations and the development of mathematical literacy levels. Formulation, employing, interpretation and validation processes used to measure mathematical literacy in the context of real-life problems are the main elements of mathematical modelling. However, it is seen that the "Mathematical Modelling" course is included in the updates made in the Secondary Education Mathematics Education Undergraduate Programs of Education Faculties of Turkey (see Turkish Council of Higher Education [in Turkish: YÖK], 2018a). Inclusion of mathematical modelling in higher education programs (see YÖK, 2018b) and emphasis on the use of mathematical modelling in secondary and primary mathematics curricula (see MEB, 2018), it is a clear indication that the importance given to mathematical modelling and thus to mathematical modelling competencies has increased.

Mathematical modelling competencies include the necessary abilities to perform different stages of mathematical modelling (Maaß, 2006; Ludwig & Reit, 2013). In other words, mathematical modelling competencies are basically based on the stages (processes) in the modelling cycle. As modelling cycles are studied in different ways by the researchers mathematical modelling competencies have been addressed by researchers in different ways (see Maaß, 2006; Blum & Leiß, 2007; Jensen, 2007; Zöttl, Ufer & Reiss 2011). In this sense, mathematical modelling competencies are considered as follows:

1. Simplifying problem: making simplifying assumptions and clarifying the goal.
2. Determining variables: assigning variables, parameters, and constants.
3. Mathematising: formulating the problem.
4. Working mathematically: mathematical operations.
5. Interpreting – validating: selecting a model, using graphical representation and relating back to the real situation (see Dede, Akçakın, & Kaya, 2018).

Many teachers believe that learning is related to experience based on "sink and swim". But experience-based learning may not always be reliable (Feiman-Nemser, 1998). In this context, in order to increase the experiences of the teacher candidates, they need to be given mentoring support. Because one of the main goals of mentoring is to develop the skills of individuals (Parsloe & Leedham, 2009). In addition, mentoring continues to increase in teaching programs and also has great potential in supporting teachers' learning (Lin, 2007). Mentoring has been recognised as an important aspect of the professional preparation of new teachers (Lai, 2010). In this context, in order to improve the mathematical modelling competencies of the students, their answers and solution papers of mathematical modelling tasks should be examined and given feedback by their teachers. However, evaluating mathematical modelling tasks are subjective because of its nature. Therefore, scoring and assessment of such tasks requires expertise. Rubrics are generally used in the process of assessing mathematical modelling tasks. However, in this case, it is difficult to expect that the scoring is completely objective (see Doğan, 2009). Therefore, it is important to give mentor support to pre-service teachers in evaluating mathematical modelling tasks in terms of developing their mathematical modelling skills. However, for pre-service teachers evaluating mathematical modelling tasks, two questions arise here. (1) Who should be supported? (2) How much support should be given? The traditional support method has no clear and plain answer to these questions. Furthermore, in order to encourage higher levels of student thinking, pre-service teachers and teachers should be supported not only about what mathematical modelling is, but also how to effectively incorporate mathematical modelling into their classes and how to present mathematical modelling in their classrooms (Gastón & Lawrence, 2015). The effectiveness of mathematical modelling teaching is related to teachers' ability to evaluate students' solutions. Because it is contradictory to say that teaching is done without evaluation. Since teaching is a very important endeavour, teacher judgments cannot be made solely on the basis of intuition, arbitrariness or tradition. Instead, teachers are obliged to obtain, analyse and use evidence that can be put forward to make the most effective decisions (evaluations) for the benefit of the students (e.g. (1) improving teaching to improve students' learning; (2) which students need remedial and advanced studies?) (Sax & Newton, 1997). As a method to support teachers at this point, Many-Facet Rasch Analysis (MFRA) analysis is a method that can answer such questions (which student, at which point, which support should be given?). In addition, recent research on mentoring reveals the importance of discipline-specific mentoring (Bradbury, 2010). Mentoring studies in mathematics education were generally conducted on the teaching processes of teachers (see Nilssen, 2003; Lin, 2007). Few studies have been conducted on mathematical modelling (see Seshaiyer, 2017). However, there are no studies in the literature on mentoring support in the process of evaluating mathematical modelling tasks. In this context, in the present study, Item Response Theory (IRT) was used to determine the students to be mentored in the evaluation of mathematical modelling tasks. In this context, it is thought that this study differs from other studies on mentoring in the literature. Because, it is not an easy process to determine the pre-service teachers to be given mentoring in scoring modelling tasks with qualitative methods and to decide exactly what mentoring support will be given. Therefore, in this study, teacher candidates to be given mentoring support were determined by MFRA based on IRT. As a result of the analysis, it was determined which stages of modelling tasks will be supported. Afterwards, interview protocol was prepared for each pre-service teacher. In particular, the pre-service teacher who needed mentoring support – who should be given mentorship support – was asked the reason for the score he gave to the modelling tasks. Other interview questions were asked according to the pre-service teacher's answer. Thus, s/he was able to determine his/her own mistakes and deficiencies related to the evaluation phase.

2   Mentoring

"Mentor was the name of a character from Greek mythology who was a wise and trusted adviser or counsellor" (Parsloe & Leedham, 2009, p. 19). The word mentor originates from the ancient Greek Homer epic and is described as "Mentor", "a trusted counselor or guide", and "mentee" as "one who is being mentored" (Mentor, 2019). "Because of common usage, Mentor is envisaged as telling

Telemachus how to go about becoming a wise leader of the city state in ancient Greece. Homer's Odyssey supports this idea to a considerable degree. It does not, however, expound Mentor's methodology in this role" (Pask & Joy, 2007, p. 7). Working definition of mentoring is "one-to-one support by a more experienced practitioner" (Hobson, 2012, p. 60). It is also stated that there are definitions that conceptualise mentoring in terms of relational, developmental) and contextual dimensions (Lai, 2010). However, when the mentioned definitions and related literature are examined, it can be seen that there is not a complete consensus on the definition of mentoring (Lai, 2010; Rik, 2010). Besides, the perspective on mentoring has important implications for how mentoring is implemented and experienced (Lai, 2010). Therefore, in the present study, mentoring in evaluating modelling tasks is considered as one-to-one support by the experienced person to the inexperienced person. In this way, it has been tried to ensure that the preservice teachers specialise in the profession.

3 Research Process

In this context, this chapter reports some data collected in a study conducted within the scope of a undergraduate course titled "Mathematical Modelling in Mathematics Education", where 18 pre-service mathematics teachers participated. The criteria for the ([A-Z])determination of the participants were to take the courses of Special Teaching Methods I-II, Measurement and Evaluation, and Introduction to Education and Educational Psychology. These criteria have been determined because the aforementioned courses enable pre-service teachers to have a certain level of knowledge about learning/teaching environment and processes, measurement approaches and thus allow them to make an adequate level of opinion and evaluation of modelling tasks.

Before the study, students were told that the data from this course would be used for a research. Then, the format of the course was decided together with the preservice mathematics teachers before the course. In other words, it was decided to give mentoring support to the preservice mathematics teachers determined by MFRA during the evaluation process of modelling tasks before the study. After determining the course format together with preservice mathematics teachers, they were asked to confirm their participation in the study. In this respect, there is no obligation to participate in the study. In addition, before the mentoring support, the preservice mathematics teachers were asked again whether they would agree to take mentoring support in the evaluation of mathematical modelling tasks.

In this study, one of the researchers teaches mathematical modelling to pre-service mathematics teachers. Pre-service mathematics teachers were provided with information about the theoretical and philosophical foundations of mathematical modelling, content, components, etc., and how to use it in teaching environments, how to assess modelling solutions etc., for nearly five weeks (three 45 min sessions each week). Then nearly for three weeks, mathematical modelling tasks were given to pre-service teachers to make them familiar with modelling tasks and to get them involved in a modelling task solving process. Then, real the solutions of the modelling tasks ("Lighthouse" adapted from Blum & Borromeo-Ferri, 2009); "Big Foot" adapted from Lesh and Harel (2003) obtained from the pre-service mathematics teachers who took the previous year's course were given to the participants of this study and they were asked to evaluate them using the Mathematical Modelling Rubric which was developed by the researchers. Eighteen pre-service teachers evaluate the solutions produced by the six groups in two different tasks. The pre-service teachers' evaluations were analysed with MFRA to determine specifically the biased evaluations of pre-service teachers. After that mentoring support has been given in the evaluation of mathematical modelling tasks to pre-service teachers that determined with MFRA. In determining the individuals who needed mentoring support, as mentioned above, MFRA analysis was used, which provides an objective assessment regardless of the characteristics of individuals, groups and raters, and regardless of the difficulty of the problem(s) (see Linacre, 1989; Prieto & Nieto, 2014). Therefore; in the scoring of mathematical modelling tasks, the MFRA technique provides an objective assessment regardless of the properties of the individuals, groups, raters, etc., and difficulty of the problem(s). Some information about the mathematical model of the MFRA is given below (Eckes, 2015, p. 30):

$$\log\left[\frac{P_{nljk}}{P_{nljk-1}}\right] = \theta_n - \delta_l - \alpha_j - \tau_k$$

P_{nljk}: Probability of examinee n receiving a rating of k from rater j on task
P_{nljk-1}: Probability of examinee n receiving a rating of $k-1$ from rater j on task l
θ_n: Ability of examinee n
δ_l: Difficulty of task l
α_j: Severity of rater j
τ_k: Difficulty of receiving a rating of k relative to $k-1$

By using MFRA, objectivity of scoring can be increased but there is a lot of expertise and time needed for raters to use this technique. In this context, it is important to give mentor support especially for the raters to improve themselves in the assessment of mathematical modelling tasks.

At this point, it was aimed to develop the competency of pre-service teachers to assess mathematical modelling solutions within the scope of traditional mentoring (Kram, 1985). With MFRA, the evaluations of the pre-service teachers were analysed by comparing the expected and observed logit scores by the Many-Facet Rasch program, and the pre-service teachers who made biased evaluations were determined. Then, in accordance with the results obtained by the MFRA, mentoring support in the process of evaluating mathematical modelling tasks was provided by a one researcher according to the interview protocols prepared by all researchers. In other words, the researchers decided together with how much and how the mentoring support will be provided by determining the pre-service mathematics teachers to be mentored with MFRA. Some of the findings in the tables are explained below.

The modelling competence scores of the groups obtained with the MFRA were double checked by two experts. In addition, the validity of the Mathematical Modelling Rubric was assessed by the MFRA. Subsequently, with MFRA it was determined biased evaluations of pre-service teachers about the solutions of mathematical modelling tasks (see Table 6.1). Mentoring support was given to judges H5 (in the table who made top biased evaluations), H3 (made biased evaluation of WM competence in more than one group) and H16 (more than one biased evaluation of multiple competencies) as they made more biased scores than others (see Table 6.1). Therefore, analysis of interviews with judges H5, H3 and H16 are given below.

When the scoring in the first line of Table 6.1 is examined, the score given by fifth judge (H5) to the mathematical (Ma) competence is expected to be 3 but it is actually 1. In this case, the fifth judge was asked the reason for this score.

H5: The variables given in the problem solving are not expressed mathematically. Variables are specified as "footprint", "depth" on the ground and "foot number". But they are not expressed mathematically and there is no mathematical expression.

Mentor: According to the results, the footprint length and body length were collected from several people (Figure 6.1), what do you think they mean?

H5: Yes, variable.

Mentor: Do you still think the same way?

H5: No, I noticed that I scored incorrectly, in fact, I have to give 3 points here. I thought wrong.

TABLE 6.1 Unexpected responses ("Big Foot" model eliciting activity)

Cat	Score	Exp.	Resd	StRes	Judges IDs	Group IDs	Trait IDs	Trait (modelling sub competencies)
1	1	3.0	−2.0	−2.9	H5	3	3	Ma
1	1	3.0	−2.0	−2.8	H3	3	4	WM
3	3	3.9	−0.9	−2.5	H18	6	1	SP
1	1	2.8	−1.8	−2.4	H3	1	4	WM
1	1	2.7	−1.7	−2.4	H5	6	2	DV
1	1	2.8	−1.8	−2.4	H9	4	2	DV
1	1	2.8	−1.8	−2.4	H14	5	5	IV
3	3	3.9	−0.9	−2.4	H18	5	2	DV
2	2	3.4	−1.4	−2.3	H6	6	1	SP
1	1	2.7	−1.7	−2.2	H3	5	4	WM
2	2	3.4	−1.4	−2.2	H8	2	1	SP
1	1	2.6	−1.6	−2.2	H8	4	5	IV
1	1	2.6	−1.6	−2.1	H3	6	4	WM
2	2	3.3	−1.3	−2.1	H6	5	5	IV
1	1	2.6	−1.6	−2.1	H13	3	1	SP
1	1	2.6	−1.6	−2.1	H16	1	3	Ma
1	1	2.6	−1.6	−2.1	H16	5	2	DV
1	1	2.6	−1.6	−2.1	H16	6	1	SP
4	4	2.4	1.6	2.1	H16	6	3	Ma
3	3	3.8	−0.8	−2.1	H18	5	5	IV
2	2	3.3	−1.3	−2.0	H7	2	2	DV
3	3	3.8	−0.8	−2.0	H18	6	5	IV

Notes: Cat (category) is the observation, Score is the category after it has been recounted, Exp. is the expected value of the Score, Resd. is the residual = Score−Expectation, StRes is the standardised residual, SP = Simplifying Problem, DV = Determining Variables, Ma = Mathematising, WM = Working Mathematically, IV = Interpreting–Validating

After mentoring support to the judge H5, a second modelling task evaluation was performed. As a result of this evaluation, it was seen that H5 scored biased Ma and WM competencies (see Table 6.2). As with the previous scoring, H5 was re-biased in Ma competency and was asked why:

H5: There are no computational and mathematical studies to solve the problem.

Mentor: Here are some drawings and evaluations (Figure 6.2).

TABLE 6.2   Unexpected responses ("Lighthouse" modelling activity)

Cat	Score	Exp.	Resd	StRes	Judges IDs	Group IDs	Trait IDs	Trait (modelling sub competencies)
1	1	3.4	−2.4	−3.9	H5	3	3	Ma
1	1	3.2	−2.2	−3.3	H5	3	4	WM
1	1	3.2	−2.2	−3.3	H18	4	3	Ma
1	1	3	−2	−2.8	H8	6	5	IV
4	4	1.8	2.2	2.8	H13	2	4	WM
1	1	3	−2	−2.8	H13	3	1	SP
1	1	3	−2	−2.7	H18	4	4	WM
1	1	2.9	−1.9	−2.6	H18	4	5	IV
1	1	2.9	−1.9	−2.5	H8	1	2	DV
2	2	3.5	−1.5	−2.5	H9	6	4	WM
1	1	2.8	−1.8	−2.4	H7	5	2	DV
2	2	3.5	−1.5	−2.4	H9	6	5	IV
1	1	2.9	−1.9	−2.4	H15	4	3	Ma
2	2	3.4	−1.4	−2.3	H5	3	1	SP
1	1	2.8	−1.8	−2.3	H5	6	5	IV
1	1	2.8	−1.8	−2.3	H7	1	2	DV
1	1	2.8	−1.8	−2.3	H12	2	1	SP
1	1	2.8	−1.8	−2.3	H13	3	4	WM
4	4	2.2	1.8	2.1	H3	2	4	WM
1	1	2.6	−1.6	−2.1	H3	6	5	IV
1	1	2.7	−1.7	−2.1	H7	1	4	WM
4	4	2.3	1.7	2.1	H16	5	4	WM

Note: Cat (category) is the observation, Score is the category after it has been recounted, Exp. is the expected value of the Score, Resd. is the residual = Score–Expectation, StRes is the standardised residual, SP = Simplifying Problem, DV = Determining Variables, Ma = Mathematising, WM = Working Mathematically, IV = Interpreting–Validating

H5:   But there is no mathematical operation.
Mentor: Well the radius is expressed. It is tried to find this radius based on a certain x value.
H5:   I didn't think there was any mathematical conclusion. But I didn't look that way. I can admit it.

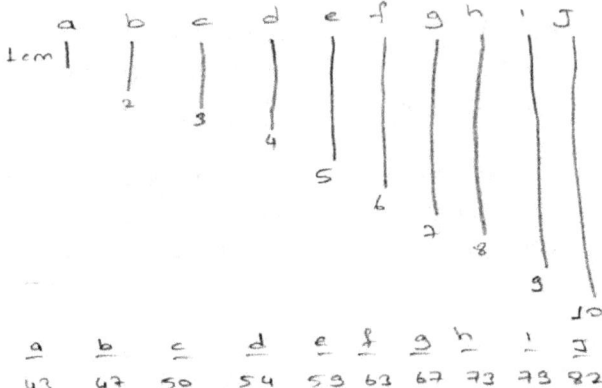

FIGURE 6.1   Solution of group 3

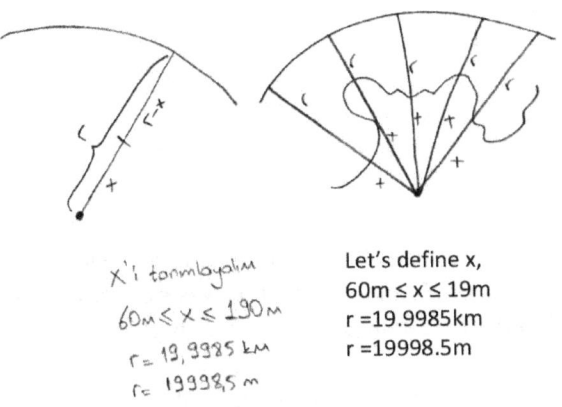

FIGURE 6.2   Solution of group 3

In the first evaluation, the H5 gave a lower score to the Ma competence than to the other competencies. When the solutions of the groups were examined and re-asked to the H5, he realised that he gave biased points to the 3rd group in Ma competency. However, in the next evaluation, H5 scored lower and biased points than the expected score in Ma competency again. In addition, H5 scored lower than expected in WM competency too. One reason for this may be that H5 is a foreign student and not fully familiar with the Turkish language or due to other individual differences.

As can be seen in Table 6.1, the third judge (H3) is expected to give 3 to third group (G3) in WM competency while he gave 1. The rationale of the score given to the third judge was asked and he responded as follows:

H3: There are no mathematical operations in problem solving.

Mentor: An attempt was made to establish a relationship between footprint length and body height and this was explained graphically (Figure 6.3).

H3: I still think there isn't any process, but what you're saying is also correct he was tried to establish a relationship between height and footprint. We can consider this as mathematical reasoning. In this case we can give points.

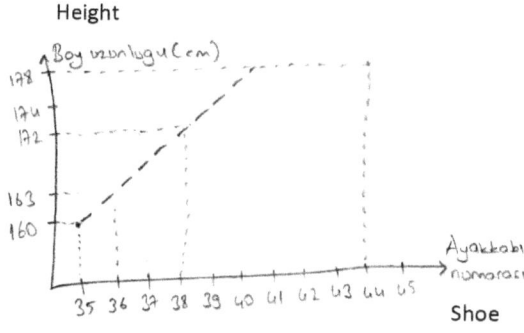

FIGURE 6.3   Solution of group 3

When the judge H3's biased scores were examined in the next task evaluation process, it was seen that WM was scored 4 points when it was expected to be given 2 points. This was asked to the H3 and received the following response:

H3: There are mathematical operations to solve the problem.

Mentor: These solutions can be some kind of solution for the problem, but are they the correct solutions (see Figure 6.5)? What do you think about it?

H3: I did not check the correctness of the solutions. So I gave the highest score in the rubric.

One reason why the H3 scored more than expected in the WM competency, can be that he did not check the accuracy of the solutions. If the solution of group 3 evaluated by the H3 is examined, it can be seen that there is a mathematical calculation but it does not lead to the correct solution of the problem (see Figure 6.4). Considering the biased scores of the H3 in the first task and the biased scores in the evaluations he made after mentoring support, it can be seen that he made less biased and more accurate evaluations in the second task. Therefore, it can be said that the mentoring support leads H3 to make more accurate evaluations.

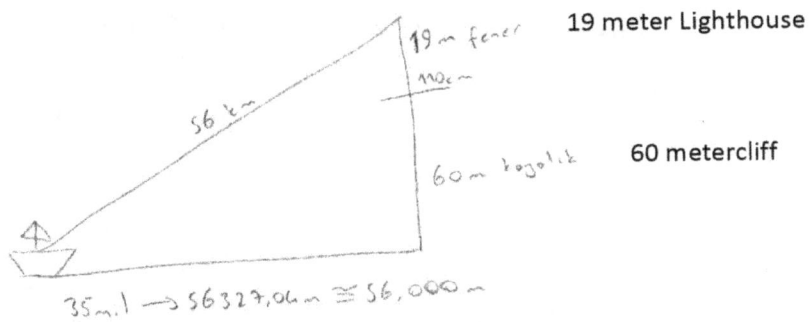

35 mil→56.327,04 meter≅56.000

FIGURE 6.4 Solution of group 2

Table 6.1 shows that the judges with the highest scores in terms of biased scores are H16 and H18. Since the H18 could not be reached in the week of the interviews, only H16 was given mentoring support. As shown in Table 6.1, H16 scored the first group lower than expected for Ma, the fifth group for the DV and the sixth group for the SP competencies and scored sixth group higher than expected for the competence Ma. Firstly, the reason of the score H16 gave to the first group for Ma competency was asked.

H16: There is no mathematical expression.
Mentor: The relationship between foot length and height, footprint depth and weight were tried to be established. Data was collected from individuals. Certain limits are defined (see Figure 6.5).
H16: I agree with you, but the variables are not represented by mathematical symbols. Variables are expressed in number intervals but no mathematical symbols are assigned. Assumptions are expressed verbally but no mathematical symbols are assigned.
Mentor: What you say is true, but what criteria are there for the lowest score in the rubric? If these exist (e.g. variables are expressed in number ranges, assumptions are expressed verbally) why shouldn't other scoring categories be considered?

After checking the rubric, H16 agreed with the mentor to give one of the two or three scoring categories. It can be seen in Table 6.2 that after the mentoring support, H16 was the least biased scorer in evaluation of second modelling task. After mentoring support given on the basis of the data in Table 6.1 and Table 6.2, it can be said that the H16 made less biased and more accurate scoring and evaluations. It can be seen that the judges (e.g. H9, H8, H13, H6 etc.) who do not receive mentoring support, perform more than one biased

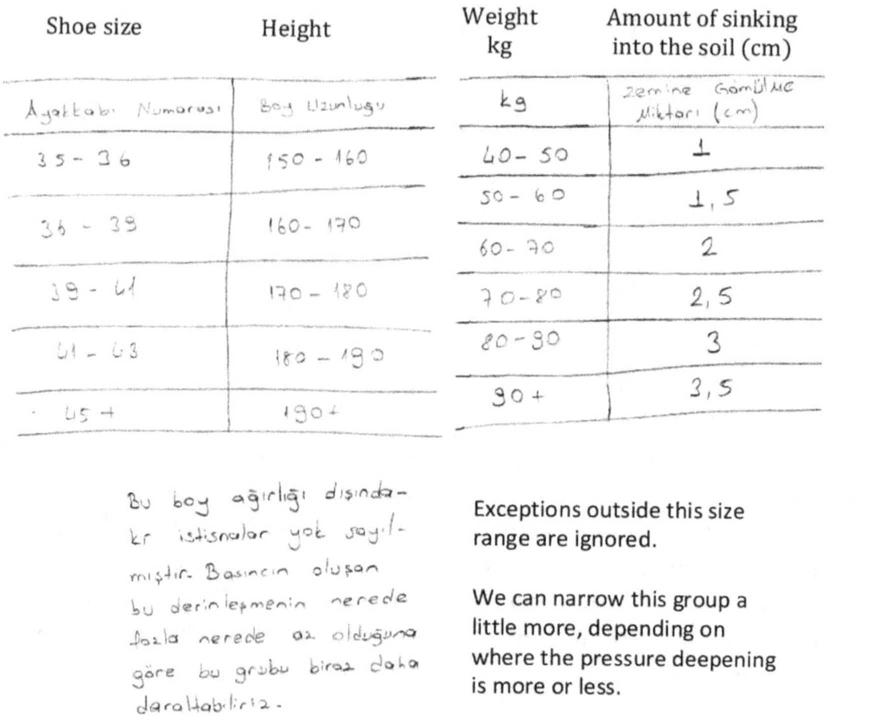

Shoe size	Height	Weight kg	Amount of sinking into the soil (cm)
Ayakkabı Numarası	Boy Uzunluğu	kg	Zemine Gömülme Miktarı (cm)
35-36	150-160	40-50	1
36-39	160-170	50-60	1,5
		60-70	2
39-41	170-180	70-80	2,5
41-43	180-190	80-90	3
45+	190+	90+	3,5

Bu boy ağırlığı dışındaki istisnalar yok sayılmıştır. Basıncın oluşan bu derinleşmenin nerede fazla nerede az olduğuna göre bu grubu biraz daha daraltabiliriz.

Exceptions outside this size range are ignored.

We can narrow this group a little more, depending on where the pressure deepening is more or less.

FIGURE 6.5   Solution of group 1

evaluation in the second evaluation or the number of biased evaluations does not change in the second task (see Tables 6.1 and 6.2). It was seen that H14 made only one biased evaluation in the first task but did not make biased evaluation in the second task despite the lack of mentoring support. This may be due to individual differences. Furthermore, it was observed that there was not much change in the number of modelling competencies that were biased. In the light of all these findings, it can be said that mentoring support for evaluating modelling tasks leads the pre-service teachers to make unbiased and more accurate evaluations.

4   Conclusion

In this study, the results of using MFRA to support pre-service teachers for evaluating mathematical modelling tasks are presented. The results show that the interaction between the mentor and mentee contributes to the skills of mentees' modelling task evaluation process and thus gives learning opportunities. The most important challenges related to mentoring support can be to decide to whom to support and to determine the scope of this support. Therefore, in this study, the pre-service teachers who would be given mentoring support were determined on the statistical basis with the help of MFRA. It is inevitable that the mentoring will be given to all participants if it cannot be determined which individual is to be given mentoring support. This can be considered as an obstacle to the optimum use of resources. Moreover, determining whether the purpose of mentoring support has been achieved has much more importance. Because the judgments of the teachers cannot be made on the basis of intuition, arbitrariness or tradition (Sax & Newton, 1997). In this respect, this study is thought to be a guide for further researches about the use of MFRA in mentoring. Mentoring was given to H3 on the WM competency which was scored biasedly. In the evaluation of first task, it was observed that the H3 gave different scores for four different groups in WM competency, whereas in the evaluation of second task, it was observed one biased scoring. While in the first evaluation he didn't consider mathematical operations as WM competency, in the second evaluation, it was seen that H3 could realise the mathematical operations which can be considered as WM competency. However, in the second evaluation made by H3, it was seen that he gave high points more than expected because he scored them without checking the accuracy of the calculations. H5 and H16 pre-service teachers were given mentoring support in SP, DV, Ma and WM competencies. In the second evaluation, it was seen that H16 made only one biased score on WM. In addition, since H5 is a foreign student and is not fully familiar with the Turkish language or because of some other reasons arising from individual differences, he didn't show improvements in evaluating other competencies while he showed improvement in evaluating Ma competency.

It is seen that pre-service teachers who were not provided mentoring support continued to make biased scores while evaluating second modelling task. In this respect, according to the findings of this study, it can be said that giving mentoring support to pre-service teachers in evaluating mathematical modelling tasks can increase their evaluating skills of mathematical modelling tasks. On the other hand, the lack of improvement about evaluating skills despite the mentorship support given to H5, who is learning the Turkish language as a second language may be an indication that language competence can be considerable factor in mentoring. In this respect, examining the effects of language competence on mentoring can make important contributions to the literature.

This study only described the mentoring approach in the process of evaluating mathematical modelling tasks. Thus, mentees were given the opportunity to improve themselves by making them to examine their own evaluating processes. Because mentors also help mentees develop their learning skills from their own practice (Barnett & Friedrichsen, 2015). Similarly, the MFRA technique can be used to monitor students' mathematical modelling competencies. In addition, more objective evaluations can be made in many areas of learning environments by using MRFA technique.

References

Barnett, E., & Friedrichsen, P. J. (2015). Educative mentoring: How a mentor supported a preservice biology teacher's pedagogical content knowledge development. *Journal of Science Teacher Education, 26*(7), 647–668.

Blum, W., & Borromeo Ferri, R. (2009). Mathematical modelling: Can it be taught and learnt? *Journal of Mathematical Modelling and Application, 1*(1), 45–58.

Blum, W., & Leiß, D. (2007). How do students and teachers deal with modelling problems? In C. Haines, P. Galbraith, W. Blum, & S. Kahn (Eds.), *Mathematical modelling (ICTMA12): Education, engineering and economics* (pp. 222–231). Ellis Horwood.

Bradbury, L. U. (2010). Educative mentoring: Promoting reform-based science teaching through mentoring relationships. *Science Education, 94*(6), 1049–1071.

Dede, Y., Akçakın, V., & Kaya, G. (Eds.). (2018). Examining mathematical modeling competencies of pre-service middle school mathematics teachers by gender: Multidimensional item response theory. Adıyaman University [Special issue]. *Journal of Educational Sciences, 8*, 150–169. Retrieved from https://dergipark.org.tr/en/pub/adyuebd/issue/40656

Doğan, N. (2009). Ölçme araçlarını sınıflama çabaları [Efforts to classify measurement tools]. In H. Atılgan (Ed.), *Eğitimde ölçme ve değerlendirme [Measurement and evaluation in education]* (pp. 119–144). Anı.

Eckes, T. (2015). *Introduction to many-facet Rasch measurement*. Peter Lang.

English, L. D. (2006). Mathematical modeling in the primary school. *Educational Studies in Mathematics, 63*(3), 303–323.

Feiman-Nemser, S. (1998). Teachers as teacher educators. *European Journal of Teacher Education, 21*(1), 63–74.

Gastón, J. L., & Lawrence, B. A. (2015). Supporting teachers' learning about mathematical modeling. *Journal of Mathematics Research, 7*(4), 2–11.

Hobson, A. J. (2012). Fostering face-to-face mentoring and coaching. In S. Fletcher & C. A. Mullen (Eds.), *Sage handbook of mentoring and coaching in education*. Sage.

Jensen, T. H. (2007). Assessing mathematical modelling competency. In C. Haines, P. Galbraith, W. Blum, & S. Khan (Eds.), *Mathematical modeling (ICTMA 12): Education, engineering and economics* (pp. 141–148). Horwood.

Kram, K. E. (1985). *Mentoring at work: Developmental relationships in organizational life*. Scott, Foresman.

Lai, E. (2010). Getting in step to improve the quality of in-service teacher learning through mentoring. *Professional Development in Education, 36*(3), 443–469.

Lesh, R., & Harel, G. (2003). Problem solving, modeling, and local conceptual development. *Mathematical Thinking and Learning, 5*(2–3), 157–189.

Lin, P.-J. (2007). The effect of a mentoring development program on mentors' conceptualizing mathematics teaching and mentoring. In J.-H. Woo, H.-C. Lew, K.-S. Park, & D.-Y. Seo (Eds.), *Proceedings of the 31st Conference of the international group for the psychology of mathematics education* (Vol. 3, pp. 201–208). The Korea Society of Educational Studies in Mathematics.

Linacre, J. M. (1989). *Many-facet Rasch measurement*. Mesa.

Ludwig, M., & Reit, X. R. (2013, January). *Comparative study about gender differences in mathematical modelling*. Paper presented at the Fifth International Conference to Review Research on Science, Technology and Mathematics Education (epiSTEME 5), Mumbai, India.

Maaß, K. (2006). What are modelling competencies? ZDM *Mathematics Education, 38*(2), 113–142.

Mentor. (2019). *Merriam-Webster's online dictionary* (11th ed.). Retrieved from https://www.merriam-webster.com/dictionary/mentor

Ministry of National Education [MEB]. (2013). *Primary and middle school mathematics curriculum*. Author.

Ministry of National Education [MEB]. (2018). *Secondary school mathematics curriculum*. Author.

Nilssen, V. (2003). *Mentoring teaching of mathematics in teacher education*. Paper presented at the 27th International Group for the Psychology of Mathematics Education Conference held jointly with the 25th PME-NA Conference, Honolulu, HI.

Organisation for Economic Co-operation and Development. (2014). *PISA 2012 results: What students know and can do – Student performance in mathematics, reading and science* (Vol. I). Author.

Organisation for Economic Co-operation and Development. (2016). *PISA 2015 results: Excellence and equity in education* (Vol. I). Author.

Parsloe, E., & Leedham, M. (2009). *Coaching and mentoring: Practical conversations to improve learning*. Kogan Page.

Pask, R., & Joy, B. (2007). *Mentoring-coaching: A guide for education professionals*. McGraw-Hill.

Prieto, G., & Nieto, E. (2014). Analysis of rater severity on written expression exam using many faceted Rasch measurement. *Psicológica, 35*(2), 385–397.

Rik, B. (2010). *The role of technology in the mentoring and coaching of teachers*. Retrieved from https://www.irisconnect.com/us/wp-content/uploads/sites/3//2014/08/the-role-of-technology-in-mentoring-and-coachingfinal-1-33.pdf

Sax, G., & Newton, J. W. (1997). *Principles of educational and psychological measurement and evaluation*. Wadsworth.

Seshaiyer, P. (2017). Leading undergraduate research projects in mathematical modeling. *Problems, Resources, and Issues in Mathematics Undergraduate Studies, 27*(4–5), 476–493.

Turkish Council of Higher Education [YÖK]. (2018a). *Matematik öğretmenliği lisans programı* [Mathematics teacher education undergraduate program]. Author.

Turkish Council of Higher Education [YÖK]. (2018b). *İlköğretim matematik öğretmenliği lisans programı* [Primary mathematics teaching undergraduate program]. Author.

Zöttl, L., Ufer, S., & Reiss, K. (2011). Assessing modelling competencies using a multi-dimensional IRT approach. In G. Kaiser, W. Blum, R. Borromeo-Ferri, & G. Stillman (Eds.), *Trends in teaching and learning of mathematical modelling* (pp. 427–437). Springer.

CHAPTER 7

The Teacher Ambassador: Mentoring Colleagues to Adopt Twenty-First Century Teaching, Learning and Pedagogical Practice

Kathy Jordan and Kathy Littlewood

Abstract

Mentoring is widespread in teaching and is often used to support pre-service teacher and in-service teacher practice, and as a strategy to support teacher capability building. Yet despite positive rhetoric around the value of mentoring in teacher education, there is a lack of clarity around what mentoring is, the roles that mentors perform and their expectations of, and experiences in, the role in teacher education arenas. In 2018 the Victorian state government launched the Tech School initiative, a state-wide initiative that aimed to build improved STEM skills and employability for secondary students. Ten technical (tech) schools have been built across the state servicing over 150 partner secondary schools. Several of these Tech Schools have appointed Teacher Ambassadors as mentors to support the implementation of the initiative at the local level. This chapter involves a case study of one of the Teacher Ambassadors and explores his motivations, challenges and experience in performing this role. The chapter aims to add to our understanding of the complex role that mentors perform in teacher education, and the importance of context in performing this role.

Keywords

Tech School Ambassador – case study

1   Introduction

Mentoring is well recognised in the literature as important to supporting the professional development of teachers (for example, Top of the Class, 2007; TEMAG, 2014). In the pre-service teacher context, mentoring is associated with the experienced classroom teacher who supports the pre-service teacher to develop their classroom teaching skills during practicum (Zeichner, 2005, 2010). In the in-service teacher context, mentoring is often associated with supporting the induction of new teachers into the profession. Mentoring of graduate teachers has been in place in Victoria for some time with graduates expected to have a mentor (a Lead Teacher or more senior teacher) to help guide and support their developing practice and identities as teachers. These mentors are also expected to help them progress from provisional registration to full Victorian Institute of Teaching registration within the first two years of teaching (DET, 2019). In the in-service context, mentoring is also used by education departments and policymakers to build teacher capability as part of wider school reform (Ellul, 2010).

Despite this perceived value of mentoring, mentoring itself can be difficult to define (Ambrosetti, 2014; Butler & Cuenca, 2012). As Jones and Brown (2011, p. 401) comment, "despite 40 years of research into mentoring, the field lacks a widely-accepted definition, single theoretical lens, and universally agreed upon model". Traditionally, mentoring has tended to be defined around the pairing of an experienced person with a less experienced one, akin to a master-apprentice role (Bradbury & Koballa, 2008); a transactional relationship, in which the older more experienced mentor, supports the younger less experienced mentee. This is certainly the case in Australian educational contexts where both supporting pre-service teachers and in-service teachers is seen as the domain of the more experienced teacher. More recently, mentoring has been defined as more complex than this simple relationship, to include more of a developmental relationship, affected by context, and the needs of the mentor and mentee (Aderibigbe, Colucci-Gray, & Gray, 2016; Hudson, 2016). According to Eby, Rhodes, and Allen (2007), mentoring involves a unique relationship between individuals, is a learning partnership, a process, involves a reciprocal relationship, is dynamic and changes over time.

The mentoring literature tends to be positive (Ambrosetti, 2014). For mentors, mentoring is perceived as leading to increased reflection, an improved work ethic, development of professional identity, renewed enthusiasm and enhanced collegiality. For mentees, the advantages include being able to share professional experiences, receive advice and feedback and develop reflective practice (Walkington, 2005; Ambrosetti, 2012). Yet while the benefits for mentors and mentees are well reported, the roles they perform are often generalised. Terms such as guide, support, advise, model and facilitate proliferate the literature (Ambrosetti, 2012). Exactly what a mentor does is also open to interpretation, as mentors conceptualise their roles in different ways, from more formal to informal ways (Davis & Fantozzi, 2016). Without such a clear understanding of the role, its expectations, duties and responsibilities, it is "difficult to know how best to support or facilitate that work" (Clarke et al., p. 3). Mentoring is also difficult to differentiate from other terms such as coaching, supervising or tutoring, as these terms are often used interchangeably and practices associated with each can blend and overlap (Ambrosetti & Dekkers, 2010; Grimmett et al., 2018).

There is general agreement in the literature that mentors require a complex set of skills (Ambrosetti, 2014). For example, when mentoring pre-service teachers, teacher mentors need to be sensitive to a pre-service teacher's "point of need" and to their development as a teacher. They need to have interpersonal skills, be able to give feedback, clearly communicate, and link theory and practice (Aderbigbe et al., 2016). They need to make "evidence based professional judgements" (Le Cornu, 2015, p. 14) about the teaching performance of the pre-service teacher against the Graduate Teaching Standards and be able to report on this in an "evidence based summative report". As well they need to build a constructive mentoring relationship with their mentee (Le Cornu, 2015).

Often though, the value of mentoring is assumed to be self-evident or a *fait accompli* through the development of learning communities, the building of relationships and the encouragement of reflective practice techniques (Le Cornu, 2012). Mentoring can be presented as a simple process, such as a simple transaction of knowledge and skill from mentor to mentee. While complexities in forming and sustaining this relationship are often iterated, solutions also tend to be readily provided. As well, while effective mentoring is often perceived as requiring a range of knowledge and skills, it is experienced particularly in the Initial Teacher Education context, and it is seniority in the beginning teacher context that matters most. While professional learning of mentors is readily identified as important to performing the role (see for example Ambrosetti, 2014; Le Cornu, 2015) lack of adequate or ongoing professional learning is also commonly reported, particularly in the ITE context. As such without formal training, teacher mentors draw on their own experiences. Yet as Nielsen et al. (2017) comment in relation to mentoring pre-service teachers, "This is problematic because unarticulated and tacitly held beliefs about one's own supervisory practices can be detrimental to preservice teacher learning whilst on practicum" (p. 347). There also appears to be a lack of attention to context. This chapter adopts the view that mentoring is a complex process and drawing on the influential work of Ambrosetti (2012, 2014), involves three components: relationship, developmental needs and contextual elements.

This chapter also adds to this understanding of mentoring through its case study of one Teacher Ambassador, whose role was mentoring teachers to implement a large state government initiative, the Tech School initiative. Understanding how mentor teachers see themselves and their role, as well as their personal and professional beliefs, and the context in which they work are all important to understanding their role.

2   Tech School Initiative

In 2018, the Victorian state government invested $128 million to establish ten Tech Schools across the state, with further funding to support ongoing operation. These Tech Schools were established as part of a system-wide effort to increase student outcomes in STEM and to support future employment in a high-tech workplace. Tech Schools aim to "deliver inspiring learning programs using innovative, high-tech spaces directly applicable to the needs of local students and educators" (DET, 2017, p. 4). Learning programs aim to engage students, by using meaningful and relevant curriculum and pedagogy. Curriculum is produced in collaboration with partner schools and industry using a co-design process, and is produced biannually to ensure multiple entry points for schools and to give them opportunities to develop and align their own curriculum. A design thinking approach is used to scaffold student learning, with students moving through the phases of empathise, define, ideate prototype and test.

The Banyule Nillumbik Tech School and the Whittlesea Tech School, both located in Melbourne's outer north are two of these Tech Schools. Each has around 15 partner secondary schools, many with high linguistic and cultural diversity. Both appointed Teacher Ambassadors to mentor teachers in their schools to develop curriculum and pedagogy in line with the broader initiative. RMIT University is a partner with these two Tech Schools. In 2018 the RMIT School of Education, in conjunction with these two Tech Schools, was funded by the Victorian Department of Education and Training to research impact on schools, teachers, students and their communities. Ethics approval from both DET and RMIT to conduct the project was gained. Interviews with seven Teacher Ambassadors in the partner schools were conducted over the year.

In this aspect of the study, data is drawn from David (pseudonym), a teacher at one of these partner schools. David had volunteered to be a Teacher Ambassador and mentor staff at his school to implement the broader Tech School initiative. David's work in this role included encouraging staff at the school to move away from a discipline-based view of curriculum and pedagogy, and adopt a more cross-disciplinary pedagogy that fostered teamwork, creativity, innovation and design thinking. He also delivered professional learning workshops, led curriculum meetings and provided one on one mentoring support. David continued in his classroom teaching role as well as his leadership role in the school while he undertook the Ambassador role. He received some professional learning time to participate in various Tech School learning activities, meetings and forums. He received no additional payment for his Ambassador role. He also did not receive any mentor training, nor a role description.

3   Objectives of the Study

This study seeks to understand how this mentor defined his role and to gain an understanding of the complex role that a mentor may perform within an educational context such as the Tech School initiative. This study had the following two research questions:
1. How does this mentor (David) define his mentoring role?
2. What motivations and challenges does he (David) perceive in performing the role?

4   Method

This chapter uses interview data to form a single case study of one Teacher Ambassador, who volunteered to mentor staff and support the implementation of the broader Banyule-Nillumbik Tech School initiative at his own school. Case study is a flexible approach that can be used to explore, explain or describe phenomena or events in settings in which they arise (Yin, 2014). A case study involves a case or a unit of analysis that enables the researcher to determine the scope of the study. It is "bounded", that is, it has boundaries around it, that are essential to ensure that the case study remains feasible (Creswell & Poth, 2018; Saldana, 2016). David was chosen as a single case study because of his revelatory comments around his role and the phenomenon of Tech School role mentoring that he had experienced. It was not a rich case study of David's total experience, but involved a single interview with David to capture a "point in time" picture of his role, and his perceptions of the motivations and challenges in his role as a phenomenon of the Tech School strategy. This study is phenomenological, in that it looks at the phenomenon of mentoring in a specific context, that of the Tech School Ambassador. Both Vagle (2018) and Van Manen (2016) have identified the value of interviews of individuals involved in a phenomenon such as the Tech School Ambassador role, as an important source of research data. An interview was selected as the best way to find out about David's beliefs. A semi-structured approach was used, whereby general questions or themes were used to frame the interview rather than a set of questions in a pre-determined order (Patton, 1990). The interview was audiotaped and then transcribed. This transcript was later reviewed and then organised for analysis using the research questions as a focus (Patton, 1990). Interview data was then categorised, with similar characteristics or properties grouped together.

David is an experienced secondary teacher of some six years. He currently teaches senior science at a large secondary school. He has mentored pre-service teachers in the past but has no formal training in this regard. David has held a leadership role in the school which involved him working with in-service teachers, particularly middle years leaders, however this did not involve a formal mentoring role. David said he "was tapped on the shoulder" by the assistant principal to take on the Ambassador role because he thought that it would suit him as he knew about STEM. David was keen to take on the role and was drawn to it as he felt that it was important for his school to be a part of such a large state-wide initiative. He also had a strong belief in the value of Tech School learning and felt that it could offer more engaging ways for students to learn, particularly through hands-on and tech-enabled learning.

David was selected to mentor because of his experience. This selection criterion is typical of that involving both pre-service and in-service teaching contexts in Australia (Ambrosetti, 2014; Nielsen et al., 2017). The TEMAG (2014) review is quite explicit in its view that experienced teachers should mentor pre-service teachers. While experience may be useful in supporting pre-service teachers, experience in teaching does not necessarily equate to skills in mentoring. Zeichner (2005, p. 118) comments that while there are "some similarities" between teaching children, adolescents and adults, "there are many important ways in which the two kinds of teaching differ and where one's expertise as a teacher does not necessarily translate into expertise as mentors of teachers". The view that mentoring of teachers is based on teaching experience proliferates a narrow view of mentoring, and encourages a master-apprentice view, rather than the more complex roles associated with reciprocal relationships.

5   Teacher Ambassador Role

David saw the Ambassador role as important to promoting the initiative at his school and supporting its implementation. As he commented about his role, "Essential. I can't, yeah, as I said, without it, the Tech School would just be guessing as to what the schools need. They wouldn't have as much support I think, within schools". He also hinted that having someone such as himself in the role who would champion the initiative was also important. As he went on to add, having, "Someone in a school. Having someone like myself who sees the benefit in this, it is really good". Yet later in the interview he seemingly contradicts himself when he comments that while many of the staff at his school would know that he was involved in STEM, they would not necessarily know that he held the Ambassador role. As he added, "It's not as if it's publicised in the school".

Arguably then, David's view about the importance of the role on the one hand and the lack of recognition for the role on the other reflects the wider literature around mentoring. Mentoring is commonly agreed in the literature as vital to supporting the professional learning of teachers. Yet, teacher mentors typically undertake the role on top of their teaching duties and if recompensed, it is for a small sum and not on par with the work involved (Ambrosetti, 2014). This tension between importance and recognition is well documented in the literature. As well, the value of mentor training is perhaps understated. Mentor training is not a simple endeavour and requires addressing numerous issues such as: suiting the needs of mentors, who can range from first timers to those who are highly experienced, from those who willingly take on the role, to those who are pressured to do it, fitting in the mentoring role on top of a teaching role, time to train, recognition and payment. However, given the importance and value of mentoring to teaching, such a prospect warrants further investigation.

When asked to describe how the initiative was being implemented at his school, David freely acknowledged that the school hadn't made clear plans, commenting for example that, "We don't have the answer to that. Currently, it's pretty ad hoc". David felt that there were several logistical issues that needed to be overcome yet he was confident that his school was well placed to do so. He spoke about how the school had been making changes to its teaching and learning programs in recent years and that these changes aligned with Tech School learning. As he commented, "It's come at a really fortunate time because at the same time as the Tech School has developed their programs, we have been working on our own programs here independently of it".

As he went on to explain in some detail, the Tech School,

> seems to be organised in terms of the experience a student has when they go over there. It seems to be very student centred. It actually comes with the expectation that during a day, students will be at different points. It's this facility there where students can move ahead. They can – they're not all stepping through things at the same time. With that requires a student

to be, have that skill set, be confident, be able to work with others. Be able to be present. Be able to understand technology pretty quickly.

David felt that changes being made to the school programs would align with this student-centred pedagogy of the Tech School. The school had for example developed an innovation subject for Year 7 and Year 9 as part of its new teaching framework. This subject has a focus on STEM and in the following year will also consider digital STEM. "It's not a whole school focus, however it sits nicely with things they were going to do". As he then elaborates,

> We say alright guys, we want you to solve the problem. Go out and find that problem. They go through the whole design thinking process so they have to learn those skills along the way, which fits in perfectly with what the tech school was doing. They have that experience at Year 7 of design thinking. The idea really is they can use those skills in the following years in other subjects. By Year 9, we're hoping that they can implement some of these things. One of our – every Wednesday we have a day long program with our Year 9s called Excel and one of the subjects offered throughout the year is a design thinking based, problem solving one. They get to apply those skills again.

And this,

> Within that is a whole bunch of skills that would be completely applicable to the Tech School. For example, for them to describe their own learning is a really important concept. For them to understand that their learning is a progression and it's on a continuum. They need to do something, actually have to learn and make those choices themselves, to go from one stage to the next stage.

David also felt that some curriculum areas in the school had already incorporated the types of learning being fostered by the initiative. As he elaborated,

> Most other subjects that I'm not involved in but know about; all our tech subjects, our electronics, woodwork, all of those have been doing this for ages. This is what they already do. They're the ones who are the most excited in the school to start working with the tech school. It's what they already do. They spend all day working on their own projects. They design it and they do it all themselves. The teachers act as facilitators for that process. They're used to it. The boys get that experience of self-guided learning the whole way through.

6 Skills Needed in the Role

When asked about the skills required to undertake the role, David was quick to comment that he thought,

> It's less perhaps a skill set and more of a mindset; really having a mindset where you truly believe that students can have a real impact, you can believe that if you empower students, they will make really fantastic things. Having that understanding, that 21st-century skills are important, and things have changed. We really should be developing students with those skills, so they can really go out into the world and do awesome things.

David thought that his role had two main aspects. The first aspect involved working with other ambassadors to co-design curriculum that would be the focus of learning in the Tech School. He saw this collaboration as important and necessary so that there was an agreed focus by the many schools and partners involved. As he went on to say, "With so many schools being involved, we all have our own differences and similarities, that I think is important to share and really focus on the needs of those particular students and come to a consensus between us all and what we believe is really important for this area and develop it".

David thought that the second aspect of his role involved mentoring other staff so as to implement Tech School learning at the school. As he commented,

> Making them aware of what's possible. That's the important thing. You can say these lofty things like students will go and have a design thinking process and they'll learn all these 21st-century skills. Really, staff want to see what it looks like on paper. They want to see that it works, and they want to see that it's worth pulling kids out of class for. It's actually – it should complement what we do here. It does, but just proving that it does is going to be a priority for me. It is important that I have the opportunity to do this. If I was just a regular teacher, I think I'd struggle.

David thought that he had been successful at doing this while noting that the initiative was recent. As he commented, "The Tech School initiative has been really successful at the school, for now, only because it's early days. It has been positive so far". He added, "I still think there's still a bit to discover about the Tech School. I mean it has recently opened". He also saw that involving school leadership was important in achieving this goal. Research supports David's view that the implementation of new initiatives is more successful when school leadership is committed to them (Le Cornu, 2015). As he commented, "Targeting leaders in schools is the way to go. Sometimes things go more smoothly when leaders have that opportunity. It doesn't have to be people right at the top. It can just be a middle leader like myself. It helps".

David commented that school staff were excited by the initiative. As he says, "We have humanities teachers really excited. We have tech teachers really excited. Science teachers obviously". He elaborated, "I have staff coming to me with existing assessments saying how do I make this better? Remember that design thinking you were talking about?" In this sense, David successfully mentored teachers across disciplines to help them develop knowledge and skills in line with the Tech School design thinking process through a learning focus that worked twofold: David kept the needs of the teachers front and foremost in his thinking with the outcome being "meaningful and effective learning for all students" (Renshaw, 2012, p. 17).

David feels he has considerable support to undertake his ambassadorial role from the school's leadership team. He comments that the principal was interested in the initiative and kept him abreast of key developments from a partner school perspective. Yet it was the allocation of a time allowance that David thought indicated the school's support most. As he commented, "Like I said before, the support means time allowance. It means I'm allowed to go to it. Every time I put a request in to do this and they've said yes … In the end it comes down to dollars and cents. You've got to pay for someone to be there". The role of school leadership in supporting mentoring has been highlighted as very important by creating "opportunities for collaboration and critical dialogue" (Le Cornu, 2015, p. 15) which works to positively affect the learning of both students and teachers.

David's view of his mentoring role requiring a mindset that has a focus on ultimately empowering students is seemingly at odds with the mentoring literature which tends to focus on mentors requiring a general skill set. For example, it requires mentors to support, advise, and critique (Le Cornu, 2015). His view perhaps signals a shift away from the traditional view of the mentor and mentee relationship as one based around a master-apprentice role and focused on specific knowledge and skills, to one more based on a way of thinking about mentoring.

David also seems to be aware that as the Tech School initiative itself will evolve over time, so too will his role. He appears comfortable with this likelihood. The literature however advocates for the role of the mentor to be clearly defined (Ambrosetti, 2012, 2014; Jones & Brown, 2011) and that lack of a clear definition is a failing. One wonders whether the mentoring role required in this instance, that is in relation to a long-term state-wide initiative, involving many schools across the state, could be clearly described. As well, one wonders whether such a clear definition, if possible, would be flexible enough to enable Ambassadors such as David to make decisions based upon the needs of his local school context.

7 Motivations and Challenges

David's initial motivation for undertaking this role was because he saw alignment with his learning coordinator role at the school. As he said, "I was really looking forward to getting involved because what was being described sounded like really what we wanted to do but to the next level". Later when he discusses that the mentoring role requires a mindset, it seems evident that he is also motivated by improving the student learning experience.

The quality of relationships between David as the mentor and the teachers he mentored is very important in the mediation of issues such logistics that may ultimately impact on the learning experience for both teachers and their students (Bennett & Carre, 1993). To overcome these issues David suggests that what is needed is "some good examples of what's possible" As he added, "what I would like to have seen from the Tech School is some kind of strategy in terms of this is what you could do at your school". He elaborated that the initiative "is new for lots of people" so having "some examples from them" would be helpful in negotiating good outcomes for his teacher mentees and their students. From these comments, it could be inferred that providing guidance about the mentoring role and what is possible within it, would deliver some clarity that would assist David, who is also new to the role.

David also has a positive view of his role and has a broad belief that he will be able to successfully mentor staff at his school as they continue to implement the broader initiative. This positive view is akin to the mentoring literature generally, wherein mentoring is most often perceived as resulting in positive benefits for both mentors and mentees including the establishment of professional learning communities, underpinned by an explicit focus on learning for all parties involved in the mentoring relationship (Le Cornu, 2010). True challenges in mentoring are sometimes presented but the overall portrayal of mentoring is a positive one. Of concern then, is that mentoring can be seen as a panacea for improving teacher capability and the complexities and challenges involved in undertaking the role can be sidestepped. This is not helpful for teacher mentors, especially when they encounter difficulties, as there is little scope for them to seek support, given the dominance of this positive narrative.

8 Conclusion

There is considerable literature around the importance and value of mentoring to teacher professional learning (Ambrosetti, 2014; Zeichner, 2005, 2010; Le Cornu, 2015). Mentors are commonly used to support pre-service teachers during placement in schools, to help them develop their teaching skills and identities as teachers. For in-service teaching, mentors are used to support graduate induction and full registration as a teacher. As well, mentors are a strategy used to support state-wide education department reform efforts, as in the recently developed Mentoring Capability Framework, created by the Victorian Department of Education (2018), to assist in the development of mentoring practices for teachers when supporting graduate teachers. For the most part, accounts of mentoring are positive, for both mentors and mentees (Le Cornu, 2010). This is despite mentoring itself being hard to define and the roles the mentors perform often lacking clarity.

This chapter provides an account of a Teacher Ambassador, whose role was to mentor teachers at his school to implement the state-wide Tech School initiative at this local level. It uses a case study of David, to illustrate how one Ambassador performed this role and provides a rich picture captured at a point in time. David saw his role involved supporting the co-design of curriculum with other Ambassadors and mentoring staff to implement changes to their practice as a result. David's view of mentoring is an optimistic one, and one that emphasised working together with staff, rather than the master-apprentice view that has tended to dominate the literature (Ambrosetti, 2014). David's position as a mentor is not clearly defined, but rather appears to have evolved and been self-determined by his perception of what is needed in the role at the time.

This examination of David's perception of mentoring and his role in the school as a mentor is of course, limited. Like much of phenomenological research, it is based upon an interview which captures a "snapshot" in time of one person's account of the phenomenon (Vagle, 2018). Without analysis of a wider range of perceptions and greater depth of historical approaches to the phenomenon it remains limited and biased to the individual and their understandings. However, as an insight upon which to build further research around defining the role of the mentor involved in long term, large scale state-wide initiatives, the detail is warranted and provides a necessary foundation for future study.

References

Aderibigbe, S., Laura Colucci-Gray, L., & Gray, D. S. (2016). Conceptions and expectations of mentoring relationships in a teacher education reform context. *Mentoring & Tutoring: Partnership in Learning, 24*(1), 8–29. doi:10.1080/13611267.2016.1163636

Ambrosetti, A. (2012). *Reconceptualising mentoring using triads in pre-service teacher education professional placements* (PhD thesis). Central Queensland University.

Ambrosetti, A. (2014). Are you ready to be a mentor? Preparing teachers for mentoring pre-service teachers. *Australian Journal of Teacher Education, 39*(6), 30–42.

Ambrosetti, A., & Dekker, J. (2010). The interconnectedness of roles of mentors and mentees in pre-service teacher education mentoring relationships. *Australian Journal of Teacher Education, 35*, 42–55.

Australian Parliament – House of Representatives Standing Committee on Education and Vocational Training. (2007). *Top of the class: Report on the inquiry into teacher education.* Retrieved December 18, 2017, from http://trove.nla.gov.au/work/26512195

Bradbury, L. U., & Koballa, T. R. (2008). Borders to cross: Identifying sources of tension in mentor–intern relationships. *Teaching and Teacher Education, 24*, 2132–2145.

Butler, B., & Cuenca, A. (2012). Conceptualizing the roles of mentor teachers during student teaching. *Action in Teacher Education, 34*, 296–308. doi:10.1080/01626620.2012.717012

Clark, A., Triggs, V., & Nielsen, W. (2014). Cooperating teacher participation in teacher education: A review of the literature. *Review of Educational Research, 84*(2), 163–202.

Creswell, J. W., & Poth, C. N. (2018). *Qualitative inquiry and research design: Choosing among five approaches* (4th ed.). Sage Publications.

Davis, J. S., & Fantozzi, V. B. (2016). What do student teachers want in mentor teachers? Desired, expected, possible, and emerging roles. *Mentoring & Tutoring: Partnership in Learning, 24*(3), 250–266. doi:10.1080/13611267.2016.1222814

Department of Education and Training (DET). (2017). *Tech schools learning programs design framework.* Personal Copy.

Department of Education and Training (DET). (2018). *Mentoring capability framework.* Retrieved from https://www.education.vic.gov.au/Documents/school/teachers/profdev/mentoringcapabilityframework.pdf

Eby, L. T., Rhodes, J. E., & Allen, T. D. (2007). Definition an evolution of mentoring. In T. D. Allen & L. T. Eby (Eds.), *The Blackwell handbook of mentoring: A multiple perspectives approach* (pp. 7–20). Blackwell Publishing.

Ellul, R. (2010). *ICT Peer coaches: Techno-pedagogues of the twenty-first century* (PhD thesis). RMIT University.

Grimmett, G., Forgasz, R., Williams, J., & White, S. (2018). Reimagining the role of mentor teachers in professional experience: Moving to I as fellow teacher educator. *Asia-Pacific Journal of Teacher Education, 46*(4), 340–353. doi:10.1080/1359866X.2018.1437391

Hudson, P., & Hudson, S. (2018). Mentoring preservice teachers: Identifying tensions and possible resolutions. *Teacher Development, 22*(1), 16–30. doi:10.1080/13664530.2017.1298535

Jones, R., & Brown, D. (2011). The mentoring relationship as a complex adaptive system: Finding a model for our experience. *Mentoring and Tutoring: Partnerships in Learning, 19*(4), 401–418.

Le Cornu, R. (2010). Changing roles, relationships and responsibilities in changing times. *Asia-Pacific Journal of Teacher Education, 38*(3), 195–206.

Le Cornu, R. (2015). *Key components of effective professional experience in Initial teacher education in Australia.* Australian Institute for Teaching and School Leadership, Melbourne. Retrieved from https://www.aitsl.edu.au/docs/default-source/default-document-library/aitsl_key-components-of-effective-professional-experience.pdf?sfvrsn=aec9ec3c_0

Nielsen, W., Mena, J., Clarke, A., O'Shea, S., Hoban, G., & Collins, J. (2017). Australia's supervising teachers: Motivators and challenges to inform professional learning. *Asia-Pacific Journal of Teacher Education, 45*(4), 346–368. doi:10.1080/1359866X.2017.1304527

Renshaw, P. (2012). *Literature review and environmental scan: Supervising professional experience students.* Australian Institute for Teaching and School Leadership, Melbourne.

Saldaña, J. (2016). *The coding manual for qualitative researchers* (3rd ed.). Sage Publications.

Teacher Education Ministerial Advisory Group (TEMAG). (2014). *Action now: Classroom ready teachers.* Retrieved from https://docs.education.gov.au/node/36783

Vagle, M. D. (2018). *Crafting phenomenological research.* Routledge.

Van Manen, M. (2016). *Phenomenology of practice: Meaning-giving methods in phenomenological research and writing.* Routledge.

Walkington, J. (2005) Becoming a teacher: Encouraging development of teacher identity through reflective practice. *Asia-Pacific Journal of Teacher Education, 33*(1), 53–64.

Zeichner, K. (2005). Becoming a teacher educator: A personal perspective. *Teaching and Teacher Education, 21,* 117–124.

Zeichner, K. (2010). Rethinking the connections between campus courses and field experiences in college-and university-based teacher education. *Journal of Teacher Education, 61*(1–2), 89–99.

CHAPTER 8

Theorising Mentoring for the 21st Century Teaching and Learning: Making Invisible Professional Growth Visible through Action Research

Huk Yuen Law

Abstract

The 21st century is an era full of complexity and uncertainty. Fostering school-children with growing awareness of life-long education has become a new demand that challenges the teacher educators to think seriously about how to prepare themselves for mentoring prospective teachers. The purpose of this chapter is to explore the way of how mentoring can be re-conceptualised and theorised by nurturing the prospective teachers' professional growth through action research. The empirical material is drawn from the case stories of two student-teachers and the methodological orientation for conceptualising mentoring grounded on the principles of action research will be elaborated through the theorising project of making invisible professional growth visible. The results show that the co-construction of the discourse between the mentor and the protégées in the form of imagined dialogue contributes to the theorisation or at least re-conceptualisation of mentoring. In theorising through the growth model, mentoring can be interpreted as encountering, as experiencing, and as relating.

Keywords

theorising mentoring – professional growth model – action research – teacher education

1   Introduction

The 21st century characterises itself by the challenge-inviting word "change" and as such the students of this new century have to prepare themselves for living in a world of complexity and uncertainty (see Karakas, 2009). In order to help the youngsters to equip themselves for coping with such a challenge, teachers need to ask themselves reflexively, "what kinds of skills ought to be taught to our schoolchildren?" Harari (2018) highlights in *21 Lessons for the 21st Century* that "reinvention" in terms of critical thinking, communication, collaboration and creativity is the best possible skill that the teachers can offer for their students and he argues strongly with such a proposal for future education by alerting us that "The now century-old model of production–line school education is bankrupt".

Guy Claxton (2007) argues that to help equip the learners of the 21st century to cope with the challenges of ever-changing world is to "expand the capacity to learn" which is in line with the advocacy of "learning to learn" and "lifelong learning" in most if not all of the educational reforms all over the globe. To expand the capacity to learn is to enlarge the *growth space* for learning. Such kind of growth space entails learning habits as anchored in social relationships that invite the learners to learn how "to ask questions, seek help, give help, and work collaboratively with other learners" (Redding, 2014, p. 26). But what kind of pedagogy would enable teachers to help the 21st century students develop their mind-set as conducive to the growth of that very learning habits? This in turn has imposed a challenging question for all the teacher educators to ponder over it.

All kinds of pedagogy involve not just the theory but also the practice. The integration of theory and practice has long been an unsettling issue in teacher education (Zevin, 2010; Oonk, Verloop, & Gravemeijer, 2015). Through decades of endeavour on resolving such an issue, John Elliott (2015) argues strongly that for those teachers who want to improve the way they teach need to "theorise" their own practice through action research so as to develop the self-understanding of their work in a particular context. And as such teacher educators would have "to undertake a second-order action research into their own teacher education practices" (Elliott, 1993, p. 177). Whether first order or second order, both the teachers and the teacher educators have their own role to play in the "meta processes" of knowledge production and in turn would have undergone the process of metamorphosis (Law, 2013; Losito, Pozzo, & Somekh, 1998). And yet, teaching teachers to think, to reflect, to theorise, and to philosophise is a risky business (Zevin, 2010). Whether what is "saying" in the lecture is meaningful or not depends on the learners' abilities to respond to what is said. In other words, it requires them to pay effort for making sense of the saying. Developing an approach of guiding teachers to theorise begins with deep thinking on directing them to see through their own experiences. The initiation of such a process would have built up a mentoring relationship even though it so happens in an informal way.

Mentoring through the adoption of action research is considered as a legitimate and yet demanding approach of contributing to teachers' professional development in the form of initial teacher training project (Iliev, Ilieva, & Pipidzanoska, 2011) and informal lifelong learning (Anagnou & Fragoulis, 2014). The challenges come from, nonetheless, the complexity behind our understanding of mentoring as the construct of which how it is defined and how the implications of the way that it is defined on the building up of the "unique relationship involving an extremely complex interplay of cognitive, affective and interpersonal factors" (Cain, 2009). In the field of management, Haggard, Dougherty, Turban and Wilbanks (2011) identified around forty different definitions used in the empirical literature since 1980 and hinted for the need of further research on the "knowledge transfer" (the exchange of what and how that kind of information happens) during the mentoring process and how mentoring fosters learning through the establishment of mentoring relationships. Drawing on professional development literatures, Smith and Lynch (2014) attempts to distinguish mentoring from coaching and yet the discussions appear to turn out to have highlighted the functions of these kinds of activities in terms of professional development itself and teacher learning rather than making a clear divide between the two constructs. As an advocate of teacher mentoring, Koki (1997) proposes that mentoring can serve as an umbrella under which the constructs such as "modeling" and "coaching" would be included in it. As argued by Irby (2012, p. 297), "mentors can coach, but coaches hardly ever mentor, and mentors and coaches can tutor but tutors rarely mentor or coach". This clearly suggests that mentoring serves as the overarching notion when compared with the constructs of "coaching" and "tutoring" as proposed by Koki. I would also adopt such an understanding of what mentoring is meant to be in terms of the establishment of sustained long-lasting and even lifelong relationships (Irby, 2018).

In this chapter, I will argue that mentoring as a phenomenon invites us to do theorising (rather than to formulate a theory) in order to make discovery of what and how mentoring relationship is and can be developed in a more interesting way through the mentoring project that I named it as "MIV" Project. It is a short form for "Making Invisible Visible" with an aim to benefit both I (as the mentor) and my student-teachers (as the protégée) from our engagement in developing the mentoring relationship through which the invisible or hidden professional growth can be made visible. Through the theorising project, I would propose the growth model of mentoring with which I depict the four stages of the teacher's professional growth by illustrating how mentoring can be interweaved with teaching in a dynamic way. And by adopting such a model, I would argue that the mentoring experiences for the protégée constitutes at least part of her life journey of becoming a mentor of the others.

2 Theorising Mentoring

2.1 The Story: My Personal Professional Growth Journey

After serving as a secondary mathematics teacher for more than two decades, I turned myself into a university educator with the intention of inspiring more young people to become professional mathematics teachers. As mathematics teachers, we cannot agree more of the slogan "teaching for understanding". But to teach with "understanding" is always challenging if not an impossible task for the student-teachers as they experience for the ever first time in life of how to do with their teaching in real classrooms. "Teaching for understanding" itself entails the demand for offering students the meaning of what they would have learned. This in turn "implies a sense of *openness* and an anticipation of *growth* that opens up the possibility for the learners to make their own interpretations of what sort of meaning is inherent in learning itself" (Law, 2009, p. 126). In my doctoral inquiry, I have developed the notion of "understanding as myth" (pp. 122–208). As a "second-order" teacher or teacher of teachers for more than a decade of my teaching in the university, I have adopted "myth" as an important indicator of growth for developing the awareness of self-awareness in my own teaching and the teaching practices of my student-teachers. Through reflection, teachers learn to define and redefine the "myth" that they create in the making of ethical choices for making learning more meaningful to the students.

"Profession" can be interpreted as "a paid profession, especially one that involves prolonged training and a formal qualification" but can also be as "a declaration of *belief* in a religion" whilst "professional" is "a person engaged or qualified in a profession" or "a person competent or skilled in a *particular* activity" (Oxford Dictionary of English, 2010, emphasis added). To me, teaching as a profession constitutes not just a paid occupation but also a declaration of belief in a religion called *education* with the faith of exploring for the well-being and meaning of our living as a human being. And as such, the teacher as a professional is more than a person engaged or qualified in a profession but a person competent in a particular activity called *obuchenie* (Vygotsky's notion for the dialectical unity of teaching/learning; see, Kirshner, 2009). To unfold the myth of our own teaching growth trajectory, we need to undertake the mystery-solving project through which we create the possibility of making our apparently invisible professional growth visible.

Ever since I began my teaching career in the university in 2002, I taught mainly the courses for both the pre-service and in-service mathematics teachers and the Action Research courses for teachers from different disciplines and teaching across various levels (from kindergarten to university) and for others who have great interest to know more of educational practices such as parents, social workers and counsellors. Before I retired officially from the university in 2015, I helped to develop a new 5-year B.Ed. Programme with double majoring in Mathematics and Mathematics Education for the holders of the Hong Kong Diploma of Secondary Education and acted as the Course Co-ordinator when it launched in 2012. Since then, I continued my teaching of the courses on a part-time basis for the Programme. In 2017, I was excited to see the first batch of graduates after their five years of endeavour in becoming mathematics teachers. It was during these five years of seeing their professional growth that I conceptualised the growth model of mentoring practice for the nurturing of my students who would desire to further with me the mentoring experiences even after they completed the course of studies.

2.2 The Growth Model of Mentoring Practice: From Teaching to Mentoring

In the context of pre-service education, Ambrosetti (2010, p. 52) concludes her discussions by offering a definition that comprises the three components of mentoring – relationship, process and context,

> Mentoring is a non-hierarchical, reciprocal relationship between mentors and mentee who work towards specific professional and personal outcomes for the mentee. The relationship usually follows a developmental pattern within a specified timeframe and roles are defined, expectations are outlined and a purpose is (ideally) clearly delineated.

Mentoring as understood from this definition shares quite a lot of common ground with what we think teaching ought to be but at the same time it can be a tricky business to make a clear distinction between these two constructs. Within the traditional school settings, teaching can hardly be regarded as "a non-hierarchical, reciprocal relationship" between teachers and students but instead it bears the power relationship between the two parties in the actual practice especially under the outcome-based culture for the purpose of accountability. The roles, expectations, and purpose for teaching in the conventional classroom are strictly defined and monitored. As such, the teacher-student relationship is so restrained that it usually follows some established social norms of developmental pattern within a specified timeframe called standard curriculum. Very often than not, the beginning teachers are susceptible to the focus on surviving in the face of the specific school culture and might not be easy for them to reflect on their stagnant experiences. As a consequence, they might get lost of the agency as required for the fostering of their professional growth on the basis of internally directed learning (Korthagen & Vasalos, 2005).

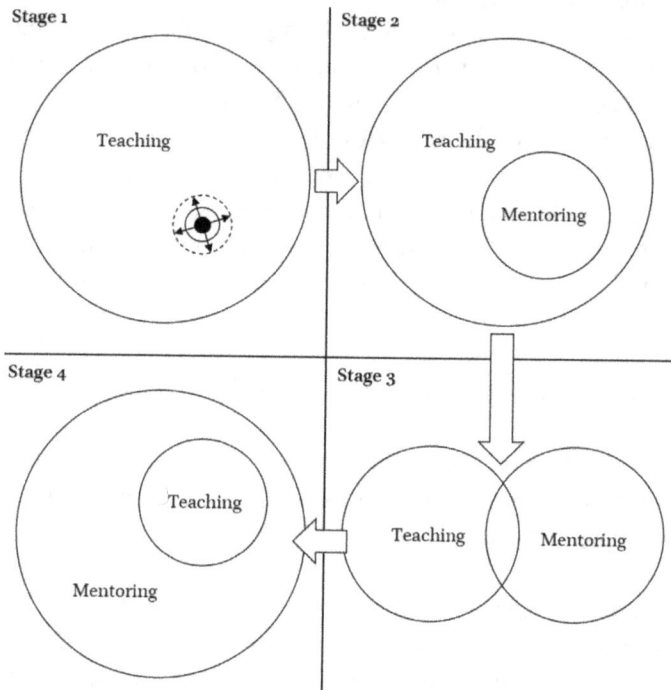

FIGURE 8.1   The four-stage growth model of mentoring practice

Drawn on the reflecting of my own professional practice, I developed a four-stage growth model (see Figure 8.1) with which I argue that mentoring itself entails teaching as a constituent of its own practice through the process of professional growth. In stage 1, teaching is the major if not the whole focus of attention when one starts one's professional practice in the classroom setting whilst mentoring if not entirely hidden remains as an auxiliary in its rudimentary state. As times go by, mentoring like a germinating seed starts to grow as the one is getting used to teaching with the practice of reflecting on one's experiencing. As shown in Stage 2, mentoring is becoming a noticeable component of daily teaching practice. In Stage 3, one is self-aware of the moment of teaching as a distinguishable from to that of mentoring and yet there would have some indistinguishable moments gaining insights into the unfolding of one's thinking, feeling and wanting for creating the possibilities of future constructive action at improving one's practice. In Stage 4, mentoring is in its fully-bloomed state with teaching being embedded in the practicing of it. When mentoring practice reaches this stage, it will not be confined by but go beyond the institutional setting of all kinds and thus would create the undefined time and space for the fostering of the ever-lasting mentoring relationship.

Upon my official retirement from the university, I have got into my stride of doing the Stage 4 mentoring practice wanting not only to help my student-teachers establish their own professional identity but also to create the growth moments of nurturing their mission and vision as the extended level of reflection for the preservation of the very spirituality as required for their life-long professional growth. Korthagen and Vasalos (2005, p. 53) identified "core reflection" consisting of five levels of reflection, namely, the levels of behaviour, competencies, beliefs, identity, and mission. I regard the level of *vision* as an extra and extended level of reflection with an orientation at developing the agency for constructive change in the foreseeable future).

In short, to theorise mentoring is to theorise the unique experiences of both the mentor and the protégée that can be shared with trust between each other in the form of open dialogue. And theorising itself is at least part of the capacity to explain what keeps us to teach with passion as times go by.

3   Methodological Considerations

3.1   *The Context of the Study*

By the end of last semester of 2019, I invited two of my student-teachers (both were studying the Diploma of Education programmes – Josephine, a full-time PGDE student and Ching, a part-time PGDP student working as a full-time Teaching Assistant in a primary school) to join in the MIV Project with the target set as a way of fostering their professional growth. Growth itself is a process that constitutes the self-reflection upon one's own experience with which one is aware of the transformation as inherent in it. As the student teachers were adopting the role of an action researcher, I wanted them to understand how to improve their practices by undertaking inquiry over the *particular* – developing some particular activity tasks as interventions (action for change) targeted at some particular learners called students in some particular space called classroom during some particular time called lesson. In line with action research principles, I see such an endeavour as *the theorising project* through which we by working together would have "a better chance to discover something new" about the ways they are practicing their teaching of the subject – mathematics, and "to say something interesting" (see Swedberg, 2016, p. 9) as they get ready to theorise their own teaching practice.

Jerome Bruner distinguished in *Life as Narrative* (1987/2004, pp. 696–697) three aspects of story, namely, fabula (theme), sjuzet (discourse), and forma (genre) – "the first two (fabula and sjuzet) … as, respectively, the timeless and the sequenced aspects of story. … A genre (forma, the third aspect of narrative) is plainly a type (in the linguist's sense) of which there are near endless tokens, … for generating different kinds of story plots". The self-told story from the student-teacher is about the timeless mystery of learning to teach with understanding and each lesson as targeted at making meaning for schoolchildren's learning entails "particularity of time, space, person, and event … reflected in the mode of the telling, in the discourse properties of the sjuzet". In short, telling the story of student-teachers' own life experiences that goes beyond time and space can embrace different interpretations of what sorts of life histories that they have undergone.

To help the student-teachers construct their own stories of practising teaching, I have arranged the meetings in the informal settings (such as in the coffee shop) with them and named such a kind of meeting as TTR (*TuToRial*). TTR serves as a special kind of tutorial that offers whoever is taking part in it the very "*Time To Reflect*" on what have been happening in the actual classroom during teaching practice and on how they would theorise their experiences through their own unique lens of seeing it. Through reflecting on their own unique experience, we would develop together the forma (genre) of their life story of their own in order to help them make sense of their growth experiences by the mode of telling who they are as an agent of having an ethical goal of teaching for supporting their students' learning with understanding.

3.2 *Methodology as Social Framing of the Ways of Doing Research*

Mentoring as a phenomenon that I make sense of it for the 21st century teaching and learning defies the divide of the two methodological traditions – quantitative versus qualitative approaches. Such a division "is counterproductive, if not outright harmful" (Moses & Knutsen, 2019, p. 295). The teacher educators who adopt the role of action researcher need to challenge themselves during the continual changing process of researching by reflecting upon not just what sorts of tools to use but also why using it. Action research as a moral philosophy (Elliott, 2015) is grounded in interpretive *contexts* serving for two main purposes: (1) to promote humanism and individual wellbeing, and (2) to make use of data for developing "interventions or practical solutions to problems experienced by people" (Moses & Knutsen, 2019, p. 292). Mentoring through action research is to hopefully serve these two purposes in terms of empowering the student-teachers with the most-needed self-awareness for developing their capacity to learn to teach. The first purpose entails the necessity of undergoing lifelong learning in the form of learning to learn whereas the second one demands research endeavour of finding tricks "that help researchers faced with concrete research problems make some progress" (Becker, 1998, p. 4). In other words, action researchers need to theorise their own experiences by assembling the pieces of trick that constitute the unique case stories of their own.

In my doctoral inquiry, I developed the notion of "liquid methodology" with which I "depict the logic or the sense of logos behind the options of the bricoleurs' toolboxes to create research space" (Law, 2009, p. 108) for interpreting action contexts. As bricoleurs, both the mentor and the protégées would develop diverse meanings by adopting diversified ontological perspectives as drawn from their ongoing mentoring experiences. Adopting the within-case approaches, I would not do cross-case comparisons but instead make use of the protégées' multiple stories as a source of the patterns to be uncovered and understood from both the ontological and epistemological perspectives (see Moses & Knutsen, 2019, pp. 225–228).

Mentoring is about encountering, experiencing, and relating. Through collaborative research with the protégées, the mentor helps them developing cultural competence and contextual knowledge to make sense not just of the mentoring events but also of the actual teaching practices they are engaging in the classroom. Reflection as an essential element for the sustaining of professional growth is not a ready-to-accomplish task for teachers at large. Adopting the role of mentor, I would make use of action research as a way of developing methodological competence for the protégées "to withstand the pressures favouring rapid occupational socialisation into the traditional professional culture" by engaging themselves with "moral experiment (generating and testing of action hypotheses) in a social context of dialogue with others" (Elliott, 2007, pp. 83–84). Such a kind of methodological competence is hopefully to empower the teachers for finding tricks of developing their own fluid pedagogy of educating the 21st century learners in coping with the changes of uncertain future.

3.3   *Procedure*

3.3.1   Data Collection

With the consensus of the student-teachers (including the use of their names and their appearances in the photo) as a way of addressing the issue of ethical concern, I regard the MIV project as a longitudinal study of how I as a mentor can help them see or theorise for themselves the professional growth that they would have gone through even after they have completed their formal course of studies. In this chapter, I would use the stories of Josephine and Ching to illustrate the way of doing my theorising of mentoring experience whilst unfolding with them the professional growth process that we have gone through.

The data were drawn from the most critical moments of their learning-to-teach experiences by addressing the question, "How has the understanding of a mathematics teacher's daily teaching practice during practicum changed over time?" (see Law, Leung, & Man, 2019). Through the first TTR, we came up with four domains (as adapted from Jaworski (1993) for developing professional development through critical reflection) as areas of concern for doing their self-reflexive inquiry. These include (1) mathematical thinking – how dialogic space can be created for facilitating the schoolchildren to think mathematically? (2) class management – how the challenge of teacher's authority (such as the handling the issues of class disciplines and students' homework copying behaviours) can be coped with? (3) learners' diversity – how ethical action would be taken to develop the learners' unique pathways of developing mathematical concepts? (4) teaching resources – how the perspective of seeing the teaching resources (including the use of iPad or other digital resources) as action possibilities for addressing the first three domains as stated above would be changed during and beyond the practicum period? The reflection logs would be the main data source for the documentation of their lived experiences during and beyond their course of studies as well as the critical reflections they did by referring to the "evidence" as drawn from the lesson plans, student works or artefacts, and field notes (the observation records of classroom interactions).

3.3.2   Data Analysis

Analysing students' thinking of what they have experienced is rooted in the emergence of new questions for further self-reflexive inquiry rather than in the production of the best strategy for answering what works in a specific context. I adopt the case story approach with which I would do the data analysis with Josephine and Ching so as to have a co-interpretation of their own data as drawn on these principles: (1) to do analysis is to understand what analysis is actually doing through dialoguing with not just the data but with the readings of the data; (2) to create an open dialogue on the interpretation of the data; (3) to write together so as to put out our own "thinking on paper" for mutual interpretations (see Freeman, 2017).

During one of our TTRs, we identified seven *"growth points"* (Johnson & Golombek, 2016) as a way of charting the growth process. The growth point is not referring to a particular time but a series of moments as emergent and contingent for capturing some critical reflections during their learning journey of becoming a professional teacher. For Josephine, the first three growth points (G1 to G3) refer to the three stages (before, during, and after) of her first TP (Teaching Practicum) and then another three growth points (G4 to G6) denote the three stages (before, during, and after) of her second TP. The last growth point (G7) refers to the moment when she was looking forward to her future teaching before she started working as a school teacher. Ching was working as a Teaching Assistant during the growth period under our discussion of the project. For Ching, the first three growth points (G1 to G3) refer to the three stages (before, during, and after) of her working experience in the first school. After having gone through these, she changed to another school to continue working as a Teaching Assistant (TA) and started her course of studies of the two-year PGDP Programme. And she would have the TP in the school during the first year of her studies. The three growth points from G4 to G6 denote the three stages (before, during, and after) of her TP that she would have undertaken and G7 is referring to the future vision that she had as she was looking forward to becoming a practicing teacher in the school. For each of the growth points, I asked them to use the 10-point scale "growth perception indices" (from 1 as the lowest to 10 as the highest) for *self-assessing* their own growth process so as to indicate the interpretations of the improvement that they had undergone across the four domains. Such a way of doing self-assessment of how well they have done in the four domains of concern is not just valid but also reliable as it serves for enhancing their autonomy of learning to teach as well as for enabling them to communicate their perceptions of their own practices (see Oscarson, 1997, 2013). And after their self-assessment, I suggested them to use the "growth web", which is a modified version of the spider web, for visualising their own professional growth.

3.4   *Results*

In the process of mentoring practice, I have many more chances to meet Josephine than Ching as the former was by that time enjoying the status as a full-time student with residence in the university campus but the latter was working as a full-time Teaching Assistant in the school. On June 1, both Josephine and Ching were able to come together for the TTR. It was in the form of a mentoring seminar (see Figure 8.2) during which they shared with each other their growth experiences. The TTR served as a special kind of tutorial through which the exchanges of discourses would help framing their social mentality and that in turn reframing the reflexive actions for improving their classroom practices. And the TTR photo serves as an "identifiable image" (see Holliday, 2004) so as to make the mentoring relationship visible to both the researcher and research participants in terms of the voice that constituted in the sustained development of reflexivity throughout the process of researching. The photographic image as shown in Figure 8.2 serves to illustrate how the TTR personalises the dialogues as tied to the specific people in specific time and space with *ontological freedom* of "saying something about their personal experience of the abstract phenomenon the story is "about" (Becker, 2002, p. 10) – about how they feel and what they think of what they have been experiencing in learning to teach a subject called mathematics. The image itself is a kind of "specified generalisation" inviting us to generalise the real instances of mentoring phenomenon which is "both specific and general, abstract and concrete" (Becker, 2002, p. 11).

I proposed to them the idea of using the "growth web" based on the four domains (mathematical thinking, class management, learners' diversity, and teaching resources) to generate the "image" for the perceptions of their professional growth. They filled up their individual "growth perception indices" in the table (Table 8.1) showing their self-assessed growth over the four domains of concern in practicing their teaching. It appears that they have similar scoring patterns across the seven growth points. And yet, it is interesting to note the subtle differences in the beginning stage of G_1–G_3 especially in the domains D_1 and D_2. For Josephine, the total scores of G_1–G_3 in both D_1 and D_2 are 12 (3 + 4 + 5) and for Ching, the total scores are 15 (5 + 5 + 5) and 17 (5 + 6 + 6) respectively. During the period of G_1–G_3, Ching was working as full-time teacher in the school for a period of one year and Josephine was doing her ever first-time teaching practicum for a period of one month. This shows that experience matters – Ching scored higher of her own self-perception of what she did than Josephine did in her scoring especially in teaching schoolchildren to think mathematically and resolving the issues related to classroom management. When comparing the perception scores of G_1 and G_7 for all of the four domains of concern, both of them have a remarkable growth of self-satisfaction of what they have experienced and have great hope of looking into the future.

After that seminar, I suggested Josephine in another meeting with her to demonstrate the computer display of her growth web (Figure 8.3) and also her "growth curve" by mapping the growth perception indices into a "curve" (Figure 8.4) to show the different growth trajectories across the four domains of concern. The growth web and the growth curve as shown in Figures 8.3 and 8.4 respectively serves the purpose of illustrating the protégées' growth trajectory in the form of graphical images rather than for that of doing a comparison of how one differs from the other.

Later, both Josephine and Ching emailed me the texts depicting the growth experiences they have undergone based on the growth table. Based on the emails that I received, I created the "imagined dialogue" (Law, 2009) and attempted to make sense of their professional growth as I interpreted from

MENTORING FOR THE 21ST CENTURY TEACHING AND LEARNING

what I read of the texts they wrote. The emails that I received serve as testimony not just to the virtuality of discourse as embodied in our interaction during the mentoring seminar (TTR) but the reality of the protégées' sensations and perceptions of their growth experiences.

FIGURE 8.2   TTR (TuToRial) as mentoring seminar

TABLE 8.1   The growth table showing the growth perceptions of the protégée (J stands for Josephine and C for Ching)

Domain \ Growth points	G1		G2		G3		G4		G5		G6		G7	
	J	C	J	C	J	C	J	C	J	C	J	C	J	C
D1 Mathematics thinking	3	5	4	5	5	5	5	6	6	7	7	7	8	8
D2 Classroom management	3	5	4	6	5	6	5	6	6	7	6	7	7	8
D3 Learners' diversity	4	3	4	4	5	5	5	6	7	7	7	8	8	9
D4 Teaching resources	3	4	5	4	5	4	6	6	7	7	8	8	9	9

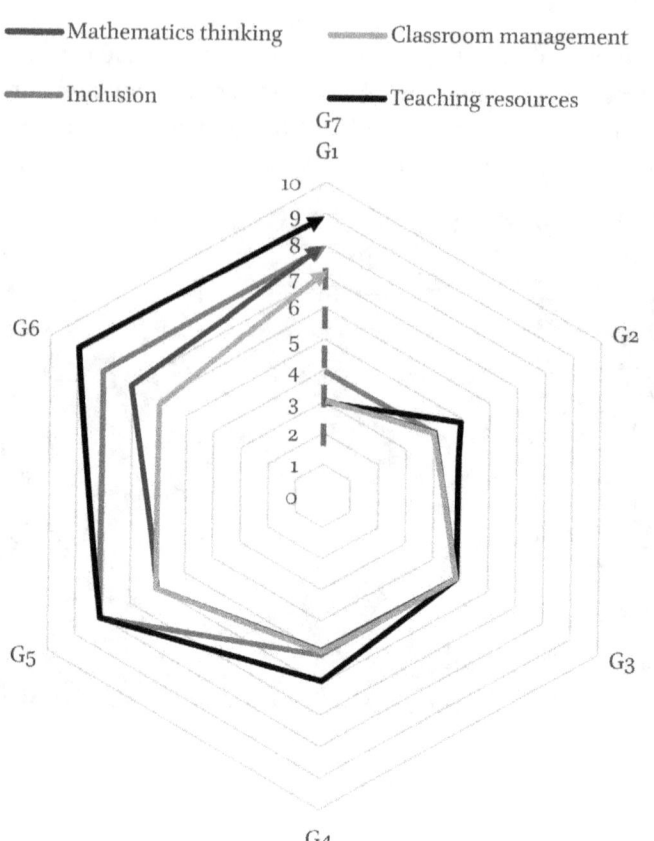

FIGURE 8.3   The "growth web" as a graphical interpretation of the protégées' continual growth process

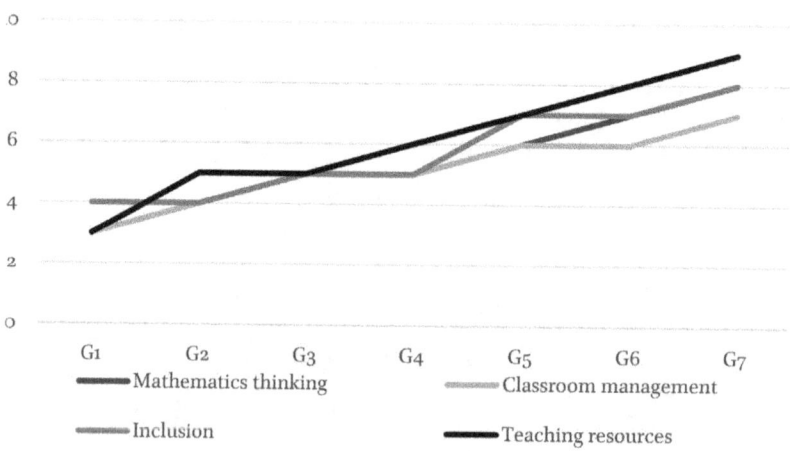

FIGURE 8.4   The "growth curve" as a graphical interpretation of the protégées' perception of performance in the four domains of concern across the seven growth points

3.5 The Imagined Dialogue

3.5.1 Stage 1: G1 and G2

Law: Would you first tell me what had happened to you in G1 and G2?

Josephine: To be honest, I got used to the teacher-centred mode of instruction when I was a school student and I had *no ideas of how to create dialogic space in the classroom for fostering the students' mathematical thinking*. During the first TP, I made use of the "Exit Slip" that you mentioned in class for the students to write down what they would have learned from my teaching.

Ching: When I worked as a TA in the first school, I lacked patience in dealing with the students.
By that time, my main duty was to help handling the SEN (Special Educational Needs) students. *With growing experiences* in working with them, I knew better of how to make individual education plans for supporting their learning. Thus, my key concern was learners' diversity in the form of inclusion without having any real challenges in my working in other domains of concern such as mathematical thinking and class management.

Law: I see.

Josephine: Class management was my key concern in the first TP. I found it hard to deal with the issue of learners' diversity as I knew not how to develop the mathematical thinking of the weak students. Perhaps, that's why they would make noise in the class. When the class was getting a bit too noisy, what I did was to use the "counting down" strategy to keep the noise within the tolerable level.

Law: Did you use some digital resources to assist your teaching?

Josephine: Oh yes, I did have used PowerPoint and visualiser for explaining the mathematical ideas.

3.5.2 Stage 2: G3 to G5

Law: What happened then?

Josephine: *I did much reflection on how to* prepare for my second TP.

Law: What did you do in doing your second TP?

Josephine: I developed much more hand-on activities for the students. With the use of worksheets and iPads, I grouped the students in pairs and asked them to do the peer discussion before writing down on the paper the thinking process they have gone through. I think that it would be good in this way to help developing their mathematical thinking.

Law:	How about you, Ching?
Ching:	I *did much reflection on my working with* the SEN children. I learned not just to have patience in helping them to learn but also the techniques of supporting their parents to learn to accept their children.
Law:	That's great! How about any teaching strategies and resources that you both did have used in doing your teaching practice? And how effective of using them?
Josephine:	This time the students were very attentive. With the adoption of group work, I did not need to have much bother of class management issue. And I think that the interactive classroom atmosphere did have good effects on minimising the learners' diversity. Besides, I used more digital resources for enhancing the teaching effectiveness such as Google Classroom and Nearpod.
Ching:	In the first TP, I did have tried using Nearpod to let the students attempt doing different levels of questions as set for them. I think that it would be a good way of dealing with the issue of learners' diversity though it might be better for some of the students to do those questions on the textbook instead of doing on the iPad. I also made efforts at using daily life problems to discuss with them how to make use of mathematical language for solving them.

3.5.3 Stage 3: G6 and G7

Law:	What were in your minds by the time you both finished your TP this year?
Ching:	I learned much after going through the TP. The most important thing that I realised was to encourage students to respond to what I was asking. But it was not easy for the SEN students. And I know that I *need to explore for more* resources in order to develop more interesting activities for motivating the students to take part in them.
Josephine:	After the second TP, I came to know that creating dialogic space in class would help much for developing students' mathematical thinking. In other words, I *need to think harder to* develop more interesting hand-on activities and to make use of a variety of resources for teaching such an abstract subject.
Law:	Sounds good! What to look for in doing your future teaching?
Josephine:	I will need to pay attention to these four domains whilst hoping for an ever-improving the way that I would teach. My teaching

	target is hopefully to make mathematics meaningful for every student that I teach!
Ching:	In the future, I wish that I could learn how to make a better collaboration with the parents in order to help me understand more of the students' learning needs. And I look forward to seeking more ways to motivate SEN students to learn Mathematics!

After completing my writing of the imagined dialogue, I have read and re-read not just the text of the dialogue itself but also the protégées' log as well. And having a touch of a kind of sensation and perception of their growth experiences, I highlighted in bold some of the idea-phrases as appeared in the dialogue to indicate my own interpretations of the mentoring experience with them that I have undergone. The imagined dialogue testifies to not just the *relationality* of mentorship but also the *interactive openness* (Law, 2009) as shared among us every time when we come to the meeting. It appears to me that I can hardly find the critical growth point of their metamorphoses through and beyond which they would have grown into a full-blown professional teacher simply by looking for the data of any form that I can possibly obtain. Perhaps, they just are professional teachers from then on and beyond awaiting us to make visible of the growth journey that they have gone through.

4 Concluding Discussions

Tramping into the 21st century, we inevitably have to face the challenges of the ever-growing complexity and uncertainty due to unpredictable outcomes and uncontrollable pace of technological advancement (OECD, 2018). Life-long learning is no longer an educational dream but a real-life demand if we want to have a self-sustaining project of pursuing wellbeing for our future life. For whatever changes that we may have in the future, it would be the teacher who should have a vital role to play in guiding the younger generations to create life options for themselves in order to face up with ever-demanding tasks for their future (Niemi, 2015). In view of the complex work as inherent in practicing mentoring for fostering the teacher's professional growth, the teacher educator adopting the role of mentor needs to undertake the life-long mentoring project with the teacher who can share the vision of transforming her life experience into pedagogical possibilities through critical reflection.

The MIV Project that I offered to my student-teachers is an attempt of fostering their professional growth through the use of action research. As a mentor, I need to undertake the action research *with* the protégées so as to generate the actionable findings for theorising their own practices (Cain, 2009). In going through the MIV Project, I did theorising not only drawn from my own professional experience but also from the interactions with the protégées. In theorising through the growth model as I depicted in this article, mentoring can be interpreted as encountering, as experiencing, and as relating.

3.6 *Mentoring as Encountering*

Mentoring is a dialectical process involving the mutuality of more than one individual. Mentoring may be seen as an ecological affordance which offers the potential protégée who acts as an agent herself the possibility to choose the pathway to act in consensus with her own goals. As argued by Gibson (1979/2015), an affordance "points to two ways, to the environment and to the observer. So does the information to specify an affordance". The TTR serves as an encountering through which the mentor creates the space of possibility for the protégée as the agent to pick up and to make use of ecological information for guiding her action. Such kind of information about the environment as perceived by the protégée involves a rather tricky process of interpretation that invites an open dialogue for exploring the subsequent actions. As a mentor, we need to be willing to enter the protégée's way of thinking in order to work together with her the problem she is struggling with.

3.7 *Mentoring as Experiencing*

Experience provides us as a human being the historical account of interactions between our own selves as an organism and the environment that we have gone through. To do theorising of what we have experienced, we as teachers need to develop the educational eye to zoom in and out on what we understand about the wellbeing of students we are teaching. The notion of "experience" constitutes Dewey's philosophical concept (Neubert, 2009) with which teachers make sense of what they do in the classroom as they "open an inquiry based on the principles of continuity and interaction" (Law, 2013, p. 105). In other words, teachers have undergone their life journey as professional growth through experiencing the experience of teaching. According to Dewey, growth is a process of both learning and inquiry through which teachers construct the meaning of their existence whilst experiencing the uncertainty (see D'Agnese, 2017, p. 75) as arisen from the actions they take within and without the confine of the classroom. And through such a process, teachers acquire not just the personal but also the professional practical knowledge through reflecting upon what they have undergone. The professional growth process is comparable or related to what the literature has revealed under various terminologies, such as "knowledge-through-experience" (Dewey, 1938), "knowledge-in-action" (Schön, 1983), and "knowledge through pedagogical experiences"

(Elbaz-Luwisch, 2007). Mentoring as experiencing serves as a splendid opportunity for both the mentor and the protégée to see their own professional growth through the mentoring practice.

3.8 *Mentoring as Relating*

Lessons are units in the classroom but the units of the learning itself are some basic factors like intentions and motivation. And thus, I would argue that it is vital to undertake the inquiry on the teacher's self as a learner rather than merely on the lesson or the learning. The differences between the components in a lesson and the components of learning are due to the fact that the lesson is a *thing* and learning is a *relation* between the teacher and the students as well as between the mentor and the protégée. As inspired by Darwin, William James argues strongly that knowledge is inherently uncertain and individuals are a real locus of agency in the world (McGranahan, 2017, p. 20). The mystery behind mentoring in terms of the notion of metamorphosis bears witness to the great miracle of growth in general and of the professional growth in particular. As teachers, we need to ask ourselves in a reflexive manner what it is that is hidden from us, what remains concealed, when the character of our own self as a unique being falls into darkness with itself.

Yeat reminded us in his poem that "we cannot tell the dancer from the dance" (as cited in Bruner, 1987/2004, p. 709). Perhaps, we cannot tell the teacher from the "teach" but at least we can let the "teach" itself affords the telling of the teacher through the mentoring practice. As a mentor, we can have an important role to play for offering protégée the chance of getting a kind of metaphysical assist (in the form of theorising) for their professional growth through the life story they are telling of how they would do with their teaching practices. Such an ontological need of telling constitutes the manifestations of what sustains the long-lasting mentoring relationship that goes beyond the constraint of time and space.

The imagined dialogue serves as a kind of "poetic representation" (McDonough, 2018) that fosters a discourse not just between the mentor and the protégée but also between the protégée and her own inner self. It provides both the mentor and the protégée ethical choices about how and why to represent the data as a way of creating action possibilities. And finally, as I interpreted the growth webs of the protégées as a modified form of spider web I was tempted to put my theorisation of mentoring in the form of poetic representation:

> No ideas of how to …?
> With reflection comes
> the growth of life experience.

And just to think harder and
Let's explore for more ...

The spider,
the philosophical creature of purpose.
And the creation of web as design of life
that enables the creature to see through it
the kind of causality that invites action
for meaning making of our life inquiry –
the change,
the transformation,
and finally,
the metamorphosis.

References

Ambrosetti, A. (2010). The interconnectedness of the roles of mentors and mentees in pre-service teacher education mentoring relationships. *Australian Journal of Teacher Education, 35*(6), 42–55.

Anagnou, E., & Fragoulis, I. (2014). The contribution of mentoring and action research to teachers' professional development in the context of informal learning. *Review of European Studies, 6*(1), 133–142.

Becker, H. (2002). Visual evidence: A Seventh Man, the specified generation, and the work of the reader. *Visual Studies, 17*(1), 3–11.

Bruner, J. (2004). Life as narrative. *Social Research, 71*(3), 691–710. (Original work published 1987)

Cain, T. (2009). Mentoring trainee teachers: how can mentors use research? *Mentoring & Tutoring: Partnership in Learning, 17*(1), 53–66.

Claxton, G. (2007). Expanding young people's capacity to learn. *British Journal of Educational Studies, 55*(2), 115–134.

D'Agnese, V. (2017). The essential uncertainty of thinking: Education and subject in John Dewey. *Journal of Philosophy of Education, 51*(1), 73–88.

Dewey, J. (1938). *Experience and education.* Kappa Delta Pi.

Elbaz-Luwisch, F. (2007). Studying teachers' lives and experience: Narrative inquiry into K-12 teaching. In D. J. Clandinin (Ed.), *Handbook of narrative inquiry: Mapping a methodology.* Sage Publications.

Elliott, J. (1993). Academics and action research: The training workshop as an exercise in ideological deconstruction. In J. Elliott (Ed.), *Reconstructing teacher education: Teacher development* (pp. 176–192). The Falmer Press.

Elliott, J. (2007). *Reflecting where the action is: The selected works of John Elliott*. Routledge.

Elliott, J. (2015). Educational action research as the quest for virtue in teaching. *Educational Action Research, 23*(1), 4–21.

Freeman, M. (2017). *Modes of thinking for qualitative data analysis*. Routledge.

Gibson, J. J. (2015). *The ecological approach to visual perception*. Psychology Press. (Original work published 1979)

Haggard, D. L., Dougherty, T. W., Turban, D. B., & Wilbanks, J. E. (2011). Who is a mentor? A review of evolving definitions and implications for research. *Journal of Management, 37*(1), 280–304.

Harari, Y. N. (2018). *21 Lessons for the 21st century*. Jonathan Cape.

Holliday, R. (2004). Reflecting the self. In C. Knowles & J. Sweetman (Eds.), *Picturing the social landscape: Visual methods and the sociological imagination* (pp. 49–64). Routledge.

Iliev, D., Ilieva, N., & Pipidzanoska, I. (2011). Action research democracy in mentoring schools. *International Journal of Humanities and Social Science, 1*(21), 58–65.

Irby, B. J. (2012). Editor's overview: Mentoring, tutoring, and coaching. *Mentoring & Tutoring: Partnership in Learning, 20*(3), 297–301.

Irby, B. J. (2018). Editor's overview: Differences and similarities with mentoring, tutoring, and coaching. *Mentoring & Tutoring: Partnership in Learning, 26*(2), 115–121.

Jaworski, B. (1993). *Mentoring in mathematics teaching*. Routledge.

Johnson, K. E., & Golombek, P. R. (2016). *Mindful L2 teacher education: A sociocultural perspective on cultivating teachers' professional development*. Routledge.

Karakas, F. (2009). New paradigms in organisational development in the 21st century: Positivity, spirituality, and complexity. *Organisation Development Journal, 27*(1). Retrieved from https://papers.ssrn.com/sol3/papers.cfm?abstract_id=1743445

Kirshner, D. (2009). Lev Vygotsky as muse to complex learning/teaching: A response to Ton Jörg's programmatic view. *Complicity: An International Journal of Complexity and Education, 6*(1), 45–55.

Koki, S. (1997). The role of teacher mentoring in educational reform. *Pacific Resources for Education and Learning*, 1–6.

Korthagen, F., & Vasalos, A. (2005). Levels in reflection: Core reflection as a means to enhance professional development. *Teachers and Teaching: Theory and Practice, 11*(1), 47–71.

Law, H. Y. (2009). *Learning to ask: The role of communication in the teaching and learning of mathematics* (Unpublished doctoral dissertation). University of East Anglia, Norwich.

Law, H. Y. (2013). Reinventing teaching in mathematics classrooms: Lesson study after a pragmatic perspective. *International Journal for Lesson and Learning Studies, 2*(2), 101–114.

Law, H. Y., Leung, Y. C. J., & Man, C. (2019). Making invisible growth visible through action research in learning to teach school mathematics: Two case stories. In K. L. Wong, Y. K. Lee, K. Y. Yau, & K. W. Wong (Eds.), *Proceedings of the Hong Kong mathematics education conference 2019* (pp. 44–48). HKAME.

Losito, B., Pozzo, G., & Somekh, B. (1998). Exploring the labyrinth of first and second order inquiry in action research. *Educational Action Research, 6*(2), 219–240.

McDonough, S. (2018). Inside the mentors' experience: Using poetic representation to examine the tensions of mentoring pre-service teachers. *Australian Journal of Teacher Education, 43*(10), 98–115.

McGranahan, L. (2017). *Darwinism and pragmatism: William James on evolution and self-transformation*. Routledge.

Moses, J. W., & Knutsen, T. L. (2019). *Ways of knowing: Competing methodologies in social and political research* (3rd ed.). Red Globe Press.

Neubert, S. (2009). *Reconstructing Deweyan pragmatism: A review essay. Educational Theory, 59*(3), 353–369.

Niemi, H. (2015). Teacher professional development in Finland: Towards a more holistic approach. *Psychology, Society and Education, 7*(3), 278–294.

OECD. (2018). *The future of education and skills: Education 2030 – The future we want*. Retrieved November 18, 2019, from https://www.oecd.org/education/2030/E2030%20Position%20Paper%20(05.04.2018).pdf

Oonk, W., Verloop, N., & Gravemeijer, K. P. E. (2015). Enriching practical knowledge: Exploring student-teachers' competence in integrating theory and practice of mathematics teaching. *Journal for Research in Mathematics Education, 46*(5), 559–598.

Oscarson, M. (1997). Self-assessment of foreign and second language proficiency. In C. Clapham & D. Corson (Eds.), *The encyclopedia of language and education* (Vol. 7, pp. 175–187). Kluwer.

Oscarson, M. (2013). The challenge of student self-assessment in language education. *Voices in Asia Journal, 1*(1), 1–14.

Redding, S. (2014). *Personal competency: A framework for building students' capacity to learn*. Center on Innovations in Learning, Temple University.

Schön, D. (1983). *The reflective practitioner: How professionals think in action*. Basic Books.

Smith, R., & Lynch, D. (2014). Improving teaching through coaching, mentoring and feedback: A review of literature. *MIER Journal of Educational Studies, Trends & Practices, 4*(2), 136–166.

Stevenson, A. (Ed.). (2010). *Oxford dictionary of English* (3rd ed.). Oxford University Press.

Swedberg, R. (2016). Before theory comes theorising or how to make social science more interesting. *The British Journal of Sociology, 67*(1), 5–18.

Zevin, J. (2010). *Teaching on a tightrope: The diverse roles of a great teacher*. Rowman & Littlefield Education.

CHAPTER 9

Mentoring Students through Global Experiences: Transformative Learning Abroad

Naomi Wilks-Smith and Darren Lingley

Abstract

International teaching practicums and field study for university students are often referred to as "transformative" experiences. This chapter reports on reciprocal teacher-guided global experiences, operationalised in the form of international education practicum and field study courses between Australia and Japan. Focus is placed upon mentoring students through the research-practice nexus as it relates to language education and intercultural understanding. The project sought pre-service teacher participants' reflections on personal and professional learning whilst undertaking a global experience. Mining students' journal data, the experiential learning of student-participants from Australia and Japan who took part in short-term teaching practice and fieldwork in the target international context is explored. The project included mentoring and support on several levels, intensive second language teaching experiences, and field study related to learning about context-specific teaching methodology at a selection of host schools. Negotiating such educational experiences in an unfamiliar language and culture played key roles in the experiential development of students. Findings will highlight the transformative experiences that students had, and the important role that mentors played in mediating their overall learning prior to and during the global experience.

Keywords

global experiences – study abroad – mentoring – journal reflections – university students

1 Introduction

Global experiences, also referred to as short-term study abroad, are increasingly common components of university programs. There is widespread rhetoric about global experiences being *transformative* (Kiely, 2005) with transformative learning defined as experiences which change individuals' ways of looking at and interpreting the world (Mezirow, 1997). This type of self-transformation is often cited as the major outcome of a study abroad experience (Doerr, 2018). Given increasing traction to encourage greater numbers of students to be involved in global experiences, it is important to understand the impact of such experiences. This chapter explores the impact that one short-term reciprocal global experience between Australia and Japan had on participating students and highlights the transformative nature of their experiences.

The current rise in opportunities for university students to participate in short-term study abroad means that greater numbers of students are having a global experience as part of their university programs. Employers and institutions increasingly expect students to possess "global competencies" which provides reason to encourage greater participation levels. Cooperation with a supporting university abroad has been found to be associated with increases in students' intercultural and global competencies (Stebleton, Soria, & Cherney, 2013) suggesting that this may increase the benefit of the experience for students. More evidence is needed however to identify whether global competencies do in fact develop over short-term global experiences and if so, how they can be measured. With significant funding directed to supporting global experiences, evidence of impact is needed to justify the use of the funds as well as the time commitment involved for participating university staff and students.

Current literature has identified that high-value programs are strongly associated with university course credit (Interis, Rezek, Bloom, & Campbell, 2018) and a good short-term program is "strongly connected to coursework and is an integral part of a larger learning experience" (Donnelly-Smith, 2009, p. 1). Short-term programs are frequently led by university staff, and therefore allow for control of the program and content so that program activities are strongly connected with university coursework. This is in contrast with programs that may be externally managed and have a larger separation from academic programs. Staff-led programs also have the advantage of providing field-based staff mentoring and opportunities to support students as they process their learning during the program. It is claimed that students get the most out of their program when it is structured, includes reflection, and includes working or studying with host-country participants (Donnelly-Smith, 2009). Deep cultural engagement with course content and opportunities for outbound students to interact with people in the host culture situates this particular study as a short-term teacher-guided global experience firmly anchored within the academic curriculums of the respective participating universities.

While obvious that global-mindedness tends to increase depending on the length of time abroad (Kehl, 2008), more research from various contexts and for differing durations is needed. In global experience programs of shorter four-week durations, the context and specific characteristics of the trip were found to be important factors that contributed to students' learning (Jones, Rowan-Kenyon, Ireland, Niehaus, & Skendall, 2012). In contrast with these findings, a longitudinal study surveying over 6,000 study abroad participants from twenty universities (Paige, Fry, Stallman, Josic, & Jon, 2009) found no significant difference in global engagement between students who participated in short-term and longer-term programs. This highlights the importance of gathering more evidence-based research from a wide range of contexts, experiences and durations in order to fully understand the impact global experiences have on participants.

The literature also suggests that global experiences develop a growth in students' intercultural competence (Salisbury, An, & Pascarella, 2013) and increases students' intercultural maturity and intercultural sensitivity, and are influential to students' attitudes, intercultural skills, and learning (Braskamp, 2009). This is further endorsed by a study of students' perceived benefits of short-term study abroad which included personal growth and intercultural development (Cheng, 2016). Global experiences have also been found to be a "value added" experience where students developed holistically and globally (Braskamp, 2009). Expanding current understandings about the impact of global experiences on participants is particularly important in the drive towards increasing global understanding in students and encouraging them to become global citizens. This is particularly important in the context of the current research because all participating students were pre-service teachers who not only needed their own personal global experiences but also needed to be prepared to embed global understandings and perspectives into their teaching practice for their future students to be global citizens (Wilson, 1993).

This range of existing literature identifies numerous educational and intercultural benefits for participants of global experiences. However, the wide range of differences between programs impacts student experiences and learning differently. For this reason, it is important to add more context-specific studies that identify the impact relevant to the learning situation and conditions of particular programs, and doing so informs our broader understanding of the experiences. A global experience can differ greatly in terms of program type, experiential and cultural contact, the level at which it is embedded within an academic course, duration, and the gap in cultural differences between home-country and target country. Each, and any combination, of these factors can impact the overall experience for participants. It is for this reason that Streitwieser and Light (2018) stress the importance of providing richly textured descriptions of individual student experiences rather than attempting to tick off sets of skills or attributes that are often claimed outcomes of transformative student experiences. Therefore, the aim of this chapter is to explore the impact of short-term reciprocal global experiences for students from Australia and Japan, to find out about their specific experiences and learning from their unique context.

2   Research Approach

The current study is a qualitative investigation using thematic analysis of journal data from participating university student pre-service teachers. The scope of the study consists of data collected from two Australian students' journals who participated in a two-week global experience to Kochi, Japan in February 2019 and two Japanese students' journals who participated in a two-week global experience to Melbourne, Australia in March 2019. Students were asked to keep journals throughout their global experience as a course assessment task that was submitted after the experience. They were asked to document their personal and professional learning whilst abroad, particularly in relation to their teaching-learning experiences. Students were invited to participate in the research by sharing their journals after the completion of their course. This process helped to distance their assessment with their free choice to participate. This study reports on the breadth of experiences, learning and reflections from these students. The data is not representative of the experiences of all participants from all global experiences but is presented to shed light on to the impact of one particular reciprocal global experience program on the participants involved.

Journals are a common source of research data when investigating students' global experiences (Doyle, 2009; Jones, Rowan-Kenyon, Ireland, Niehaus, & Skendall, 2012). They provide a tool for guided reflection by capturing an understanding of the impact of an experience on participants (Stebleton et al., 2013) and provide students with the opportunity to share their experiences and what they are learning, as well as to reflect on it (Smith-Paríolá & Gòkè-Paríolá, 2006; Vande Berg, 2007). The current study uses journal data that includes student observations, experiences, insights, questions and reflections, which provides qualitative, context-specific evidence to address the impact of the global experience on students and details the nature of the experiences and learning.

Thematic analysis was carried out on the journals. The analysis involved searching across the journals to identify repeated patterns of meaning (Braun & Clarke, 2006). An inductive approach (Braun & Clarke, 2006) to thematic analysis was used, whereby the themes were derived from the actual data. A strong focus was on the semantic level of thematic analysis (Boyatzis, 1998) which involved the identification of patterns in the semantic meaning content of the journals. Ethical approval to carry out this project was granted from each university. The university student participants received plain language statements and signed consent forms agreeing to participate.

3 Description of Reciprocal Global Experiences

The mentored global experiences described herein aimed to nurture a spirit of "global mobility" in education and placed a strong focus on the ecological validity of working closely with undergraduate students on international teaching practice and fieldwork. A central aim was for students from both universities to develop a global outlook through an experiential study about education while based in the target international context. Such international field study courses afford students with opportunities to do teacher training, examine education and cultural issues in international contexts, gain intercultural insights, and build basic research and data collection skills. This collaborative education project between the cooperating universities emphasised specific course content and prioritised the praxis between research and education. The priority for this project was focused on creating authentic learning opportunities for highly motivated undergraduate students to do practice teaching and carry out guided field study abroad.

The global experiences were operationalised in the form of reciprocal teacher-guided credit-bearing education courses. Project members from each university guided their students on pre-service teaching and field study courses, with academic and ground support from the cooperating host institution faculty members. Such content-specific student mobility programs encourage outbound students to think about education from a global perspective. Participating students can learn experientially about context-specific language education in other parts of the world and draw on their findings to make applications to their own context when they become practicing teachers. These student experiences and learning opportunities were supported by a multi-faceted mentoring network consisting of university lecturer-mentors who guided students throughout the global experience, the lecturer-mentors from the host-university, teacher-mentors in schools, and peer mentors. There was one lecturer-mentor from one university, two lecturer-mentors from the hosting university, five teacher-mentors from one city and six teacher-mentors from the other city, as well as a group of six peer mentors which included same-university peers and host-university peers. The impact of these mentors on students' learning throughout the experience were identified in students' journals, and is described in Section 4.

Mentoring, guiding and working together with students as they navigated their authentic global experiences was a pillar of this global education project. As guiding lecturer-mentors, we were understandably the primary mentors for the participating students and much of the data generated from the student journals identified our role as central in positively mediating their global experience. As lecturer-mentors, whilst also being researcher-authors reporting the research, this creates a dilemma of sorts for us. We have made a conscious effort to de-emphasise ourselves in mining the reflective journal data from our students, but it was nevertheless a central part of the global experience for each student. We refer to it only as needed in an effort to distance ourselves in reporting the findings and, instead, we make every effort to place primary focus on the data related to the learning experiences and mentoring that students received from cooperating classroom teachers in the international context.

No reciprocal program is a perfect mirror in meeting the experiential education needs of the respective program participants. For the outbound Australian pre-service student teachers, the primary aim was to do practice teaching in Japan while learning about education in the host culture. For the outbound Japanese students, the primary focus was on field study and data collection towards an undergraduate thesis. This included class observations, teacher interviews and, where possible, some practice teaching. The two Australian students were both taking the same education course and worked together in the field, while the two Japanese students worked separately, one on teaching Japanese as a foreign language (JFL), and the other on the teaching and preservation of indigenous languages in Australia. While all four participants were pre-service teachers, the two Australian students were preparing for a career as general primary school teachers, while one Japanese student was preparing for a career as a JFL teacher and the other was in preparation to be a high school teacher of English.

4 Findings and Discussion

Student journals identified the significant impact that the global experience had on them. It was evident from the journal data that one major area of growth was in personal learning and development.

4.1 *Personal Learning and Development*

Students' personal learning and development related to navigating themselves in an unfamiliar context and culture, especially with regards to social interactions in a new cultural environment. Students felt varying levels of comfort in their new social interactions, some expressing this as a major area of growth. In their new cultural context, students commonly reflected on the shift from their "comfort zone",

> … with each new experience I found myself stepping out of my comfort zone. [These experiences] … helped me grow and change throughout the small space of two weeks.

Social interactions also often included navigating meaning in an unfamiliar language. This was particularly challenging for the Australian students in Japan who had no previous Japanese language learning. By contrast, the students travelling from Japan to Australia had each studied English throughout their schooling and during university so the shift to English was more familiar to them and they each had relatively high levels of English fluency enabling smoother interactions during their Australian fieldwork. There is evidence, however, that social interactions for the Japanese students, especially in the form of interviewing teachers was challenging. As first-time interviewers new to a challenging data collection method, students noted the value of having their accompanying teacher present:

> When we couldn't catch up with what the interviewee was saying, he interrupted as needed to summarize or re-phrase, or gave additional follow-up questions between the talk to help us gain the exact detail. We greatly improved our interviewing techniques over the two weeks.

At other times,

> he massaged the communication between us and teachers when it was hard for us to understand the language or to speak up. This enriched the social aspect of the field study for us.

4.2 Professional Learning

Journal data also identified significant growth in the professional learning of participating students. Each of the students are current pre-service teachers who had a stated goal of experiencing language education abroad as a major focus of their global experience. For the Australian students, this involved experiencing the teaching and learning of English in Japan, and for the Japanese students, this involved researching language education in Australia (Japanese and indigenous languages). There were two categories of professional growth evident from the journal data: (1) new learning and new experiences related to teaching pedagogy, and (2) reflecting and learning from pre-service teachers' own teaching in context. Importantly, arising from these two categories of professional learning was the reconstruction of new knowledge for future practice.

4.3 Teaching Pedagogy

There were numerous specific examples of learned teaching pedagogy and practice. Each pre-service teacher compiled notes and explanations about new strategies and techniques that were used by teachers in the schools they visited. One commented that "the most interesting and valuable experience to me was seeing a variety of different teaching strategies implemented into each lesson". One of the specific strategies observed in schools in Japan for teaching English was the use of a lesson schedule. The schedule consisted of word cards with images of the meanings to show the sequence of teaching-learning activities that would be done in the lesson. The schedule was familiar to students and was displayed on the board at the front of the class so that all students knew how many activities there would be and what they were.

> This allowed students to really concentrate on the content, rather than spend a long time receiving instructions. As they were familiar with the schedule, [the teacher] enabled the students to feel comfortable when learning this new language, a key component of teaching EAL [English as an additional language]. When planning a sequence of lessons, I will keep this strategy in mind and hopefully will be able to do it as well as [the teacher] did!

The Japanese student involved in JFL observations made particular note of how effectively her mentor teacher dealt with challenges in the Australian Japanese language curriculum in her pedagogy.

> In Australia, some schools have no JFL classes, so if students move to a school which has JFL, it's hard for them to adapt and join in with classes

because of their lack of exposure to Japanese, and there is a possibility that many don't know Japanese at all ... I wondered how they catch up ... In Japan, there is a common national curriculum for everybody with prescribed English textbooks, so there are no big differences. The teacher told me that there are a lot of new students in her grade three and four classes, so she teaches them the basics while the other students are doing group activities. I was amazed by how flexibly she managed.

Another effective teaching strategy that was observed by the Australian pre-service teachers was the use of visuals to portray the meaning of words. Visual cues were also provided through the use of gestures by teachers. Teachers used "body language for emphasis" and often "communicated through gestures". Gestures were a particularly helpful strategy when there was a "language barrier". Prior to arriving in Japan,

> We all had the misconception that teachers would only speak Japanese when teaching English. This couldn't be further from the truth ... lessons were strictly in English! Immersing students in English was fantastic for their English comprehension and their communicative ability.

Using such an approach meant that teaching strategies such as using visuals and gestures were particularly important. A similar strategy was identified by the student who observed indigenous language lessons. She was impressed by a strategy used by the teacher to help overcome the reality that English pronunciation had affected the pronunciation of the Woiwurrung language making it hard to preserve or fix because of insufficient materials:

> The class started with "Letter & Sounds" by using the Indigenous letter chart, and that day's focus was on the letter 'a' and 'u'. Then a two-group team match spelling game "Tic Tac Toe" started. First, the teacher says the word in English, and makes students guess the spelling in Woiwurrung that includes 'a' and 'u'. She also used a Woiwurrung phrase for praise and children seemed to understand the meaning very naturally.

There are clear connections here in how pre-service teachers learned the value of language and communication and how these are enhanced through strategies to meet a particular learning context.

A very important element of the professional experience was when pre-service teachers demonstrated their awareness of their learning. One commented

> I set out to teach students English language skills – but I think I learnt the most! I was provided a once in a lifetime opportunity to teach overseas and I will use these strategies in my future classroom for all students in my class.

There was even an awareness that there would be an ongoing impact of the experience into the future with one pre-service teacher commenting

> There were so many things I learnt that will help me become a better teacher. There are probably techniques I won't even realise I picked up on until I have my own classroom and think back to the amazing times in [the schools]. I'm confident that I grew as a pre-service teacher and as an individual, and for that I am so grateful.

For one of the Japanese students, evidence of awareness of learning was explicitly identified by the following entry:

> Attending [teacher's] classes, I realized that she always praises the students, and this is one of the key points to manage a language classroom well. She is trying to be positive all the time, and not negative, such as "Hey! Don't do that". She said, "Everything I have learned is from what other teachers do". Communicating with other teachers and sharing information such as what actions are working well or not, is really important to improve teaching skills. I learned this important concept about mentoring.

4.4 Pre-Service Teachers' Own Teaching in Context

A central component of the global experience involved teaching. Pre-service teachers had opportunities to observe and teach in a number of schools, with a focus on the second language. It was a challenge for pre-service teachers prior to the global experience to plan for a context they had never experienced before, for students they had never met, and for language lessons where the language levels were unknown. In order to undertake this, the emphasis was placed on planning a wide range of open-ended activities that could be adapted and modified to suit varying language levels. There were uncertainties about how relevant the planning and resources would be prior to attending the schools. One pre-service teacher thoughtfully recorded her wonderings about

> … what might be important and relevant to the lifeworlds of the students in these schools. I started to worry that my teaching resources were made

without much knowledge of what would interest the students and were irrelevant to what they were learning in school.

The worries were set aside when pre-service teachers familiarised themselves during classroom observations and could make connections between the students, their language levels, and their own planning and resources. Not everything went smoothly all the time. One student commented

> I really appreciated the work I had put into developing such a broad range of activities because there were times where the class didn't respond well to certain lessons. I was quickly able to guide the activities towards a new path, changing the course of lessons so that students would learn best.

Teaching in a new cultural context where the pre-service teachers' language was a foreign language for students created a steep learning curve but one that was embraced and enjoyed.

> I loved having responsibilities and having the spotlight on me when taking my own lessons, simply because these were the moments when I learnt the most!

A wide range of teaching strategies that were new to the pre-service teachers were used to suit their new context for second language teaching. One pre-service teacher discussed what it was like to teach in a classroom context where their language differed from that of students,

> ... a key learning of mine was adapting to having a language barrier. ... I was able to use my body expression to gain certain responses from the students. Yet a major issue about the language barrier was that while I wanted everyone to understand me clearly, I didn't want to change my voice, tone or vocabulary in order to communicate ... I learnt to control what I said and how I said it. This was a wonderful experience for me to have because I know that in every classroom of mine, there will be at least one student who speaks another language ... This taught me how important the use of our voices is in teaching ...

There were opportunities for pre-service teachers to teach classes often with little or no prior warning.

> I was forced to plan and improvise on the spot for many activities. The practice of adapting lessons based on the students' understanding is

perhaps the main professional learning I acquired during this global experience.

One successful strategy that pre-service teachers adopted was creating "quick bullet-point lesson plans". Another related aspect of learning that was very valuable was "improvising with and without materials". One pre-service teacher provides an example of this explaining that

> A valuable lesson I learned was how to adapt the resources you have to suit your class. For example, I read a picture book, Wombat Stew, to a Grade 3 class. The book contains Australian slang and words that would not be familiar to the students. To ensure the students could still enjoy the text and engage with it, I adapted my reading on the spot. I kept the storyline simple, maintained repetition and rhyme and kept the focus on the Australian animals. This is a strategy I will apply again. I think being flexible around your students' needs is key!

Learning from what didn't work at first was also particularly valuable. Pre-service teachers could actually see the difference in the impact of their teaching over just a few short days in the new teaching context. One pre-service teacher shared that early in the teaching experience

> The students struggled to understand my questions and I had some help from the homeroom teacher in Japanese. I think the way I was wording the questions in a different way to the ALT [assistant language teacher], they were a bit confused and hesitant to answer ….

Over time, strategies were developed. "As I talked more and more, I got the hang of showing body language and changing my wording to suit the students". Personal reflections such as the abovementioned example about what didn't work, and why, led to a change in pre-service teachers' practice and the adoption of new strategies for the new context.

4.5 *Reconstructing Knowledge for Future Practice*

An ongoing impact of the global experience was evident in pre-service teachers' journals when reflecting on experiences that have changed the way they think about something and reconstructing their new knowledge to shape their planning for future practice. Such growth was evident in students' professional learning about teaching pedagogy in a new international context. This was particularly apparent for one Japanese participant who was introduced to the concept of "growth mindset" during her teacher interviews.

> One idea that I was very impressed with is 'growth mindset'. [Teacher] told me that growth mindset is very big in Australia. It's especially important in language classes. This was a new idea of education for me and I thought about how Japanese education could benefit from this. I think that the growth mindset should penetrate deeper into Japanese education. In Japan, students are often told they must all be the same level but in [teacher's] class, she accepts that students are not all the same level. I want to bring this to my teaching practice.

For the Japanese pre-service teachers who were just about to embark on extended teaching practicums in their home country, such kind of mentored global education experience can thus be potentially profound.

For the Australian pre-service teachers, one reflection about future practice related to the importance of the learning environment.

> Something I'm passionate about as a future teacher is having a calm, decluttered learning environment. A theme I noticed throughout all schools in Kochi was the simple learning environment. Classrooms were resource rich – but it didn't feel crowded. Students and teachers only had out what was being used for the lesson at the time and afterwards it was put away and the board was cleared for the next lesson. The rooms were filled with natural light, each window displaying beautiful scenery and nature. A thought I will hold onto and put into practice in my classrooms – Were the clean classrooms, natural light, clutter free environments part of the reason for the student's excellent classroom behaviour and focus?

The impact of experiencing a new learning environment has the power to ignite new ways of thinking about environments and shape future practice.

After having a teaching experience that was in their students' second languages for the first time, pre-service teachers made connections with the possible experiences of students in their home country who would similarly be learning in their second language. Journal data identified a new awareness of the needs of second language learners and the development of strategies to interact with and teach these students. One pre-service teacher commented that based on her experience

> I would always strive to provide ESL [English as a Second Language] students (and all students in my future class) with a variety of ways to interact with language. Having activities that are relevant to students' interests are engaging and will help students to develop conversational language

skills so they can apply them in real life situations, not just within the classroom.

Another pre-service teacher reflected on the use of power-point for vocabulary learning, together with the repetition technique,

> ... now I want to incorporate this throughout a series of lessons, investigating how well the strategy works. It could be introduced within EAL [English as an Additional Language] classes but could also be used in other subjects such as science, maths and geography. A unit could be reviewed by using this PowerPoint technique, teaching maths terms such as "multiplication", "addition", "multiple of", "therefore", "product", along with their symbol.

This example clearly demonstrates the reconstruction of new knowledge for future practice that extends beyond the experience of teaching a second language to other areas of the curriculum.

4.6   Role of Mentors

A strong theme that arose from the journals was the important role that mentors provided in preparing students for the experience, navigating the experience, and providing role-modelling and guidance. The mentors included university staff who accompanied the global experience, staff from the host university, teacher-mentors in schools, peers sharing the global experience, and host university students who were participants in a "reverse" global experience.

4.7   Mentoring Provided Pre-Experience

For both parts of the reciprocal global experiences, mentoring commenced with pre-departure meetings with the accompanying university staff and participating pre-service teachers which included language and cultural information and information about teaching in schools and pedagogical considerations. The pre-trip meetings were not just a one-way delivery of information. The Australian pre-service teachers were actively involved in the preparations and had choices in the range of teaching experiences they would have. A major area of focus of the pre-departure meetings was planning for teaching in the new overseas context, which included an unfamiliar language and culture. Meetings provided

1. Time to look through resources, discussions about what would be useful to take or make, how many resources were needed and the age/level of English language to target the resources at.

2. Being mentored through this process eased any pre-trip anxieties around feeling unprepared to teach in another country.

With field study and data collection through interviews and observation as the target activity for Japanese students visiting Melbourne, the pre-departure mentoring objectives meant working with students in developing basic research skills in these methods. This included working with students to draft a research proposal in their area of interest, guiding students to relevant background readings in JFL and indigenous languages, and co-constructing semi-structured interview questions. As a teacher-guided field study course, the premise of the course was that the accompanying teacher would work closely with students while in Australia to introduce them to what is involved in field research. This proved intuitively appealing to students. One highlighted the value of this in her journal:

> The position of learning together was very helpful. We discussed and revised what we learned every day after interviewing people. This helped me to understand the study deeply, even before we left, which wouldn't have happened if I was doing it alone. As someone who aims to be a teacher, I felt that showing an attitude of learning together is important to motivate the learner's interest and improve skills.

Similarly, another student comment related to preparations, included

> He gave me some suggestions about books and research papers for my research area to prepare pre-departure study. It was very helpful because it is hard and takes a lot of time for me to choose good materials in English.

4.8 Mentoring during the Global Experience: By Accompanying University Staff

Mentoring by accompanying university staff during the global experience was critical to the experience. One pre-service teacher documented that the university staff member

> ... provided support in so many ways during our stay ..., helping with everything from language barriers and cultural insights, to serving as a role model teacher in the primary schools we visited. She ensured [university students] felt safe, comfortable and excited for this experience, preparing us from our very first meeting! ... [Her] assistance in the classrooms was invaluable. [She] provided written feedback after our lessons and gave

verbal encouragement between lessons, and each night about our teaching plans for the following day.

One pre-service teacher said

> ... it really helped me have a mentor teacher give me some comments and things to improve on as well as things I did well. Feedback is an essential part of the learning process and I am really appreciative that [university staff] provided us with feedback ...

Another commented,

> Just having my teacher there with me during an interview or in the classroom observations was comforting to me. He told us what to expect, supported us during interviews, and we also had many de-briefing sessions after school each day. This helped me when I gathered my data to write my report.

4.9 Mentoring during the Global Experience: By Teachers at Host Schools

The teachers at each school served as a great inspiration and as the primary mentors during this project. They provided information about their school, explained their language programs and classes, and also provided lots of class observation and teaching time. The important role of teacher-mentors in providing support was evident throughout the experience for both teams.

> The determination, care and enthusiasm they demonstrated towards teaching was so inspiring and left a huge mark on me. At each school, they went out of their way to make us feel welcome ... I learnt so much as a pre-service teacher and as an individual and cannot thank those wonderful teachers enough for that.

> I am appreciative of the teaching time I received and the support from the classroom teachers ...

One student remarked,

> [Teacher] is the busiest teacher I have ever met. Her Japanese classes start at 8:30 in the morning then one class after another without taking a break. However, she looked so full of energy. She included us as assistant

> teachers, so although I was observing I was also participating. She taught us things such as class features, what materials she uses, her personal theory of Japanese teaching. I felt no distance with her at all.

The Australian team were likewise moved by one special teacher-mentor.

> We met one teacher in particular, ... who was one of the most generous, selfless people I have ever met. ... She moved from classroom to classroom, teaching English with so much enthusiasm and passion that students couldn't help but respond positively to. By the end of each day, after teaching for hours, she somehow still had so much energy to give.

> [This teacher] ... became a huge inspiration ... showing us what passion really looks like in the classroom.

> [This] ... passionate and humble teacher taught me my biggest lesson of this trip – that my attitude, excitement and presence in the classroom has a large impact on students and how much they will engage and learn from the lesson ... My career long goal as a teacher is to be enthusiastic about all of my lessons, create a stress free and comfortable learning environment and engage students in their learning.

> I spent my entire time ... thinking about how I want to be that kind of teacher, who is clearly passionate about her work and inspires others to be the best they can be.

5 Conclusion

This chapter reported on reflections of pre-service teachers who participated in reciprocal teacher-guided global experiences between Australia and Japan. Findings showed a broad range of both personal and professional growth arising directly from the global experiences, including in areas such as teaching pedagogy and pre-service teachers' learning from their own teaching in context. Through this growth, participating students developed and reconstructed their knowledge for future practice, particularly in relation to building a sense of self-efficacy as young teachers, understanding issues in language education, and respecting the value of intercultural learning. The role of mentors before and during the global experience was paramount in the realisation of these outcomes. This crucial role that mentors played in helping navigate the authentic global experiences and in mediating professional learning by working together with students in the field was highlighted. Findings from this study contribute to the notion of global experiences as transformative in nature for the university students involved, and support advocacy for future experiences, particularly joint reciprocal projects where the mentoring process can be enriched by partners in the host context. The value of collaborating with a partner university was found to be highly beneficial, which adds to the existing literature in this area. Further, the multi-faceted mentoring support for students during their challenging international field study contributed to the overall success of students' experiences as they negotiated professional training and learning in a foreign context in an unfamiliar language and culture. Our description of how multiple mentors helped to pedagogically mediate authentic experiential learning contributes to an under-represented area of mentoring research as it relates to study abroad. For researchers and practitioners interested in conducting and mentoring similar international practicums and field study, it is hoped that our study can inform and support planning, pedagogy and practice in effectively convening future global experiences.

References

Braskamp, L. (2009). Assessing progress in global learning and development of students with education abroad experiences. *Frontiers: The Interdisciplinary Journal of Study Abroad, 18*, 101.

Cheng, A. (2016). Students perceived benefits of short-term study abroad programs: A case study of Hong Kong higher education. In D. Velliaris & D. Coleman-George (Eds.), *Handbook of research on study abroad programs and outbound mobility* (pp. 163–187). Information Science Reference. Retrieved from https://ebookcentral.proquest.com

Doerr, N. (2018). *Transforming study abroad: A handbook.* Berghahn Books. Retrieved from https://ebookcentral.proquest.com

Donnelly-Smith, L. (2009). Global learning through short-term study abroad. *Peer Review, 11*(4), 12–15.

Doyle, D. (2009). Holistic assessment and the study abroad experience. *Frontiers: The Interdisciplinary Journal of Study Abroad, 18*, 143–155.

Interis, M., Rezek, J., Bloom, K., & Campbell, A. (2018). Assessing the value of short-term study abroad programmes to students. *Applied Economics, 50*(17), 1919–1933.

Jones, S., Rowan-Kenyon, H., Ireland, S., Niehaus, E., & Skendall, K. (2012). The meaning students make as participants in short-term immersion programs. *Journal of College Student Development, 53*(2), 201–220.

Kehl, K. (2008). Differences in global-mindedness between short-term and semester-long study abroad participants at selected private universities. *Frontiers: The Interdisciplinary Journal of Study Abroad, 15*, 67.

Kiely, R. (2005). A transformative learning model for service-learning: A longitudinal case study. *Michigan Journal of Community Service Learning, 12*, 5–22.

Mezirow, J. (1997). Transformative learning: Theory to practice. *New Directions for Adult and Continuing Education, 74*, 5–12.

Paige, R., Fry, G., Stallman, E., Josic, J., & Jon, J. (2009). *Study abroad for global engagement: Results that inform research and policy agendas.* Paper presented at the Forum on Education Abroad Conference, Portland, OR.

Salisbury, M., An, B., & Pascarella, E. (2013). The effect of study abroad on intercultural competence among undergraduate college students. *Journal of Student Affairs Research and Practice, 50*(1), 1–20.

Smith-Paríolá, J., & Gòkè-Paríolá, A. (2006). Expanding the parameters of service learning: A case study. *Journal of Studies in International Education, 10*, 71–86.

Stebleton, M., Soria, K., & Cherney, B. (2013). The high impact of education abroad: College students' engagement in international experiences and the development of intercultural competencies. *Frontiers: The Interdisciplinary Journal of Study Abroad, 22*, 1–24.

Streitwieser, B., & Light, T. (2018). Student conceptions of international experience in the study abroad context. *Higher Education, 75*(3), 471–487.

Vande Berg, M. (2007). Intervening in the learning of U.S. students abroad. *Journal of Studies in International Education, 11*, 392–399.

Wilson, A. (1993). Conversation partners: Helping students gain a global perspective through cross-cultural experiences. *Theory into Practice, 32*(1), 21–26. doi:10.1080/00405849309543568

Epilogue

Tania Broadley

Education, and in particular teaching, is characterised by a journey of continuous learning where a raft of knowledge and skills are accumulated to foster the growth of teachers and indeed, their learners. This characterisation is underpinned by the continuous development of a strong body of professional knowledge. This book expertly illustrates the important process of mentoring in the construction and dissemination of this educational knowledge. One of the key strengths of this book is the diversity of contexts in which the various aspects of mentoring are evidenced and discussed. The various chapters, all built upon current national and international action research in diverse educational settings, highlight how the role of mentoring continues to be multifaceted and thus, how the contribution to professional development of educators may be characterised across a range of contexts. The chapters presented here illustrate the lessons to be learnt from these diverse contexts and across various "walks of life" in education – professors, students, student-teachers, teachers, peers and PhDs. They also illustrate the mentoring journey – from teaching "inductions" through to senior mentoring roles.

The benefits and characteristics of successful mentoring relationships have seen mentoring adopted across a wide range of professions, including education, so it is not surprising that the various chapters in this book are deeply steeped in a range of theoretical purposes underpinning teaching, learning and professional relationships. The authors explore the dynamic relationship between context, mentors and mentees and contribute to a widening of our understanding of this complex relationship.

Mentoring itself is based upon beliefs about how individuals learn and what is important in the learning process for professionals. It is often difficult to define and there are many interpretations of how mentoring may be approached. Kochan and Pascarelli (2012) define mentoring in three distinct ways noting that each can be affected by cultural purpose:

– traditional mentoring involving the transmission of the culture and values of the context,
– transitional mentoring involving a collaborative process, respecting both the culture of the context and the identity of the mentee and
– transformative mentoring involving shifting roles for both mentor and mentee, laying emphasis on mutual growth and development.

EPILOGUE

The diversity of contexts and insights into mentoring within that context is at the heart of each chapter. For example, central to the heart of Mena and Clarke's work in this volume is the discussion of transitional mentoring as it relates to pre-service teachers. In outlining the role of mentoring in pre-service teacher education, they draw upon a model that both respects the role of the mentor, the mentee and the context of the workplace. In presenting the four profiles of mentors, they distinguish roles that encompass the work of cooperating teachers within the context of mentoring: partner, advocate, nurturer, and facilitator. Through analysing and coding the roles they provide profiles on mentors that will enable greater professional development and learning to occur, thus addressing the complex relationship skills required in mentoring in different workplaces. This idea of "codified" knowledge (Eraut, 2014) and transitional mentoring is also evident in the interaction between the mentors and mentees in Saunders, Chester and Xenos' work, which examines peer tutoring for higher education students using two models – Class Wide Peer Tutoring, Supplemental Instruction and Peer Assisted Study Sessions. Their work illustrates successful intentional curriculum design and transition pedagogy in a tertiary education context and creates insights into the diversity of both the context and the mentees. Their conclusions have significant propositions for future development, where the identity of the mentee is central to the relationship.

Providing professional development to teachers on mentoring can help to build capacity in two ways: improved quality mentoring of pre-service teachers, and reflection on teaching practices for mentors' own pedagogical development. In the ever-changing initial teacher education space between universities and schools, the role of the mentor and their contribution to professional knowledge development becomes increasingly significant. However, the role of the mentor has been only vaguely defined by policy makers. The relationship has been seen as a process of supporting the mentee to reach a particular goal, notably the standards for fully qualified teacher status. Littlewood and Jordan in this volume outline a traditional approach to mentoring drawing heavily upon the Australian Institute for Teaching and School Leadership which recommends that teacher mentors need access to professional learning in order to develop mentoring skills, to enable the provision of high-level support to pre-service teachers. They examine the professional learning provided by the Institute and the scant uptake by the mentors in their study. What is exciting and diverse in their conclusions is the evidence that any mentoring approach relying upon narrowly focussed professional development was unlikely to be successful and a greater reliance upon communication and transformative mentoring may be advantageous. This is a much reviewed space – with a number of apposite models defining the uptake of professional learning about mentoring against other professions (Grimmett, Forgasz, Williams, & White, 2018). Although these authors have chosen to focus upon the relationship as integral to success of any mentoring professional development programme, their findings make for ongoing discussion and debate – which in itself is a healthy start to the role of mentoring in initial teacher education. Similarly, Jordan and Littlewood, in a later chapter explore the mentor identity and their feelings and perceptions about a particular model of pre-service placement. They present a personal insight into the challenges and complexities of the relationship, further endorsing the traditionalism of the current policy approach in Australia. This chapter contributes to their previous work and complements the overall context of initial teacher education mentoring prevalent in other chapters – it is an astute and perceptive description of a personal approach and the mixed, complex feelings of mentors involved in this context. As such it value-adds to our wider understandings and theories of mentoring in initial teacher education.

That the mentoring relationship can move between traditional and transitional and to a lesser extent transformational relationship, is evident in the rarely explored area of doctoral supervision. Gradovski highlights the opportunities such mentoring provides for the development of participants' professional agency. His critique interrogates the concepts of professional agency and authorial agency and thus provides insights into a rare relationship that also shifts across different contexts and cultures.

A range of researchers have characterised mentoring as developing a deep understanding of professional identity and role (Ngara & Ngwarai, 2012; Taylor & Neimeyer, 2009). Huk Yuen Law in "Theorising Mentoring for the 21st Century Teaching and Learning" in this volume allows us fresh insights into this development of identity and the subsequent changes in the traditional mentoring model as mentees move beyond the transmission of knowledge to active discourses around their identity.

In the final chapter of this book, Wilkes-Smith and Lingley examine the transformational nature of mentoring where roles and cultural contexts frequently shift in reciprocal teacher-guided global experiences, in the form of international education practicum and field study courses between Australia and Japan. With an emphasis upon language education and intercultural understanding, it is inevitable that the aspects of mutual respect and growth are key outcomes of their work.

What is evident within each of these chapters and is a constant ongoing theme throughout this book is the constant search to articulate the mentoring relationship and to explore within each diverse context the effect of this relationship upon those involved. This thread of intentional discovery is both exciting and exhaustive. What is clear when the totality of chapters are now examined and the key lessons to be learnt are derived, is that the adoption of any one approach and theoretical framework for mentoring in educational contexts is likely to be fraught. That is – the authors have expertly explored both the challenges and advantages of their specific context and the powerful lessons within each context – clearly illustrating the relevance and interrelationship of the context to the mentoring approach.

This prevailing message presents significant challenges for educators, setting up a tension between the various aspects of mentoring such as nurturing, imitation, reflective practice and disruptive challenging. When overlaid with the possibility of a shifting transformational role between the mentor and the mentee, the challenges appear vast. But the passion and spirit of the search is also evident in each of the chapters presented here and the overall conclusion of the combined chapters making up the authority of the book is the ardour and voice of educational contexts and diversity, framed in the professional development and learning scaffolds supplied by each of the authors. It is this commitment that will sustain education and mentoring well into the future.

References

Eraut, M. (2014). Developing knowledge for qualified professionals. In M. Eraut (Ed.), *Workplace learning in teacher education* (pp. 47–72). Springer.

Grimmett, G., Forgasz, R., Williams, J., & White, S. (2018). Reimagining the role of mentor teachers in professional experience: moving to I as fellow teacher educator. *Asia-Pacific Journal of Teacher Education*, 46(4), 340–353.

Kochan, F., & Pascarelli, J. (2012). Culture and mentoring in the global age. In S. J. Fletcher & C. A. Mullen (Eds.), *Handbook of mentoring and coaching in education* (pp. 184–198). Sage.

Ngara, R., & Ngwarai, R. (2012). Mentor and mentee conceptions on mentor roles and qualities: A case study of Masvingo teacher training colleges. *International Journal of Social Sciences & Education*, 2(3).

Taylor, J. M., & Neimeyer, G. J. (2009). Graduate school mentoring in clinical, counselling, and experimental academic training programs: An exploratory study. *Counselling Psychology Quarterly*, 22(2), 257–266.

www.ingramcontent.com/pod-product-compliance
Lightning Source LLC
Chambersburg PA
CBHW052045300426
44117CB00012B/1986